"A must read for all vets."
Sgt. William Robb, Korean War Veteran, USMC

"Having had two tours in Vietnam during the height of the conflict, I can directly relate to the frustrations characterized in 'Unglorious War.' Not being allowed to take the battle to the enemy due to purely political considerations was the direct result of the heavy casualties suffered by the United States of America. I found this book to be a good read and could not put it down."
Captain Robert D. McIntosh, Vietnam Veteran,
US Army 1962-1970

"As a WWII veteran, I am unaware of any politics which were used to keep the United States and our allies from winning WWII. We pulled together and sacrificed as a nation. 'Unglorious War' showed that the Vietnam War was a war we didn't fight to win. How sad because we lost over 58,000 men fighting a limited war. The goal of fighting any war is to win."
Staff Sgt. Donald T. Baker, 21st Weather Squadron,
8th Air Force, U.S. Army Air Corp 1942-1945

"This is a story with very human characters filled with fears and ghosts from the past. They lead complex lives as their conscience dictates with a realization of who they are and what their role in life should be, overcoming the past enough to keep it from interfering with their present duties and from coming to grips with their faith. This book is a fine mixture of factual, relevant work combined with raw emotions and great empathy. It is a book well worth reading."
Reverend Robert Baker

UNGLORIOUS WAR

MAXINE FLAM

Flamingo
Publications
Los Angeles

Cover design by Maxine Flam and Bruce Heinsius
Cover photo by Bruce Heinsius Photography
Cover Layout by Bruce Heinsius

Background front and rear cover permission to reproduce photographs by PaPaGrizz. Photographs are from "Remembering the Vietnam War CD-ROM-over 1,000 Photos." Used by Permission.

Scripture quotations marked (GNT) are from the Good News Translation in Today's English Version – Second Edition Copyright © 1992 by American Bible Society. Used by Permission.

Manual for Courts-Martial United States (2000 Edition) including Appendix 2, Uniform Code of Military Justice by Joint Service Committee on Military Justice, a public domain document, was used as reference for the military trial.

ISBN 978-0-9821174-0-8

Flamingo Publications
12748 Bosworth Street
North Hollywood, CA 91606
818-980-1602
Visit our Web site at www.flamingopublications.com

Acknowledgments

Writing is a solitary experience. From the formation of the idea to the research to the writing and rewriting experience, I was alone in my creating experience. However, once I finished my book and talked about it with others, I was no longer alone. Friends and co-workers expressed an interest to help any way they could. There are several people I need to thank at this time.

Gary Kaye, for his permanently borrowed laptop and technical assistance; Gary Kinsman, for additional technical assistance and printing services when my printer was temporarily down; Eddie and Ryan from CDW, for sending me a mouse and back-up drive; Ralf Weissenberger, one of my bosses, who came through with internet sites to help me in my research and for agreeing to be the hero on the cover the book; my mother, G.G., Bob and Warren's advice with the preproduction phase of printing; B.R. and Robert for proofreading; Bruce Heinsius for his cover photography work and cover layout design skills; Eric White and Glynn Gilchrist, for putting together my website; Carl Elkins, CIO of my company, for allowing me to use the conference room for the photo shoot; the Los Angeles City Libraries and librarians Linda Moussa and Cindy McNaughton for their research assistance; Pastor Bob who gave me the emotional and spiritual support I desperately needed to keep going including suggesting the title of the book based on the synopsis and the anonymous people who believed in me by investing in this book. Without their support, "Unglorious War" would never have been published.

I dedicate this book to my late father, Sidney Flam, (1919-1995) WWII Veteran, (1941-1945) Sergeant, U.S. Army, 5th Armored Division, 75th Medical Battalion who received Five Unit Bronze Stars, the Silver Star for bravery, Combat Medics Badge with Bronze Star and Good Conduct Medal. A man who saw much, said little about it, and was the greatest dad a girl like me could have ever had.

And to all veterans who have served this great nation: past, present and future.

"The greatest love you can have for your friends
is to give your life for them."

John 15:13 (GNT)

"If it wasn't for God, you wouldn't have a country;
if it wasn't for the veteran, you wouldn't
have a country either."

George "Georgie-baby" Jacobs, Veteran U.S. Navy

UNGLORIOUS WAR

Chapter 1

I arrived at the Hickam Air Force Base at 8:30 a.m., 30 minutes before the court-martial was to begin. I didn't sleep a wink last night. My mind was racing. Everything I worked for over the past 15 years was coming to a conclusion. My close friends and co-workers said they would meet me here. The only one I couldn't get in touch with was Steven. I left a message at his office with all the details of where to meet. Chaplain Cook changed his Bible study to attend. What a sweet man. I have known him for 25 years; the entire time I had been in the Navy. He was a source of spiritual inspiration even in my darkest hour of despair. Whenever I sought advice, he would stop what he was doing to make time and counsel me.

Chaplain Cook wasn't tall. He stood about 5'9", slender with dark blond hair. Clean shaven and dressed in his chaplain uniform, he inconspicuously carried his Bible, hymnal and prayer stole wherever he went. He once told me that he was a boy scout and believed in their creed, "be prepared."

I checked my watch. It was 8:33 a.m. I hoped the Sergeant at Arms would open the double doors early so I could sit down.

I started to pace. It had been a long time since I felt this much anxiety. I could take one of my pills but I don't want to dull my senses. I wanted, no, no, I needed to be alert. I don't want to miss one moment of the trial.

8:40 a.m. Maria and George arrived. I've known each one over 20 years. I waived to them. They saw me and walked over.

"How are you holding up?" said George.

"Nervous," I replied.

"Well, that's to be expected. Everyone will be here to support you. Don't worry about that," he said confidently.

8:45 a.m. The Sergeant at Arms opened the doors to the court-martial room. It looked like a regular court room. As I entered, I noticed five rows of pew seats on each side of the aisle which seated 10 people per pew. About a 100 people could sit comfortably with space in the back for the overflow crowd. There were two tables in the front, one on each side of the aisle, made of dark wood, maybe cherry wood. One was the prosecutors table; the other, the defense table. At the front of the room was the judge's desk. It was three steps off the floor on some kind of podium and made of the same wood as the other two tables. To either side of the judge's chair were two chairs for the members of the panel to sit. Those chairs were used if the court-martial was a member trial which was similar to a civilian jury trial. The accused could opt for a trial by a judge only. In that instance, the members of the panel would be dismissed.

8:50 a.m. The cameras were being set up. The court-martial would air on closed circuit TV throughout the entire base. Too many people wanted to attend so the only way to oblige the officers and enlisted personnel was to televise it on closed circuit TV. The officer's club was open to everyone. I was told by upper brass they expected standing room only. Another TV link was set up in the barracks closest to the court-martial room. The bunks were taken out and 200 chairs were set in blocks of ten to a row.

8:52 a.m. Chaplain Cook arrived. I waived to him to come and sit by Maria, George and me. He walked over to us, shook hands with George, gave Maria and me each a reassuring hug and sat down.

8:54 a.m. Steven finally arrived. I waived. He walked over and sat on the other side of me.

"I meant to be here earlier but I got caught up in some things at the office," he said apologetically.

"No problem. You made it. That's all that counts," I said smiling.

"There was no way I would have missed this," he replied.

8:58 a.m. The Sergeant at Arms announced that the doors would close in one minute. The court-martial would begin as scheduled at 9:00 a.m. The prosecution attorney arrived through a door on the right side. The two defense attorneys arrived through a door on the left side. After they were seated, the defendant was brought in by the military police.

8:59 a.m. The Sergeant at Arms closed the court room doors. I felt my heart pounding; my hands, sweating. Justice was coming. After 15 years of fighting the Government for every inch of documentation, the truth would be known. I closed my eyes for a moment giving thanks to God for giving me the strength to get to this day, thanking Him for His support and not letting me give up.

9:00 a.m. The judge walked in from a door behind his desk followed by the four men who were the members of the military panel.

Chapter 2

"All rise. This Article 39a session is called to order. The Honorable Colonel Johnathan Beecham, presiding," bellowed the Sergeant at Arms.

"Be seated," said Military Judge Colonel Johnathan Beecham as he banged his gavel once.

"Will the court reporter please read the convening orders?" said Judge Beecham.

"Yes Your Honor," replied the court reporter.

"Today is July 19th, 1984, 0900 hours.

Pursuant to paragraph B1, General Order Number 2, Department of the Army, a General Court-Martial is convened with the following members at Hickam Air Force Base:

Colonel Johnathan Beecham presiding.

Members:

Lt. Colonel Matthew Johnston

Major Paul Baker

Captain Donald Rogers

First Lieutenant Joseph Rodriguez.

This court-martial is convened by General Court-Martial, Convening Order Number 84-0176, Headquarters of the Army of the United States of America. Copies of which have been furnished to the military judge, counsel and the accused and to this reporter for insertion at this point in the record."

The court reporter continued, "The charges have been properly referred to this court-martial for trial and were served on the accused on June 27th, 1984 more than the required five days notice needed. No continuance can be granted.

There are no corrections noted on the convening orders.

The accused detailed to this court-martial is present: Colonel Anthony Joseph Lambello Jr. formerly known as Lt. Anthony Joseph Lambello Jr." The court reporter finished and sat down.

"Let the record state that Lt. Anthony Lambello Jr. and Colonel Anthony Lambello Jr. are one in the same person. Is there any objection by counsel?" said Judge Beecham.

"No objection, Your Honor," stated each counsel.

The court reporter replied, "So recorded. There is no one else detailed in the court-martial."

"For the record," said Judge Beecham, "state your rank and name," addressing the court reporter.

"I am Private First Class Richard Williams. I am the court reporter for this court-martial."

"The oaths will now be administered," instructed Judge Beecham.

"Trial counsel will administer the oath to the military judge," said the court reporter.

"Do you swear that you will faithfully and impartially perform, according to your conscience and the laws applicable to trial by court-martial, all the duties incumbent upon you as military judge of this court-martial, so help you God?"

"I do," replied Judge Beecham.

"Trial counsel will administer the oath to the members of the court," said the court reporter.

"Do you swear that you will answer truthfully the questions concerning whether you should serve as a member of this court-martial; that you will faithfully and impartially try according to the evidence, your conscience, and the laws applicable to trial by court-martial, the case of the accused now before this Court; and that you will not disclose or discover the vote or opinion of any particular member of the court upon the findings or sentence unless required to do so in due course of law so help you God?"

"I do," said each members of the court in unison.

Judge Beecham administered the oaths to the prosecution and defense counsels.

"Do you swear that you will faithfully perform all the duties as prosecution or defense counsel in the case now hearing so help you God?"

"I do," said the attorneys in unison.

The court reporter said, "All members of the prosecution are qualified and certified under Article 27(b) and have now been sworn under Article 42(a).

No member of the prosecution has acted in any manner which might tend to disqualify him or her in this court-martial.

Primary Prosecutor in this case is Captain Trent West.

All retained members of the defense are qualified and certified under Article 27(b) and have now been sworn under Article 42(a).

No member of the defense has acted in any manner which might tend to disqualify him or her in this court-martial.

Primary Defense Counsel in this case is Major David Parquet. Consulting Defense Counsel is the Law Firm of Birnbaum and Miller, Roger Miller Esq.

Qualifications of Defense Counsel: Major David Parquet is a 20 year veteran who has been part of over 300 military defense counsels. Roger Miller Esq. is in private practice with

30 years experience as a consultant to the Judge Advocate General for both the prosecution and the defense.

The court reporter finished speaking and looked at the judge.

Judge Beecham began:

"Colonel Anthony Joseph Lambello Jr., you have the right to be represented in this court-martial by a Judge Advocate General, a General Flag Officer, or Military Counsel of your own selection, if the counsel you request is reasonably available. If you are represented by military counsel of your own selection, you would have the right to have court counsel appointed to help you in your own defense. However, you may request that a student at a university or a professor to act as associate counsel with the military counsel you select, and the United States Marine Corp., the detailing authority, may approve such a request. Do you understand?"

"Yes sir," Colonel Lambello replied.

"In addition, you have the right to be represented by civilian counsel, at no expense to the United States Government. Civilian counsel may represent you alone or along with your military counsel. Do you understand?"

"Yes sir."

"Do you have any questions about your rights to counsel?"

"No sir."

"Whom do you want to represent you?"

"Private Counsel only, sir. Roger Miller Esq.," replied Colonel Lambello.

"As stated earlier, counsel for the parties have the necessary qualifications and have been sworn in."

"State the charges against the accused," said Judge Beecham to Captain West.

Captain Trent West stood up and began to read the list of charges against Colonel Lambello.

"The general nature of the charges in this case are:

Article 99 – Misbehavior before the enemy.

Article 107 – False official statements.

Article 119 – Manslaughter with Article 134 – Negligent homicide as a lesser charge.

These charges were preferred by Colonel Alan Becker, Commanding Officer of Colonel Lambello's current unit, forwarded with recommendations as to disposition by Admiral Hargrove due to extenuating circumstances in bringing this case to trial which will be addressed shortly.

Your honor, are you aware of any matter which may be a ground for a challenge against you?" said Captain West.

"I am aware of none," stated Judge Beecham flatly.

"The Government has no challenge for cause against the military judge," replied Captain West.

"The defense has no challenge for cause against the military judge," said Roger Miller Esq.

"Colonel Lambello, do you understand that you have the right to be tried by a court-martial composed of members including if you request in writing at least one-third enlisted persons and that if you are found guilty of any offense, those members would determine a sentence?" said Judge Beecham.

"Yes sir."

"Do you also understand that you may request in writing or orally, here in the court-martial trial before me alone, and that if I approve such a request, there will be no members and I alone will decide whether you are guilty and, if I find you guilty, determine a sentence?"

"Yes sir."

"Have you discussed these choices with your counsel?"

"Yes sir."

"By which type of court-martial do you choose to be tried?" asked Judge Beecham.

"A trial by Your Honor alone," replied Colonel Lambello.

"The court reporter shall note that the accused requested a trial by military judge only," said Judge Beecham.

"Have you discussed this request and the rights I just described with your counsel?"

"Yes sir."

"If I approve your request your request for trial by me alone, you give up your right to trial by a court-martial composed of members, including if you requested, enlisted members. Do you wish to request trial by me alone?"

"Yes sir."

"Your request is approved. The court-martial is assembled. I thank the members of my panel. They are excused from further duty."

The four members of the panel rose from their seats and walked to the first row of the public gallery.

"The accused will now be arraigned," said Judge Beecham.

"All parties and the military judge have been furnished a copy of the charges and specifications. Does the accused want them read?" said the court reporter looking uncomfortable.

"Yes, Your Honor," said Attorney Roger Miller, "the accused wants the charges read."

"So be it. The court reporter will now read the charges into the record," said Judge Beecham.

"Article 99 – Misbehavior before the enemy. 'Any member of the armed forces who before or in the presence of the enemy –

a3 through disobedience, neglect, or intentional misconduct endangers the safety of any such command, unit, place or military property;

a5 is guilty of cowardly conduct;

b3 endangering safety of a command, unit, place, ship, or military property;

b3b that the accused committed certain disobedience, neglect or intentional misconduct;

b3d that this act occurred while the accused was before or in the presence of the enemy.

c1b 'Enemy' includes organized forces of the enemy in time of war, any hostile body that our forces may be opposing, such as a rebellious mob or band of renegades, including civilians as well as military organizations.

c1c 'Before the enemy' – whether a person is before the enemy is a question of tactical relation not distance.

c5a Cowardice is misbehavior motivated by fear.

c5b Fear is a natural feeling of apprehension when going into battle. The mere display of apprehension does not constitute this offense.

c5c Refusal or abandonment of a performance of duty before or in the presence of the enemy as a result of fear constitutes this offense.'"

"Extenuating circumstances as stated earlier relates to Colonel Lambello's service in Vietnam which caused these charges to be brought forth now and not 15 years ago. The delay is due to Article 107 – The filing of false official statements."

"Article 107 – False official statements – Any person subject to this chapter who, with intent to deceive, signs any false record, return, regulation, order or other official document knowing it to be false, or makes any other false official statement knowing it to be false, shall be punished as a court-martial may direct.

b1 that the accused signed a certain official document or made a certain official statement;

b3 that the accused knew it to be false at the time of signing it or making it; and b4 that the document or statement was made with the intent to deceive."

"Article 119 – Manslaughter – Any person subject to this chapter who, without an intent to kill or inflict great bodily harm, unlawfully kills a human being by culpable negligence, lesser offense is Article 134 – (Homicide, negligent).

b1 that a certain person is dead;

b2 that this death resulted from the act or failure to act of the accused;

b4 that the act or failure to act of the accused which caused the death amounted to simple negligence; and

b5 that under the circumstances the conduct of the accused was to the prejudice of good order and discipline in the armed forces or was of a nature to bring discredit upon the armed forces.

c1 Nature of offense. Negligent homicide is any unlawful homicide which is the result of simple negligence. An intent to kill or injure is not required.

c2 Simple negligence. Simple negligence is the absence of due care, that is, an act or omission of a person who is under a duty to use due care which exhibits a lack of that degree of care of the safety of others which a reasonably careful person would have exercised under the same or similar circumstances.

Simple negligence is a lesser degree of carelessness than culpable negligence.

d Lesser included offenses. None."

As the charges were read aloud, tears ran down my face. I wasn't bawling. The days of screaming and crying had passed but I couldn't stop them from flowing nor did I want to. Chaplain Cook looked over but before he could give me his handkerchief, Steven had already pulled out his and handed it to me. I dried my eyes and continued to listen intensely to the proceedings.

"The charges are signed by Colonel Alan Becker, a person subject to the code, as accuser; are properly sworn to before a commissioned officer of the armed forces to administer oaths, and are properly referred to this court-martial for trial by the United States Marine Corp., the convening authority." The court reporter sat down.

"Before receiving your plea, Colonel Lambello, I advise you that any motions to dismiss any charge or to grant other relief should be made at this time. Colonel Lambello, how do you plead?" said Judge Beecham.

"Your Honor, the defense has one prior motion already presented to the court under Rule 910 RCM (Rules of Court-Martial)," said Roger Miller.

"So noted," said Judge Beecham.

"Colonel Lambello, how do you plead?" repeated Judge Beecham.

Roger Miller rose on behalf of Colonel Lambello to speak."

"On behalf of the accused, Colonel Anthony Joseph Lambello Jr. pleads...."

Chapter 3

General Sherman called Admiral Lewis and told him there was a patient coming in from Japan with a top-level clearance. This patient needed the Navy's best nurse to give 'round the clock care. Admiral Lewis suggested me without hesitation. He knew of Captain Smith and his covert involvement in Laos over the past few years. Admiral Lewis also knew that Captain Smith was listed as Missing In Action (MIA) and was reclassified after six months to Killed In Action (KIA) even though no remains were found only to find out that he had been held all this time in a jungle prison as a Prisoner Of War (POW). The military desperately needed to know what Captain Smith knew about the Vietcong (VC), North Vietnamese Army (NVA), the terrain, the prison camp and anything else. Information was scarce despite Captain Smith and his men being rescued alive. Because only Captain Smith spoke Vietnamese, only he could provide the vital information needed for security in the region.

Admiral Lewis said he would set everything up. When Captain Smith arrived in Hawaii, I would be his caregiver.

I was sitting at my desk buried in paperwork. This was how I started most days, with a stack of files in my in-box. My office was near the front steps of the hospital. To my right, I had a window with a view of the main entrance to the hospital. I saw anyone who entered and left but I rarely looked out due to my enormous workload of 12 hours a day, 6 days a week. On the occasions when I was at my desk late in the evening, I saw the lights of the hotels on the beaches of Oahu. My mornings were spent doing paperwork and attending meetings and my afternoons were spent in the physical therapy room with the hard patients, the ones that were difficult to rehab for a variety of reasons. I saved the early evenings for prioritizing my workload for the next day.

My office was tiny by managerial standards, yet functional. I didn't require much space. My desk was made of oak with three drawers on each side and a drawer in the middle. There was a three-tier bookcase against the wall to my left and a small two-tier bookcase behind me. An ancient dark brown sofa sat opposite my desk for visitors or staff to sit on while conversing with me. It had a rip on the side when I received it. I originally covered it with tape. A few months later I purchased a throw roughly the same color to cover up the entire sofa. Since there was no money in the budget for a new one, I made do with this.

Chief of Staff, Dr. Peter Fong visited every morning with coffee in hand, in addition to calling me six times a day. Peter was 42, a thin man of Chinese descent, 5'6", black hair and brown eyes. He was young to be Chief of Staff but it was not something he went after. It was something he fell into. Six months ago, the last Chief of Staff died suddenly of a heart attack.

Peter and I were colleagues and long time friends. We went back eight years to when I first came to Oahu General after completing my Bachelors in Nursing. Peter was very supportive of me when my parents died. This drew our friendship closer and we stayed close when he married and had a son.

"Hi," I said.

"Hi, you look buried as always," Peter replied as he handed me my usual cup of Joe.

I took the coffee from him and replied with my usual sigh, "I am."

I took a sip and said, "Yuk! Couldn't you have made this any stronger? Never mind, don't answer that. I've tasted some of your past stuff. It could put hair on a Chinese Crested Hairless Dog." I put the cup down and continued, "You've got to get a Director of Nursing. I'm at wit's end."

I had been doing double duty as Peter's Director of Nursing and Administrative Head of Physical Therapy Nursing for a few months and things were piling up fast.

"I've narrowed down the search to five candidates but you need to interview them," Peter said.

"When can your secretary set up the interviews?" I asked.

"I'll have her get right on it." Peter said.

"Listen, I got a call from Admiral Lewis," Peter continued. "He's on his way to see you. It sounds urgent. He'll be here in 20 minutes."

"Well, it can't be good news," I exclaimed.

I jumped up from my chair not knowing what direction to go in. Peter found this amusing. I, on the other hand, was beside myself.

"Oh my God, I need to change. He can't see me in greens! I'm supposed to be wearing white which I stopped doing two years ago along with that silly hat."

"Relax," said Peter. "He knows you're on shift. If he says anything, tell him greens are more comfortable. Just remember to salute," he said jokingly.

Peter and I made small talk about his son while I nervously looked out the window. The Admiral's staff car pulled up. I rose from my chair. As I made my way to the front of the hospital, Admiral Lewis was entering the building. Peter remained behind.

I saluted Admiral Lewis.

"At ease, Lieutenant. Will you please accompany me to my staff car? We are due for a briefing at 0900 hours," said Admiral Lewis.

I accompanied the Admiral to Hickam Air Force Base. We were escorted by two military policemen to a secure room. As I entered, there were several people waiting including General Jackson Sherman.

I sat down in the back of the room. Admiral Lewis spoke, "As of this moment, Lt. Bristol, we are increasing your clearance to the maximum possible. You have always been on active duty with the Navy but your assignment for the past eight years has been at Oahu General. Your ideas for rehabilitating patients have been reviewed by doctors, physical therapists, and other professionals around the United States. We even had some interest from the French and British. The Navy thinks very highly of your skills.

I know you are wondering what is going on. This meeting is to brief you about your role in nursing a special patient back to health. He is on his way from Japan and when he arrives from that moment on, we want you to care for him. Not just rehabilitate him but physically care for him 'round the clock. His clearance is the highest level of top secret. He just spent six months as a POW and another two weeks or so wandering in the jungles of Laos in an effort to make contact with a recon party. His condition is serious. Before he arrives, you will have access to all of his medical records. You will be working closely with his doctors; however, you will be the primary one-on-one caregiver. I know that you have not done one-on-one in years, since nursing school according to your records – your specialty being rehabilitation nursing but we need you to do this. Captain Smith is extremely important to us."

"Of course, sir, I will do whatever needs to be done," I replied.

"Captain Smith will soon be promoted to Major Smith. His paperwork is in process. I stress the fact that he will be your only focus. I will have my driver return you to the hospital so you can reorganize your duties. You won't be going home anytime soon so if you have an animal, you will need to make arrangements to have it taken care of in addition to any domestic issues such as bill paying, etc. You will delegate all your present work. Dr. Fong will be briefed on a limited basis. I realize he is a close friend but, as you know, there is only so much you can tell him. Since 90% of your time is spent at Oahu General with the other 10% flying to Maui, Kauai, and the other hospitals, you will need to delegate your managerial work to other managers and supervisors. You will be living in the same room as Captain Smith. Arrangements are being made for a private room as I speak. You will have a cot to sleep on; a desk to write your notes on. Captain Smith will be arriving within the next four hours and that is all the time you have to get ready. Are there any questions?"

The room was silent for a moment.

"Admiral, sir, I can't think of any right now but if I do, I will contact you immediately," I said in a monotone voice.

My mind was spinning with all the information that had been thrown at me but I knew that Captain Smith must have knowledge that very few men possessed to have Admiral Lewis and General Sherman working side by side.

"Does anyone else have anything to add?" said Admiral Lewis.

"I have been told you are the best in your field. I need you to give 100%, Lt. Bristol," said General Sherman.

"Yes sir," I replied. "I promise I will."

With that, the meeting was adjourned. I saluted all the officers and left.

As I was being driven back to Oahu General, I kept thinking about everything that was said in the meeting. Why me? There had to be other nurses better qualified to give Captain Smith the bedside care he needed now. I can understand them selecting me do his rehabilitation when he is stronger but why pick me for one-on-one nursing – something I haven't done in years. I guess my qualifications matched their requirements otherwise they wouldn't have chosen me. I decided not to dwell on it.

When I arrived back at the hospital, I called Peter to come down to my office.

Peter no sooner stepped into my office before I said, "Well, you better get a Director of Nursing as soon as possible. I have a special patient due to arrive at 1:00 p.m. and that's all the time I have to get my desk in order."

Peter picked up the phone, called his secretary, told her to call a temporary nursing service and have some candidates for the Director of Nursing position sent over to Oahu General as soon as possible.

I called personnel. I asked them to send another secretary to my office so I could clear out my in box before Captain Smith arrived. I must have written a hundred notes on every file. I had writer's cramp before I was finished.

Now the only problem was who would assume the State Physical Therapy Nursing position while I was on special assignment. I asked Peter not to do anything right away in filling the position. He would have to convene a board within a week but he would recommend everything stay as it was for now. I contacted each PT Nursing Manager and told them that for the next month the weekly staff meeting would be canceled but to mail their status reports to my office. Nobody asked any questions. They knew if I could tell them, I would. My group was the best. They would pick up the additional work as long as it was necessary.

I was ready to meet Captain Smith.

Chapter 4

It was just past 1:00 p.m. when Captain Smith arrived at Oahu General. Green colored identification badges were issued to any personnel having access to the room. Two guards were posted at his door. I walked by to get a glimpse of what was going on and each time I passed, the guards saluted. After the 5ᵗʰ time, I told each of them to please drop the formality. I appreciated it but it was not the time or the place plus it made me crazy.

After Captain Smith was settled in his room on the first floor, I was paged to meet him. I started to enter the room but Dr. Richard Jacobs stopped me and introduced himself.

"Lt. Bristol, my name is Dr. Richard Jacobs. I will be Captain Smith's primary doctor. I am here to see what kind of extensive surgery he needs on his leg. After I determine the extent of the damage, I will schedule a team of surgeons to correct the problem. The doctors in Vietnam stopped the hemorrhage. He was airlifted immediately to Japan. The doctors in Japan saved the leg from amputation but the bone was shattered in the mid-shaft area. I anticipate surgery will be needed to insert a metal rod with metal pins at each end to take the place of the femur.

I was about to meet Captain Smith but nobody could have prepared me for what I was to see. Captain Smith's condition was far worse than I expected. I had taken care of Vietnam Veterans since the start of the war but he was my first POW.

The former muscular Special Forces Officer weighed a mere 137 pounds. He looked like pictures I had seen of Holocaust survivors from WWII. His wrists and ankles were infected where the thick ropes that bound him tore the flesh off his bones. Above the infections were bruising the likes of which I had never seen. His back had welts and scabs from the continuous beatings he endured. He had skin lesions and suffered from malnutrition and dehydration.

For four years, the vast majority of my patients had been men injured in battle. Their injuries ranged from the loss of a limb to blindness to deafness to paralysis but all were battlefield injuries. Oahu General never had any POWs. Here I was assigned as his one-on-one nurse. I didn't like one-on-one nursing because I found myself being drawn into that person's personal life and I needed objectivity when dealing with my patients. The shifts were 8 hours but with the shortage of nurses in school, I was always asked to work a shift after my hospital rotation. After 16 hours of patient care, I had to go home, study and hope I got 4 hours of sleep.

I loved the physical therapy rotation in nursing school. I found that interacting with someone a few hours a day made me a better nurse in one skill than trying to do it all. As I went up the administrative ladder, my time with each person decreased thus limiting my emotional attachments. I made the most of the limited time I spent with my patients. Time constraints helped me become more objective. I believe this objectivity helped me provide the best treatment possible. My techniques were recognized by upper brass which was why I was selected to help Captain Smith recover from his injuries. Now, the nursing as I had practiced it for so long was about to change.

I stood behind Dr. Jacobs and watched as he examined

Captain Smith. The room was large, about three times the size of my office. The bed was to the left with machines on both sides. My cot was located closer to the window touching the far wall. My desk was against the wall opposite Captain Smith's bed. It wasn't as nice as my normal desk but functional. It looked like a government surplus metal desk with a metal chair that was painful to sit on. I removed that ugly chair and had my chair brought over from my office. My in-box sat on the left side; my desk lamp on the right. There were no pictures on the wall which made the room depressing. I called Bill in maintenance to find something to hang on the wall.

After Dr. Jacobs left, I was left to tend to Captain Smith alone. He had IVs in both arms and a central line located just under his left collarbone. A Foley catheter hung on the right side of the bed. Aside from his emaciation and captivity injuries, his right femur was stabilized in a temporary cast and metal cradle.

Captain Smith had not regained consciousness since he went into surgery in Japan. The military was glad to have him back in Hawaii because with the knowledge he possessed and the physical condition he was in, Captain Smith was a potential National Security catastrophe but it was apparent from the severity of the beatings he received, he never uttered a word.

Chapter 5

The rest of the first day was uneventful. By late evening, I took Captain Smith's vitals and recorded them. I adjusted the monitors to go off at the slightest change of blood pressure, pulse, and respiration. I asked security to call me at 6:00 a.m. The first night I worked on files until midnight. Then I slipped off my reading glasses, laid down on my cot and went to sleep.

Captain Smith slept through the night. He was on a morphine drip which kept the pain under control but the first night would be one of the few nights he would have peace for the next two weeks. Dr. Jacobs and the team decided to operate immediately. They scheduled the operation for the 3rd day after his arrival. It was the consensus of the team that a metal rod would be inserted to create a new femur. The only concern was the accuracy of the measurement so that the right leg would not come out shorter than the left.

Surgery was scheduled at 6:00 a.m. Preparation was at 4:00 a.m. The second night I slept four hours and was up at 4:00 a.m. to help prep Captain Smith. At 5:30 a.m., the surgical team arrived to wheel him into surgery. Peter showed up early and told me that I might as well go back to bed for a few hours. It was hard since I was already up and worried about my patient. I never felt for a patient what I was feeling for Captain Smith. Was it pity? Was it some need to keep him safe from everyone and everything considering his recent ordeal? Was it something more – how could that be? I just met him. I put this out of mind and took Peter up on his offer to get some sleep. I went upstairs to his office and put in a wake-up call for 11:00 a.m.

As Chief of Staff, Peter had the best office that the hospital offered. His office was about 700 sq feet, the size my living room, dining room and bedroom. He had a large maple desk that was always immaculately polished with all his files neatly stacked in their proper in/out boxes. The carpeting was a cream color which beautifully offset the furniture. There was a black leather sofa against the left wall and two chairs opposite his desk. He had a small conference room off to the left. His private bathroom was on the right. He had a shower, sink and commode but no bathtub. Housekeeping always had it fully stocked with fresh towels, shampoo, soap and washcloths. The funny thing was Peter hardly used anything but the commode. It was everyone else who used the shower. All anyone had to do was ask permission. Peter was the quiet type and never said no.

I slept on the sofa until my wake-up call. At 11:00 a.m., I showered, grabbed a bagel from the breakfast cart on the first floor and was there to meet the gurney as it emerged from surgery at 11:45 a.m. Dr. Jacobs looked worried. He pulled me off to the side and told me that I needed to help bring Captain Smith out of his medicated sleep tomorrow. It was necessary so they could gauge his pain threshold.

The leg was a mess. The doctors implanted the rod with one end inserted two inches below the head of the femur and two inches above the knee. The shatter was extensive. The metal rod took the place of the femur. If this didn't work, the doctors would have no choice but to amputate the leg.

The surgeons took intricate measurements to ensure there would be little difference between the right and left leg length. The healing time was estimated at three to four months but with Captain Smith's emaciated condition it could be as long as six. General Sherman was anxious to have Captain Smith back as soon as possible and when they heard it could take at least three to four months for the leg to heal, he nearly had a stroke. I smiled and said that three months was extremely optimistic because it didn't include the minimum three month physical therapy time. After 8 years in nursing with my specialty in physical therapy, I knew how long Captain Smith would be at Oahu General.

I went to recovery. The surgeon was with Captain Smith. This gave me some time so I called Peter and asked if he had a few minutes.

"Sure," replied Peter. "Come up."

I was anxious and concerned.

"What's up? You sounded like this was urgent," Peter said.

"It is. I have an idea how I am going to write my nursing assessment but Admiral Lewis isn't going to like it. I don't care. My duty is to my patient. But Peter, I have another problem. I am worried my own personal problem will rear its ugly head. I got out of one-on-one nursing because of the long hours and intense patient care."

I felt bad to think of myself but I had to. I had a duty to my patient and myself. I couldn't be of use to anyone if I didn't take care of myself. It wasn't a premonition but I had a bad feeling of what might be coming if I didn't get the sleep I needed.

"As far as your nursing assessment is concerned, you were picked because of your experience and your knowledge. The military wants you to give him the best care possible. This is a temporary assignment. As far as your problem is concerned, it is in the past but if it comes up, we will deal with it. Don't worry. Just do your job and everything will be alright," Peter said.

I gave Peter a weak smile and thanked him. I went back to recovery and asked one of the recovery nurses when Captain Smith would be taken back to his room. I was told in about an hour. I returned to his room, sat down and began to write his assessment. Within the hour, Captain Smith was back in his room. The next 48 hours would be painstakingly long. Dr. Jacobs was optimistic. The surgery went according to plan and no additional surgeries would be needed.

That was wonderful news. Unfortunately, that would be the only good news for the next two weeks.

Chapter 6

It was 9:00 a.m. the next day when Captain Smith started to stir. I went over to his bed to take his vitals. His face was drawn and pale. I took a washcloth, wet it with cool water and wiped his forehead and cheeks.

Captain Smith opened his bleary eyes and said, "Where am I?"

"Oahu General Hospital, Hawaii," I replied.

"Who are you?" Captain Smith murmured.

"Lt. Marla Bristol."

"How long have I been here?"

"Three days."

"Why was I brought here and not to a base hospital?"

"Security and other reasons."

"What other reasons?" he inquired.

"General Sherman and Admiral Lewis wanted you cared for by someone who had a high clearance level and nursing skills that would get you back on your feet quickly." Any other questions, sir?" I asked.

Captain Smith looked me up and down and said, "You are definitely a sight for sore eyes."

"Thank you, Major."

"Major? I think you have the wrong patient," replied Captain Smith.

"Oops, well you will know soon enough. You've been promoted to Major."

The newly promoted Major Smith did not say anything for a moment.

Then I spoke, "Are you in a lot of pain?"

"Some but I have endured worse."

"I know. According to your records, you were a POW for the past few months."

When I mentioned POW, Major Smith immediately changed the subject.

"I remember being shot in the leg as the helicopter took off. I don't remember much after that. The medic gave me a morphine shot. What can you tell me about my condition?"

"You were shot twice in the right leg. One bullet passed through but the other hit the bone and shattered it. Triage was done in Khe Sanh to stop the bleeding. You were stabilized in Japan and brought to Hawaii for your final surgery. A metal rod with metal pins was inserted to hold the two pieces of remaining leg bone together. The rod will take the place of your right femur. The top of the femur near the hip socket and the bottom near the knee joint are intact. The rod was inserted into remaining bone below the hip socket and the bone above the knee. You will need calcium and protein supplements to strengthen and build bone density. You have numerous skin infections, some on your wrists and ankles but many are on your back. I have dressed them with topical antibiotics. You have two IV bottles. One is to keep you hydrated and one is antibiotics to treat the infections internally."

I tried to be as precise and as positive as possible.

"You mentioned earlier that you were chosen for your security clearance and qualifications. What are your qualifications?"

"I am a Lieutenant in the Navy. I have been a nurse for

8 years. I have been assigned to you for your entire stay at Oahu General. Whether it takes one month, six or a year, my orders are to help you return physically to where you were before you were a POW. My orders came directly from Admiral Lewis and General Sherman."

Major Smith listened intensely. Before he could respond to all this information, he made the mistake of trying to move and winced in pain. I began my pain assessment and then quickly gave him a morphine injection as per Dr. Jacobs's standing orders. After the injection took effect, I outlined his treatment plan. I mentioned that General Sherman wanted to speak with him as soon as possible.

"My friends call me Bear," Major Smith responded. "It looks like we will be spending a lot of time together so I would like it if you would please call me Bear."

"Sure but why do they call you that?" I replied. I knew that most Vietnam Vets had nicknames, some quite unique but there was always a story behind it and I was curious what Major Smith's story was.

"Well, it's kind of funny you asked because there were two reasons I was called that. The first reason is I have a talent to imitate celebrities.

"Like who?" I asked.

"Humphrey Bogart, Jimmy Cagney, and James Stewart but the one I did that got me my name was Yogi Bear from the cartoon. 'Hey Boo Boo, there is a picnic basket just waiting for us over there.' The other reason I was called Bear was that I am very protective of my men the way a mother bear is protective of her cubs. I wouldn't send someone to do something that I wouldn't do myself."

At that moment I should have adopted the nickname "the Lioness." I looked at Bear and saw him vulnerable to everything, a feeling I never had before with other vets but a feeling I had early in my career. It was this feeling that caused me not to become a regular duty nurse and focus on the specialty of physical therapy nursing. An overwhelming feeling of protectiveness hit me like a mother lion feels when protecting her babies. Bear brought this feeling to the surface and it concerned me. I was responsible for the hard therapies that no one else could handle. This was going to be one of the hardest therapies of my career. That didn't concern me as much as the demand of being a 24 hour a day nurse. After being out of floor nursing since nursing school, I had a six sense that I was going to need help but for now I had to follow orders.

As a floor nurse, there are more emotional and psychological demands. It's different working with multiple people day in and day out versus working with a few patients in a section, like an ICU or small ward. In nursing school, the teachers preach not to let your personal feelings interfere with your duties or you will become a detriment to your patient. I can't forget the whole picture like why I became a nurse. I wanted to make a difference in a person's life. I didn't join the Navy because I was poor and needed a way out like some people. I'm not judging and saying that's bad. That wasn't my reason. I wasn't in it for the pension or life time medical benefits. I wanted to serve my country. The Navy was a way of life for me; it was the path I chose.

I thought all of this when Bear spoke in one of his voices, Humphrey Bogart. Despite the scratchiness from the anesthetic, he said, "Penny for your thoughts, kid."

"Nothing important," I said trying to complete my work.

Bear wouldn't leave it alone. He imitated Jimmy Cagney from one of his gangster movies, "You dirty rat, I know you're hiding something. You can't get away. No, I won't let you get away."

I started laughing.

Bear smiled. "Now, why the serious look before," he said in his normal voice.

"I was just thinking about nursing and why I was picked for this assignment. Nothing else."

"I've known General Sherman a long time, even butted heads with him on more than one occasion. If he didn't think you were the right person, he wouldn't have chosen you. Relax, everything will be ok," Bear said confidently.

"I should be saying that to you."

"I already know it because you are my nurse; I am in a good hospital with excellent doctors so I have nothing to be concerned about." He paused a moment to catch his breath.

Wearily Bear whispered, "I know General Sherman is anxious to talk to me so I am ready to begin the debriefings."

"I need Dr. Jacobs's approval on this. If he says it's alright, I will contact General Sherman after I have done my nursing duties."

"You know that they are anxious to talk to me," Bear repeated.

"I heard you the first time," I said sternly. "This is a decision that is out of both our hands. Besides, are you in any condition to talk to them after all you have been through? Don't you think this could wait another day?"

"I know the information they want." Bear said persistently.

"It's been a long time. Another few hours can't make a difference," I said knowing what his response would be.

"You would be surprised," he retorted.

"Let me call Dr. Jacobs and get the ball rolling." I picked up the telephone and called Dr. Jacobs. He came down and examined Bear. Dr. Jacobs asked to see me in the hall.

"I don't have a problem with him talking to the brass," he said like he was telling me a secret. "They are breathing down my back to have a debriefing as soon as possible. However, you are his caregiver and you have to be the one who decides how much is too much. Marla, as strange as these sounds, you call the shots with his day-to-day activities. Start with whatever you think is ok and work it up to whatever feels right for him." replied Dr. Jacobs.

"Thanks, Dr. Jacobs."

"I'll be in to check on him later."

Dr. Jacobs left. I entered Bear's room.

"Bear, I need to do my nursing duties. If you feel up to a meeting after I finish, I will call General Sherman.

Bear responded this time as Jimmy Stewart, "You do what you need to do. When you are done, I will tell you how I feel. Howze about that? By the way, have you seen Harvey?" Bear said smiling weakly. He looked exhausted and it wasn't even noon yet.

"Good. Harvey stepped out for a moment." I said smiling.

I knew Major Smith was different than anyone I had ever encountered. I was having feelings for a man I just met. How was this possible? I felt deep in my soul that this man wasn't going to be an average case. No, not at all. Bear wasn't an average man. He was a man who had been to hell and back, a Special Forces Officer who endured time as a POW and God knows what else. I knew it when he first opened those baby blue eyes and stared at me, he was unlike any man I had ever taken care of. As his battered and bruised body lay there in the bed like a shattered doll, I looked into his eyes and I saw his soul. At that moment, I realized I loved him. But wait a minute, I must be nuts. How could I love him? Love at first sight? For me, rational Marla? No! I just met the man but these feelings persisted. They wouldn't go away. I couldn't let my personal feelings jeopardize my professional caretaking. He needed the best the military had to offer.

The brass thought it was me. I was flattered but if I couldn't control these feelings....

I told myself I have to stop thinking these thoughts and concentrate on my job. It was time to start my morning routine.

I changed the bed by rolling the sheet from the side to side careful not to disturb Bear's leg. When I put the new sheet on, I rolled him the other way. The top sheet and blanket were not difficult to change but I had to keep Bear's leg as still as possible. Not an easy thing for one person to do. There was a triangle bar above the bed for Bear to grab on to but Dr. Jacob cautioned me that he should use it as little as possible the first two weeks. I removed the dressings on his back, bathed his beaten, scared body, applied antibacterial ointment and redressed his wounds. His wrists had scabs that I left alone. I helped him brush his teeth and gave him some ice chips to suck on. I changed the surgical dressing on his leg and put a new gown on him. My last chore was to empty the catheter bag.

Lunch had come and gone for both of us. Bear was on a liquid diet. After 6 months in captivity and another 2 weeks in the jungle subsisting on God knows what, his body needed to be reacquainted with food. Chicken broth or beef broth, and tea with honey and lemon were all he could have. Everything had to be measured because he was on intake and output. Every ounce of liquid including the water he drank had to be measured against what was in the Foley to make sure his kidneys functioned correctly.

I had a tray brought up from the cafeteria. I had a sandwich, chips and an ice tea. Freddy was on duty. He knew how to make sandwiches just the way I liked them. He was my favorite cook.

It was mid-afternoon by the time all the hygiene and cleaning was completed. Bear was shivering. I called housekeeping requesting extra blankets be sent to his room. During the interim, I pulled the one blanket and sheet up to his shoulders. He was dozing on and off.

"Are you finished with all your nursing duties?" he said sleepily.

"Yes, how do you feel? Are you in any pain?"

"A little."

"Do you want something for it?"

"No."

"If you want, I will call General Sherman and schedule a meeting for tomorrow 11:00 a.m.," I said.

"Ok," Bear replied in a near whisper.

I sat down in the corner of his room and made the call. Bear was half-awake when I told him that Admiral Lewis and General Sherman would be here at 11:00 a.m. tomorrow sharp.

Bear dozed on and off until early evening. I helped him with his dinner tray which was chicken broth and tea in addition to cherry Jello requested by the Major himself. Bear went to bed at 10:00 p.m. I kept busy reading some PT reports until midnight. Before I retired, I checked the monitors and recorded Bear's vitals. Three times that night, the monitors went off. At 7:00 a.m., I had only three hours sleep. It was time I requested some help.

Chapter 7

The breakfast tray had arrived. Bear began semi-solid food today. His food consisted of two soft boiled eggs, applesauce and a small container of oatmeal. Anywhere I could, I mixed-in non-fat dry milk for added protein. After breakfast, I helped Bear wash his face, comb his hair, brush his teeth, etc. With his personal hygiene completed, I called Peter and asked him to meet me outside his room.

"Peter, I need help," I said exasperated.

"What do you need?"

"You need to remind Admiral Lewis about my problem from nursing school."

"Wouldn't you be a better person to do that?" Peter said not wanting to be put in the middle of a fight.

I was upset that Peter wouldn't go to bat for me. Was it that he didn't want to confront Admiral Lewis? I had heard rumors that Peter didn't back up his staff but I never believed it. Now it made sense that he inherited his position of Chief of Staff instead of actively pursuing it when the rumor circulated that the old Chief of Staff was considering resigning due to health reasons. Peter wasn't a person who actively pursued fixing what was necessary. He was as passive as a cow grazing in a field.

"I would except he might not believe me. I got three

hours sleep last night and not much more the night before. Besides, you're Chief of Staff here."

"Yes, that's true but this is a direct order from the military, not an administrative assignment. I sympathize with you but I don't know what I can do."

He pushed it off as something between the military and me.

"Peter, that's why your input as an outsider is important. Even on a rush basis, it's going to take time to get someone cleared. I really need George."

Reluctantly, Peter replied, "I'll talk to Admiral Lewis when he gets here."

"Peter, you know my file and you know what happened when I didn't get enough sleep in school. I'm not proud of what happened. Thank God my father placed me in rehab and for the Navy honoring its commitment to take me. Despite whatever happens, I may work 12 hours a day at the hospital but I am always able to get at least 7 hours of sleep a night. This is a different situation. Until it is rectified, I am going to need the pills."

"Marla, you just said we both know what happened when you took the pills. I can't risk you getting hooked again," Peter said sternly.

"Precisely my point, but no one is giving me a choice. In order for me to do this job, I need the pills in the interim until I can get some relief. Admiral Lewis knows my record. That is why I went into physical therapy nursing and away from floor nursing."

I paused and looked Peter directly in the eyes and said, "Well, are you going to give me the pills?"

"After I talk to Admiral Lewis and explain the circumstances, we will work on clearing George. Then I will give you a few pills to get through this but only under my strict supervision."

"You don't understand. I need them today. So you better stop him before his briefing with Bear. He will be here at 11:00 a.m."

"I will be here at 11:00 a.m. also." Peter walked away.

"Hey, aren't you forgetting something?" I screamed back.

"Come up at 11:30 a.m. I will have a couple of day's worth of pills for you but that's all," Peter said firmly.

At 11:00 a.m., Admiral Lewis and General Sherman entered Major Smith's room. I started to leave the room but Admiral Lewis stopped me. He wanted me present because the purpose of being Bear's private nurse was to know that he had knowledge of sensitive information in case Bear ever inadvertently spoke of it.

"Permission to speak freely, sir?" I said.

"Permission granted," responded Admiral Lewis.

"Meaning no disrespect, Admiral, but I am a nurse not a soldier. My job is to help people recover from their injuries. You don't need me to listen to the briefings. I need to spend this time doing personal things."

"What things?" he asked.

"Take a shower, wash my hair, shave my legs and armpits for starters," I said without emotion.

Bear tried not to laugh but General Sherman couldn't contain himself and said to Admiral Lewis, "You asked her James and she gave you an honest answer."

Admiral Lewis was not happy with my response but allowed me to leave. Peter was outside the room preparing to knock when I opened the door first. He handed me a bottle with four pills in it. I looked at the bottle before putting it in my pocket. It brought back memories I cared to forget. I needed another solution that did not come in the form of a pill. That solution was a great guy named George.

Everyone called him George but his real name was about

20 letters long. He was 25 years old, 6'5", 265 pounds, and a mixture of black, Hawaiian, Jamaican and about half a dozen other cultures. He was everyone's favorite orderly. He came to Oahu General from Maui six years ago.

Dr. Fong knocked on the Bear's door. Admiral Lewis answered.

"We are about to start a high level briefing, Doctor." "Yes I know," replied Dr. Fong, "but I need to speak to you."

"Can't this wait?" said Admiral Lewis impatiently.

"No it can't. Can you please step into the hall?" said Dr. Fong firmly.

Admiral Lewis got up and walked out of the room.

"Ok, what is it?" he grumbled.

"I'm concerned about Marla," said Peter.

"Concerned about what?"

"Her providing quality nursing care alone to Major Smith."

"Why wouldn't she be able to? She's the best."

"Sleep depravation for one."

"I explained that she needed to give 100% and she agreed."

"Begging the Admiral's pardon, but you probably ordered her. There's a difference," replied Peter rather sternly.

"Major Smith possesses certain information that few people are privy to. Marla possesses extensive nursing skills that few nurses possess. It was a perfect match. We need her to get him back on his feet."

"Eight years ago, Marla almost didn't make it into the Navy because of her addiction to amphetamines. With no sleep, she will be unable to complete her assignment. If I give her uppers for the entire time she is assigned to rehabilitate Major Smith, then she will no doubt have a relapse and be of no use to anyone. It would only take about two weeks of no sleep and pill popping before she is back to where she was in nursing school. This time, it will be a minimum 30 day trip to rehab. She needs help. You don't have to bring in another nurse. Bring in an orderly to help her do the heavy duties such as turning Major Smith, making the bed, bathing him. While he is awake, he doesn't pose a security risk or am I reading the situation wrong? The time you truly need Marla is at night when the Major is sleeping."

Admiral Lewis pondered what he heard for a few moments and then asked, "Do you have someone in mind?"

"I do but you would have to clear him."

"Give me his information and we will start clearance procedures immediately."

Admiral Lewis took George's information and returned to Bear's room.

At 12:30 p.m. Dr. Jacobs broke up the meeting and said that if Major Smith was up to it they could continue again tomorrow at 11:00 a.m. They all agreed to reassemble tomorrow.

It took two weeks for George's permanent clearance to come through. He was assigned to work exclusively for me. When it happened, I received a long needed break. I was grateful when George's temporary clearance came through in a week. The only condition was that George was not to be left alone with Bear. The two days worth of amphetamines were not enough but given the temporary circumstances, and under Dr. Fong's tight monitoring, I was given a one week supply with a one week refill. I used them for two weeks but not the maximum dosage. The pills helped me survive the interim. Even lying down on the cot in the room while George made the bed and turned Bear gave me the additional rest I needed.

Four days after surgery, Bear was weaned from his IV's except the antibiotics. They stayed in for the full 10 days.

Pain was another issue. His pain would be excruciating;

he screamed out like a wounded animal. I never felt as help-less in my career as I felt now. It wasn't just physical pain but psychological pain as well. Even though Bear had a high tolerance for physical pain, at night he would cry out sud-denly like a wolf with its paw caught in a trap. I spoke to Dr. Jacobs about this. He wrote an order to adjust the morphine for each episode but it was a hard thing to watch. It ripped me up inside.

I tried other methods to alleviate the pain. I had an egg crate brought in for Bear to sleep on. This eased the pressure on his back, legs and arms but the pain persisted. I ordered a special pillow for his head but this didn't help either. His body was too battered and abused. Only time would heal Bear's wounds.

Chapter 8

I called my friend, Chaplain Cook who came to Oahu General once a week to visit the veterans in the physical therapy ward.

"Chaplain Cook, do you think you could see my new patient, Major Thomas Smith?" I asked.

"Did he ask to see clergy, Marla?" replied Chaplain Cook.

"No, but I thought that it would be nice for him to have another person to talk to."

"Sure, I'll stop by the next time I am at the hospital."

"Thanks, Chaplain Cook."

I kept thinking to what end would this work out? When Bear was better would he go back to Vietnam? Would he go to the mainland? Does he have a family? A girlfriend? A wife? I put everything out of my mind with the purpose of making him whole again. I didn't know any personal information about Major Smith but I knew one thing, that my feelings for him were genuine. I loved him but how could I love a man I just met? I wasn't sure. Was it sexual? No, not now. It was a love for one human being to another. Major Smith touched my soul which was something no man had ever done. I felt kind of silly to think such a thing but it was true. In 8 years of nursing, I never saw anyone who had suffered so much physical and psychological pain and yet in our talks I would never had known it. If I hadn't been there at night, lived through the nightmares and watched him writhe in pain, I wouldn't have believed he had survived the most horrible atrocity a person could ever know: being held as a prisoner of war, enduring torture, beatings, malnutrition and situations too unimaginable to ponder.

Chaplain Cook dropped by as promised. I left the two alone and waited outside Bear's room until they were finished. He introduced himself to Bear and stayed for 5 minutes. They talked about cars and chess. I didn't know Chaplain Cook liked to play chess and I knew the man for 8 years. Bear asked Chaplain Cook to come back for a game or two and he agreed.

Slowly, the infected welts on his back started to heal. After 10 days of massive IV antibiotics and ointments, I saw some progress but the road to recovery was long and hard. How much scarring there would be was unknown.

The first two weeks at Oahu General were like a yo yo for Bear. For every step forward, he would take two steps back. Aside from the horrible pain, there was the psychological anguish of what he looked like and the physical anguish of not being able to do the smallest things for himself. He hated the fact that he couldn't use a regular toilet. The Foley and the bed pan were an embarrassment to him. He despised the situation of having someone else bathe him in bed, especially a woman. I asked Dr. Jacobs if I could remove the catheter when the IV antibiotics came out and he said yes. He told me if Bear needed help urinating, I would have to help him with the urinal because his leg could not be disturbed.

The majority of my patients were men. My experience over the years has been that men had to be independent. It was difficult for any man, especially one as resourceful as Bear, to be totally dependent on a woman for the smallest of needs. I sensed he had issues with this but he never said a word to me. That's why I wanted George to help me, especially to talk to Bear, man to man and let him know he could ask George for help with anything and he would do it. I knew Bear was Special Forces. I read the file. I met many Marines, Army, Air Force, Navy, Army Rangers and Green Berets in therapy. Of course I was just their Physical Therapy nurse. The ego/macho thing was there but at a lesser level. These men were more independent with taking care of their physical needs. They knew they had to listen to me and my nurses because we were the ones who would get them back on their feet and out of the hospital. For them, the hospital was their temporary hell which kept them from going forward with their life.

Bear's situation was different because he was lying in a bed recuperating from surgery and other wounds. He had been through six months of hell in a prison camp plus two weeks wandering in a jungle. This made the hospital look like a vacation. The reality was it was no vacation. It was another prison that Bear needed to escape from.

Bear continued his debriefing for two weeks following the surgery. It was hard to make Admiral Lewis and General Sherman see the same man that I saw the other 22 ½ hours a day when I was alone with him. All they were interested in was information and to hell with what he had been through. That steamed me to no end but this was life in the military; a path which Bear and I chose to walk in our own way.

During one of the briefings Bear asked Admiral Lewis, "Tell me a little about Marla."

Admiral Lewis replied, "Well, son, if you want to know about her personal life, ask her. Even though she is a private person, she is one of the most forthright persons I have ever met, if you come right out and ask her."

"Come on, can't you at least tell me if she is seeing someone?" said Bear almost pleading.

"Sorry Major but if you want to know anything about Marla, you will have to ask her yourself."

On the 10th day, the IV antibiotics were removed and now it was time to remove the Foley. I have done many catheter removals over my career but this was different. As much as I tried not to be uncomfortable, I was. I had already seen every inch of Bear's body. I had feelings for him which I knew were love. This love was real and not pity but my love for him could not interfere with my professional nursing duties. I had a job to do. I felt that if this situation was not handled correctly, this could be extremely embarrassing for Bear and me.

I decided to wait until after dinner. George was now assisting in Bear's bathing and bedpan needs but removing a Foley was a nursing duty. Trying to be extremely professional, I went over to the bed with my tray.

"Bear," I began, "Since the IVs have been disconnected, you are not going to need your Foley any more so I have been given orders to remove it. A urinal will be put on the side of your bed for your use. George or I can help you if you need assistance.

"No offense, but is there any chance Dr. Jacobs could take it out?"

"No offense taken but this is considered a nursing duty. If you want, I will call Dr. Jacobs and ask him to come down." I turned and headed for the phone.

Bear called out. "No, never mind. I've been stuck, probed, cut, beaten, whipped, tortured, burned, hung by my arms and legs tied together in front of me, what the hell is a catheter removal going to do?" he said resigning himself to another humiliating procedure.

Bear shot me a quick glance. I tried to hide how

uncomfortable I was but he had already seen my face so all I could say was, "I'll be quick."

I went over to the bed with my tray and within 15 seconds I had cleaned the area and removed the catheter.

"That's it." I said as I took my tray away from the bed.

"That was fast. Thank you."

"You're welcome," I replied as I left the room. I couldn't have left fast enough.

On the 12th day, Bear received a call from his mother in Connecticut. She had been traveling in Europe and just got word her son was injured. She wanted to be on the next flight out but General Sherman asked her to wait at least another three weeks. She reluctantly agreed. Too bad General Sherman didn't say four or six.

I had outlined a nutritional plan – vitamins, minerals, protein and calcium. Dr. Jacobs reviewed the plan and approved it. I wanted Major Smith to gain weight so I devised a good tasting nutritious protein drink. At lunch it contained blended fruits with vitamin, mineral and protein supplements. At dinner, it contained blended vegetables with added protein powder. I asked Freddy to find the best fruits and vegetables each day, blend them together and send them up. The guy was a genius. He found the best fruit that never ever made it to the cafeteria such as pineapples, mangos, apples, bananas, grapes, peaches, pears, oranges: the list went on and on. He even surprised me with blueberries, strawberries and raspberries.

I had already started Bear on range of motion exercises in bed along with some stretching exercises to keep the muscles of the unaffected limbs from atrophying but I knew that without everyday movement there would be some decrease in mobility when he was ready to progress to physical therapy. The next goal was to tailor a small weight lifting program for his arms and upper body that would help him look and feel better. This was a bit more of a challenge but I attacked the problem head on. At this point, George had been on board almost a week.

With George's help, Bear was now able to do some hygiene for himself. This was a great morale booster. He still couldn't use a shower which bothered him a great deal and since he wasn't able to get out the bed, he wasn't able to go down to the smoking room to enjoy a cigarette. This was something he desperately wanted. These problems were about to be solved.

Chapter 9

After a meeting with Jose Ramirez, the physical therapist assigned to the case, Dr. Jacobs and I met with Bill from engineering. Bill could fix or design just about anything. I described my idea of a special wheelchair and he sketched something out. I asked Bill if he could build it and how long it would take. He said a week. I told him I needed it in three days and three days later, I had my chair.

I knew that this would make a tremendous change in Bear's attitude. I told George that when he came tomorrow not to bathe Bear but to transfer him to this special wheelchair. The wheelchair was just like any other except the right leg was bolstered in a steel cage to keep Bear's leg straight out and reinforced at the foot. The seat was set slightly higher than a regular chair, reinforced to be firmer, and the wheels were made of wider rubber than other wheelchairs to allow it to go into the shower and give extra support against slippage. This allowed Bear to shower in the wheelchair without trying to transfer him to a shower chair which could not support his healing leg. I asked Dr. Jacobs to sit in the chair before Bear tried it because Dr. Jacobs and Bear were almost the same height but Dr. Jacobs was 40 pounds heavier. I knew if it would support Dr. Jacobs, it would support Bear. The support from the top of his leg to his foot was solid. Bill agreed to check the wheels once a week and lubricate as necessary. To solve the drainage problem, a few small holes were drilled into the hard seat material. After showering, the seat was changed to a regular wheelchair seat with an egg crate used as padding.

The next day George came in and told Bear that he wasn't bathing him. It was time he went to the showers like any other patient. The chair was placed parallel to the bed. George picked up Bear like a normal person picked up a sack of potatoes and put him in the wheelchair. When George arrived at the shower room, I was waiting at the handicapped stall. I pulled out three large garbage bags I got from housekeeping. I pulled back Bear's gown exposing his right leg. To keep the injured leg from getting wet, I wrapped it in the garbage bags from the foot to the groin area. Then I removed the bandages on Bear's back. I left while George undressed him and wheeled him into the shower. George handed him the removable showerhead, a bar of soap and wash cloth, reached in, slowly turned on the warm water, then a little higher till he found the right pressure. I came back with two bath towels, two hand towels, four wash cloths, a clean gown, a robe, and a bottle of hair shampoo. I left them on the bench next to the stall.

"George, page me when you're done so I can remove the garbage bags from his leg," I said as I walked away from the shower area.

George stood guard. Bear asked for his help once to wash his back. Due to the scabs, George said he couldn't actually do that. All he was allowed to do was put a cool trickle of water on it. George told him I would be taking care of that area. Twenty minutes later, George paged me. He had put a bath towel around Bear's waist. When I returned, only his upper body was exposed. I washed my hands. I took the 2nd bath towel, dried Bear's hair, face, neck, and chest area.

I opened the steel cage, removed the garbage bags, took a clean wash cloth with soap and washed Bear's lower leg and foot. I dried the area. I grabbed another washcloth and washed and dried his upper leg and applied a clean surgical dressing. I took another cloth to wash his back. I dried it being careful not to disturb the scabs and dressed the open wounds. I used the 4th cloth to wash my hands from the anti-biotic ointment. I left and waited by the PT door. I tried to give Bear as much privacy as I could even though I knew every time I helped him, I felt like I was invading his personal space. It was important to have George help Bear do as much of his personal hygiene as possible. This was one time being on the sideline was fine with me. Five minutes later, the three of us went back to his room.

George put Bear back in bed. I dried off the wheelchair with Bear's bath towel. Bill came down to check the chair. All was well. Bill put the regular seat on the chair and I put the egg crate on the seat. George transferred Bear back into the chair. That first week Bear spent a few hours a day in the chair gradually working his way up to a full day. The fact that he could now shower made him feel less dependent on me. Bear needed to feel independent. George wheeled him to the day room to have a smoke after showering and then outside for a ride around the grounds. Bear began meeting with a soldier I never saw before in the smoking room a couple of days after he became mobile. The two would chat for 20 or 30 minutes every day, exchange notes and then the man would leave. This man visited everyday throughout Bear's recovery. I hoped Bear would tell me who he was but I never asked. A man needs some secrets. God knows, he hasn't had any since he came here. If this was something he wanted kept private, I respected that.

The fresh air and opportunity to have a couple of cigarettes immensely improved Bear's outlook. When he returned to his room, he pulled his bedside tray table over to his wheelchair and offered to give chess lessons. George took Bear up on his offer and spent at least an hour a day "competing" with him.

By the end of the first month, Bear's pain became more manageable. His leg was healing slowly considering his general health when he arrived.

At the end of the 5th week, I finally had control of his daytime schedule. He was down to only one pain episode per night and he seemed more rested in the day needing only a nap before dinner. His schedule was:

7:00 a.m.	Wake up, vitals taken
7:15 a.m.	Breakfast
8:00 a.m.	Shower with George's assistance
9:00 a.m.	Break time, play chess or checkers or cards on the patio, smoke
11:00 a.m.	Military briefings if scheduled
12:30 p.m.	Lunch with protein drink, smoke
2:00 p.m.	Physical therapy beginning with light weights
3:00 p.m.	Nap
6:00 p.m.	Dinner
7:00 p.m.	Watch TV, talk, write letters, smoke
11:00 p.m.	Vitals taken, lights out

Chapter 10

Things had begun to settle down until Bear's mother insisted on visiting.

Mrs. Patricia Smith was the widow of William Smith, Bear's father who had retired as a full-bird Colonel in the United States Army. At 60 years old, she stood 5'8" tall, with blond hair, steely blue eyes and an attitude as rough as any military man I had ever met. As beautiful as she was tough, she knew how to get what she wanted from the system. She busied herself with the military wives' auxiliary groups but her son was her primary concern. Not long after I met her, I found out that the pit-bull attitude was just a façade. When it came to her son, she was like melted butter.

Mrs. Smith arrived at Oahu General only to be held back by General Sherman until Dr. Jacobs could prepare her for how her son looked. Dr. Jacobs introduced her to me before she went into his room. I felt sorry for her because she was about to see what kind of hell her son had endured. I kept thinking no mother should see her son like that.

Bear had regained some color in his face and put on three pounds but was about forty pounds off his previous weight. The bruising from the IVs had healed but his back was still a mess. I made sure Bear was dressed in pajamas rather than the standard issue gown. This lessened the scariness of his appearance by covering his healing leg. He shaved but his face was drawn and gaunt. The one thing that never diminished was the sparkle in those sea blue eyes. Mrs. Smith needed to see that and forget the rest but I knew that was impossible.

Even though Mrs. Smith was told everything, she didn't understand the gravity of her son's injuries until she saw him.

"Hello Thomas," she said walking over to the bed, trying to hide her tears.

"Hello mother."

"I'm so happy to see you," she replied as she reached her hand out to his.

"I'm happy to see you too," as Thomas took her hand. "I can see that whatever they said to prepare you as to what I look liked wasn't enough. I can read it in your face."

"I'm sorry, Thomas. You were always the one person I couldn't keep my feelings from."

"It was worse a month ago. You probably wouldn't have recognized me at all. I really have improved," Thomas said trying to sound optimistic.

"Son, are you in any pain?"

"A little at night but it is getting better. I never realized the things I took for granted until I couldn't do them for myself but I've made progress since I've been here," Thomas replied trying to sound upbeat.

"Is there anything I can do to help you?" asked Patricia fighting back the tears.

"No mother I have the best care anywhere. Maybe, if you think of it, you can pick up some magazines. That would help pass the time. You know I like any of the car magazines, or Time, or Newsweek."

"Anything for you," Patricia said. She bent down and gave Thomas a kiss on his forehead. "I know you are on a schedule. I'm going to be in town for as long as you want me here. General Sherman's aide is taking me to my hotel. I'll see you again tomorrow."

"Mother, call first. Every day is different when it comes to doing the simplest of things."

"Ok, I will."

Mrs. Smith put her hand up to his face. Thomas reached out and pulled her hand toward his lips and kissed it. She put his hand down, turned and left the room. I followed her out and went over to see if she was alright. She grabbed me and started to cry.

I held her for a few seconds until she backed away.

She dabbed her eyes and said, "I'm sorry. I wasn't prepared to see Thomas like that. I know you told me but I didn't understand until I saw him."

"It's alright," I said trying to reassure her that what she felt was normal.

"Lt. Bristol, is he getting the best care? Please be honest with me," said Mrs. Smith. She had gained her composure and was back in control of herself.

"Yes, Mrs. Smith, he is getting excellent care here. General Sherman wouldn't have him here if he wasn't. If you are still concerned, I could arrange a briefing for you."

"No, that won't be necessary. I can see in your demeanor that you are very efficient and Thomas is receiving the care he needs. I don't know how much more I could do to help him."

"You could get him the magazines he wanted. It's pretty boring watching TV or listening to the radio and the hospital library doesn't exactly have the greatest book selections. The magazines would cheer him up immensely."

"Thank you Lt. Bristol."

"You can call me Marla."

"You can call me Patricia."

Whatever preconceived notions I had from conversations with General Sherman disappeared. Patricia was a mother concerned about her son. Period. End of discussion.

Two days later, Mrs. Smith returned with ten magazines. She went in to see her son.

"Thomas, here are some magazines you wanted. I told the man at the book store that if you want more, he should deliver them and send me the bill. General Sherman has asked me to return home but has promised to keep me updated about your condition. I agreed because I can't be of any use to you here and I don't want to get in the way. I love you so much, son."

"I love you too, mother. You are doing the right thing. You belong with your friends running your charities. I have a long healing time ahead of me and there is nothing you can do to shorten that."

Patricia kissed Thomas' forehead. As she turned to leave, she said, "Thomas, you have a beautiful nurse who cares about you very much. You are very lucky to have her."

"I know mother, I know," Bear replied smiling.

Chapter 11

About the 6th week, Bear and I were spending every evening watching TV and talking after dinner. Since we both enjoyed Frank Sinatra, Dean Martin and jazz, we would take turns picking music for the following night together. I had a large collection at home but since I wasn't able to leave the hospital, George stopped by my house and picked up my records. Peter had a record player in his office that I permanently borrowed for the evening's music.

We also enjoyed watching westerns and Humphrey Bogart movies. Movie night was once a week in the cafeteria. Two of Bogies' movies were on the agenda: "Casablanca" and "To Have and Have Not." Bear couldn't get enough of "Bonanza." There we were – the two of us – watching the Cartwrights (Little Joe, Ben, Adam, and Hoss and don't forget Hop Sing, the cook). Each week, it was a different crisis on the ranch. For that one hour, once a week, we were transported to a simpler place and time.

Bear loved chess but I didn't know how to play so he taught me. We also played cards and scrabble. Dr. Jacobs, Bear, George and I enjoyed a lively game of 7-card stud one evening. I felt that anything to stimulate the mind was therapy for Bear.

Chapter 12

I received an emergency call about a patient I had rehabbed two years ago. He was threatening suicide. I had permission from Admiral Lewis to leave Bear to try to defuse the situation. I called George to cover for me. I also made Dr. Jacobs aware of the situation and he was on-call should any medical situation arose.

"So Bear, what shall we do today?" Do you want to go to the smoking room? Play some cards? Chess?" said George.

"How about we get to know each other?" replied Bear.

"Fine with me. What do you want to talk about?"

"Marla."

George squirmed in his seat.

"I'd rather not if you don't mind," he replied.

"Why not?" said Bear inquisitively.

"I just don't."

"I want to know more about her. Please tell me."

"You need to ask her yourself," said George wishing he could leave the room.

"I can't."

"Why not? She's easy to talk to. She will tell you anything you want to know."

"I heard that from someone else. You don't understand, George. I love her. She is unlike any other woman I've ever met. Those compassionate brown eyes and reassuring smile told me that I would get through this fiasco from the first day I regained consciousness. I looked like hell but despite my physical appearance her eyes confidently conveyed that everything would be ok. She is sweet and kind but there is an incredible strength to her. When she speaks, people jump but at the same time, she is a team player devoted solely to the care of her patients. Lt. Bristol's devotion to her profession is rare. Until I met Marla, I had only seen it among my Special Forces buddies.

George, before this hospitalization, I was wounded in the shoulder and recuperated in Japan. The care was excellent but not like what I received from Marla. I realized my rank, security clearance and possession of certain knowledge caused a change in my status and Marla was chosen to drop everything to nurse me back to health. Maybe that makes it fate. I don't know things like that. All I know is that I love her. What do I do or say to her? Maybe she has a boyfriend or husband. I don't see a ring but that doesn't mean anything. Is she seeing anyone?"

"No, but please realize that Marla is a very private person but if you ask her, she will tell you whatever you want to know. I don't like to talk about her without her knowledge." George started to bite his nails, something he hadn't done in years. "Can we please change the subject?"

"No, I need to talk to someone and you are the only one I can confide in. These feelings I have for her are real. You believe me, don't you George?" Bear said.

"Yes, I believe you but I have seen men fall in love with the nurses that help them get well. It happens all the time. Once they are well, they return to their lives. It turns out to be a temporary feeling."

"Not with me, no, no, not me. I don't fall in and out of

love. Do you think Marla could have feelings for me? Maybe not now but when I am well?”

“Bear, this is something you need to talk to her about.”

“I don't even know anything about her except her qualifications as a nurse. I don't know where was she born, does she have any brothers and sisters, you know stuff like that.”

“You need to have a conversation with her. She will answer any and all questions you ask. Just pick some evening when the two of you are alone and start talking. I guarantee she will tell you what you want to know.”

“Thanks George. Now how about a game of chess?”

The boys played chess for the next four hours until I returned. I managed to talk the suicidal veteran into receiving some psychiatric help.

I was about to find out what happened while I was gone.

Chapter 13

It was time Dr. Jacobs ordered an x-ray of Bear's leg. I didn't expect much healing and I was correct. I figured at least another 6-7 weeks and it turned out Bear was right on schedule. Bear was gaining 1-2 pounds a week but was still 35 pounds off his old weight. With the consent of Dr. Jacobs, I now had Bear lifting 10 pound weights in his wheelchair to begin strengthening his arms. His back was almost healed. Dr. Jacobs gave me the green light to do massage therapy on that area. Because the scabs were still an issue, I did the massage. I couldn't risk someone else accidentally knocking them off early plus I had experience working around damaged areas.

After 6 weeks of being together day and night, Bear initiated small talk with me but I knew there were more questions he wanted answers to.

I answered his questions but I had some of my own which I wanted answered. I didn't want to press the situation so I waited a couple more weeks before I asked him my questions.

Early one evening during our 8th week together, I returned with a stack of reports to review. Bear eyed me as I walked across the room. I saw him out of the corner of my eye watching me from the moment I entered the room but

I focused on the reports I carried. I put them down on the desk, turned on the desk lamp and reviewed each of them one at a time. Bear was much more interested in an in-depth conversation than TV.

"Marla, I'd like to talk instead of watching TV tonight? Do you think you could review your reports later?"

"Tonight is 'Bonanza.' Are you sure?" I replied in a surprise tone of voice.

"Yes, I'm sure," he said laughing.

"Ok, what do you want to talk about?" I got up from my desk and pulled my chair close to the bed.

"I don't know. Nothing in particular."

"Well, I… I need a topic. You go first," I said.

"Ok, but I don't know what to say," replied Bear.

"Neither do I. Look, it was your idea to talk instead of watching 'Bonanza,' so something has to be on your mind?"

"You have been my nurse for two months now and I only know a few things about you. I'm sure you know everything about me."

"Not everything Bear." When I said that, I looked up and I caught Bear staring at me.

"Please call me Thomas."

"Alright, Thomas. Where do I begin? I like to play scrabble, 7-card stud and now chess. I enjoy exercising. I try to ride the stationary bike in the therapy room when I can. I read mostly fiction books, especially mysteries. I enjoy crossword puzzles but I do the easy ones. I don't have time for the hard ones. I study Karate. I am currently a brown belt and have participated in a couple of tournaments. I was working toward my black belt but it's currently been put on hold.

"Because of me?"

"Yes, for now, but that's ok. I was overwhelmed with

work and other issues before you entered the picture. Not participating in tournaments right now is fine with me."

"Why Karate?"

"Uh, it's great therapy. It also helps establish balance in the body. When you are able, I will show you some balance movements. I know you are a Special Forces Officer and you probably received top defense training. For me, I use Karate as a means of applying myself in body, mind and spirit. Balance is necessary in all areas of life. So changing the subject, tell me what do you like to do?"

"I like to fish and play golf. It's been a long time since I have done either. What about food? Let me guess. You are a vegetarian," Thomas said.

"Not by a long shot," I said with a half smile. "I eat just about anything. I'm not a fan of mussels, oysters or poi but aside from those three things, I can't think of anything else I wouldn't eat. I stick mostly to fish, fruits and vegetables but I don't mind a good steak now and then. What do you like?"

"I'm not into poi either. Growing up I was a finicky eater but after being in the military and eating their food, everything is good." When I went fishing, I would catch trout and cook it right there at the lake. There is nothing better than fresh caught trout pan fried over an open flame. I also enjoy a good steak when I can get it."

"Well, when you can walk, we will celebrate with special food. You get to pick the place," I said trying not to sound excited.

"Sounds delicious. The only thing that tastes good around here is your protein drinks. At least you vary the flavor."

"Thank Freddy for that. I'm sorry the hospital food isn't great but if it's any consolation, I'm stuck with it too."

We looked at one another and laughed for a moment.

"It really feels good to laugh again after such a long time of pain and darkness," replied Thomas.

My heart ached for something to say but all I could do was nod. We talked for a while about what kind of sports and movies we enjoyed. Bear started doing his imitations for me. What a talent he had for imitating the great ones.

Jimmy Cagney – "You dirty rat."

Humphrey Bogart – "You played it for her, now play it for me. If she can stand it, so can I."

Yogi Bear – "Hey Boo Boo, give me that picnic basket."

Jimmy Stewart –"Has anyone seen Harvey?"

I thought for sure that when he left the military, he would get a job in Hollywood doing imitations of famous people.

"Marla," Thomas said inquisitively, "I noticed you don't have a ring on your finger so I assume you are not married?"

"I'm not," I replied wondering where this was going.

"Boyfriend?"

"No time for that. I'm married to the military." Quickly turning the questioning around I said, "And you Thomas, are you married?"

"No."

"Girlfriend?"

"No, not with spending 3 tours of duty in NAM."

The two of us looked at each other without anything else to say so I turned on the TV and we watched the last half hour of "Bonanza" together.

Chapter 14

It was now the 10th week and Dr. Jacobs wanted another x-ray to see if Thomas had made any substantial progress. The x-ray showed 85% healing. Dr. Jacobs was pleased. At the 12th week, the x-ray showed 95%. At the 13th week, the bone was as close to 100% healed as it would be on either side of the metal rod.

Now Thomas's biggest challenge awaited him. Rehabilitation! I would be doing what I was best at.

The special wheelchair was history. George took Thomas for a shower in a regular wheelchair. No garbage bag today. As soon as he came out of the shower, I worked on massaging his leg. I wanted to get an added jump on physical therapy. The warm water helped to stretch the muscles. The PT plan had been outlined and approved by all parties. Thomas needed to progress slowly. The right leg muscles had substantially atrophied and needed to be brought back to normal but this had to progress slowly or there would be possible muscle or ligament tears. The left leg was in fair condition but after three months of non-use, it, too had atrophied. Thomas would begin therapy with massage then on to the whirlpool. Eventual light weight bearing machines would be added. Thomas's stamina would be the barometer of how much therapy he would receive per day.

It was at this time that I proposed to Admiral Lewis that Thomas stay alone at night. His pain was being controlled these days by aspirin with more intense pain controlled by codeine. I was deeply concerned about Thomas' mental state, specifically issues regarding his POW days but I had no basis to bring such concerns to Admiral Lewis or General Sherman. Since the early days, there has been no screaming at night, no calling out. He did have an unusual physical movement of shaking his left leg while sleeping but that could be a number of things. It didn't mean it was a reaction to his captivity.

Admiral Lewis balked at my proposal to leave Thomas alone at night not explaining to me that he was thinking the same thing. I told Admiral Lewis either George or someone else who was cleared like Dr. Jacobs would be on call. At some point, Thomas would have to be left alone. After a discussion with Dr. Jacobs, Admiral Lewis spoke to Thomas and informed him I would be off from 11:00 p.m. to 7:00 a.m. but someone would remain on call. Thomas seemed fine with the new arrangement.

The second night after his therapy began, I said good night to Thomas and left for the evening. Before leaving, I spoke to George.

"If you need me, I am a phone call away," I said as I walked out of Thomas' room.

I took my pager and left.

I don't know why I took the pager. George was there. Dr. Jacobs was there but for some strange reason I took my 'electronic leash.'

For the first time in three months, I was going home. It felt a little strange so I stopped off at the Tiki Bar. I had so many good times there with my nurses. I just needed to unwind and home wasn't the place to do it.

It was 11:10 p.m. when I walked in. I looked around like it was my first time in the place. After three months of being cooped up in a hospital 24 hours a day, 7 days a week, the shock of seeing humanity was overwhelming. Scantily clad women were sipping their tropical drinks; men in their outlandish tropical shirts gawking at them. There were a few service men on leave drinking beer and laughing. I went over to the bar and ordered my usual 7 and 7. Kono, the regular bartender, welcomed me like his long lost sister. He even came from behind the bar and gave me a hug.

"Long time stranger," said Kono.

"It's been a while," I said as I pulled the barstool close to the bar.

"Heard you were working on a special person, a real VIP Major?"

"Now Kono, you know I can't talk about it," I said as I grabbed a handful of peanuts out of the bowl.

"I understand. Are you hungry?" Kono asked.

"Definitely, can you order me some poppers?"

I loved jalapeño poppers. Poppers were jalapeños stuffed with cheese and deep fried. Not the healthiest dish to eat but then I didn't eat it every day.

"Sure, anything for you girl." Kono yelled to the runner to get an order of poppers brought to the bar.

"At this hour?" said the runner.

"Just do it; it's for a special customer," Kono replied.

"You little flirt. Kono, I need to be out at midnight. I've got an early shift so will you call me a cab?"

"No problem."

It was weird sitting alone, having a drink without my girls whooping it up with me. I turned to the left and saw part of the daily paper lying on the stool next to me. I reached over and picked it up. It was the first paper I had seen since the day Thomas entered my life.

The poppers came hot from the oven just the way I liked them. I was reading the paper and eating when my pager went off. I had only been gone 45 minutes so I turned it down to see if I would be paged again. George was on-shift. I was sure it was a mistake. If it wasn't, I would know soon enough. Two minutes later it went off again.

"Kono, I have to go. How much do I owe you?"

"Nothing, I'll take care of it. You get back to work now."

I ran out of the bar, grabbed a cab and went back to Oahu General. George was waiting outside Thomas' room. Dr. Jacobs was inside.

"George, what happened?"

"Dr. Jacobs will tell you. I just couldn't handle it. I'm sorry, Marla." George was visible shaken.

"Calm down, just tell me," I said trying to comfort George.

"Bear cried out. You could hear him down the hall," George said.

Dr. Jacobs came out of Thomas' room. "This was out of George's league so he called me. I sedated him. Then I paged you. This wasn't a pain type of scream like physical pain. This was different. You know what I mean?" Dr. Jacobs stared intensely at me waiting for the answer he already knew was coming.

"Yes, like psychological pain. He hadn't shown all the signs to me. I wasn't sure if he was having flashbacks relating to his time in NAM. I needed to test my theory by leaving him with someone else. I had to see if this would happen. As long as I was here all the time, I was his security blanket." I paused, "I hoped this wouldn't happen. I want him to get some psychological therapy. Dr. Jacobs, can you help him get some counseling?" I asked with great concern.

"He may resist. I could be wrong because I don't know him as well as you do, but I do know one thing. If he opens up to anyone, it would be you. You will have to be there to bring whatever is bothering him to the surface."

"Dr. Jacobs, I'm not a psych nurse. I'm not even a critical

care nurse. I was assigned to this case because the Navy felt I was the best person to handle the situation and they upped my clearance," I replied exasperated.

"You are and have been the best person to handle this job. Even though you aren't a psych nurse, you are a human being. Get him to open up. Start when the opportunity presents itself and stop when he says stop. I can't help you gauge this. Admiral Lewis, George, General Sherman, even his mother can't help him. It has to be you. After three months of 'round the clock care with the man, there isn't anybody who knows him better or he has felt safer with." Dr. Jacobs grabbed me by the shoulders and gave me a reassuring tap.

"You're right," I said reluctantly.

"By the way, where were you when I paged? You weren't home. I called there first."

"I stopped at the Tiki bar to have a drink."

"First night away from this place and you picked the Tiki bar?" replied Dr. Jacobs with surprise. "Well, I don't think I would have gone home either especially if I were single."

"I found it hard to go to a place I haven't seen in three months. Good thing Dr. Fong had his accountant take over my bill paying and his housekeeper came over and emptied the fridge or who knows what kind of things would be growing in there. It would be Biology 101 all over again," I said with a smirk.

Dr. Jacobs smiled.

"Now, I need engineering to bring my bed back," I said as I headed to the phone.

"It's on the way. I called them after I called you. Good night, Marla."

"Good night, Dr. Jacobs."

I went into Thomas' room. He was sound asleep.

Chapter 15

I woke up just before 7:00 a.m. Thomas was still asleep. I went over and took his vitals. At the touch of my hand, he opened his eyes.

"Good morning," I said.

"Hi."

Thomas turned his head and saw my bed was back in the corner of the room. He looked back at me and said, "When I went to sleep, your bed was gone. Now I'm awake and your bed is back. What gives?"

"Let's talk over breakfast. I'm famished," I said changing the subject.

Breakfast came and I was upfront with everything. Carefully and with much compassion, I asked, "Do you want to talk about anything that might be bothering you? If not, I can find someone else for you to talk to. Maybe Chaplain Cook?"

"No, I don't want to talk to anybody. I don't even know if there is anything to talk about," replied Thomas in an irritated tone of voice.

"I know that I can't possibly understand what you've been through and I won't sit here and patronize you and say I do. One thing I am is a good listener. For my nurses, I have been like a sister or a mother when it comes to boyfriend or husband problems. For my patients, I have been their mother, father, brother, sister and even pastor because I know that to heal the body, the mind has to be healed too," I said calmly.

"I know you want to help me let go of my demons from NAM but unfortunately, they will never leave me. They are ingrained in me permanently. Only I can deal with them, face them and slay them like a warrior slays dragons. I appreciate your concern, Marla. I really do," said Thomas ending the subject.

Thomas finished speaking. Nothing further was said between us. I paged George to take him down to the shower area.

I went upstairs to Dr. Fong's private bathroom and took a long hot shower and washed my hair. It felt good to let my thoughts wander and my body relax under the pulsing showerhead. After I finished, I went downstairs and met Thomas in the therapy room. I had George take Thomas to the whirlpool machine after his shower. Thirty minutes later, Thomas went over to the massage table and I gave him a gentle massage. Then on to light weights. It would take time but Thomas would finally be able to see the progress he was making on his body. It wouldn't be long before his physique would return to the way it was before he was a POW. His mind – that would be another problem. Maybe a visit from Chaplain Cook would help. It certainly wouldn't hurt. I went to see Chaplain Cook the next day.

Chaplain Cook was in his office reading when I knocked on the study door.

"Come in," he said in his polite tone of voice.

In 8 years of friendship I never heard Chaplain Cook get angry, yell or say a disparaging word about anyone. If anyone lived the way a religious person was supposed to live – follow the Ten Commandments, not hurt anyone, be kind and considerate, love your neighbor as yourself – it was Chaplain Cook.

"Yes Marla, what can I do for you?" said Chaplain Cook smiling.

"Thomas is over in the smoking area which gave me the opportunity to come see you. I know you play chess with him a couple times a week. I was wondering if he opened up to you about what happened earlier this week?"

"No, he hasn't said anything to me."

"He's been having nightmares from his time in NAM. He won't open up to me. I thought he might say something to you."

"Marla, I play chess with Thomas. That's as far as our relationship has gone. I don't think I'm the person he's going to open up to. If he does decide to speak about that part of his life, I believe it would be you he would choose."

"Any chance of you putting a bug in his ear? I am here to help him physically, mentally and emotionally."

"I can't make any promises but if the opportunity presents itself, I will put a bug in his ear as you so eloquently put it. Don't worry, Marla. It will work itself out. It always does."

"Thanks, Chaplain Cook. I appreciate your time."

"That's what I'm here for."

Chapter 16

As the days passed, Thomas continued to put on weight and the therapy time was extended a little longer each day. I watched Thomas regain his muscular stature over the weeks of physical therapy and my eyes went beyond a professional interest to pure fantasy. I saw a body that went from skin and bones to rock hard muscles: rippled-abdominal muscles, arm muscles that had tripled in size and legs muscles had regained their former stature. He looked like the Greek God, Adonis.

Thomas had not discussed the outburst with me or anyone else. I would not be able to sleep at home until the issue was resolved. After three years of working with injured Vietnam Veterans, I felt deep down that Thomas would never open up. There would always be that wall between us.

Chaplain Cook continued to play chess twice a week with Thomas. One particular day, Thomas had a horrible therapy session and came back to the room very depressed.

"Knock, knock. Thomas, it's Chaplain Cook. Are you up for a match?"

"I'll try. Things didn't go well for me today in therapy."

"Maybe you are due for a change of luck."

"Maybe."

As the game progressed, Chaplain Cook decided to

chance it and let Thomas know he was more than a chess partner.

"I know I haven't known you long and our acquaintance has been confined to chess but if you need someone to talk to, I'm always available," said Chaplain Cook waiting for an answer. "Marla is a great listener too. I've known her since the beginning of her military career and even though she is only 28, her job has matured her beyond her years."

"And who does she talk to when she needs an ear?"

"Usually me. That's what Chaplains do; they listen and then give advice when asked."

"Well Chaplain, what words of wisdom do you have for me today?" said Thomas trying not to sound sarcastic.

"It depends. I know you aren't religious. I am not a Chaplain who crams religion down a person's throat but if you would allow me to drop off a book later, you might find some comfort in it."

"And what book is that?"

"The Book of Psalms. Is that ok?"

"Sure."

Nothing more was said and the chess game continued.

The next day Chaplain Cook dropped off the book while Thomas was in therapy.

Chapter 17

As Thomas became more independent, I had more time to catch up on my PT reports and other problems that happened during my absence. Due to everyone's pitching in, I was able to maintain my position as the State of Hawaii PT Nursing Director. My staff was the best in the business. The problem cases were brought to me for review and the balance of the cases were handled by the PT nursing managers at each hospital.

It had been almost five months since Thomas was brought in. Therapy was going well; his weight was returning to normal. His leg muscles had improved as he did his curls. He started out bench pressing 40 pounds and eventually he was doing 200. As he progressed on the machines, I worked with him on maneuvering around on crutches. During therapy, he would use the parallel bars. He still used the shower chair as a preventive measure to keep from falling. Thomas' spirits seemed high at times but once in a while, I would see his concentration break for a moment. He seemed distant but when I called his name he would answer and continue with what we were doing. I sensed that during that break he was back in NAM, thinking about his captivity, the beatings and his escape from the camp but without him opening up, I didn't know for sure.

The further along Thomas proceeded in his recovery, the harder it became for me to contain my feelings for him. My love for him grew more each day. I tried to squelch those feelings but it was obvious to my co-workers how I felt. These feelings disrupted my concentration which led to errors in my reports. When these errors were pointed out, I made up excuses that I was tired or not feeling well.

Thomas asked Dr. Jacobs for permission to leave the hospital because he wanted to have dinner with me alone. Admiral Lewis sent a staff car to pick us up. Admiral Lewis suggested an Italian restaurant near the hospital. Thomas wanted to go later so we could watch the sun set on the patio. Since it was summer, sunset was around 8:30 p.m. Thomas "heard" I liked white carnations so he asked Admiral Lewis to buy me one.

Thomas told me that he wanted to talk but not at the hospital. I had promised a special meal and now he wanted to cash in on that promise. General Sherman stopped by the hospital with a casual outfit for Thomas to wear: black slacks and a white polo shirt. Thomas had just transferred to the walker and tried not to let using this contraption bother him as he left the hospital. He invited me to dinner at the "Villa Sorrento" for the following night. Pick up time was 8:00 p.m. I could hardly wait.

The next day arrived. At 8:00 p.m. the two of us left in the Admiral's staff car. We arrived at the restaurant at 8:15 p.m. A warm breeze greeted us as we crossed the patio toward a table on the balcony that overlooked the ocean. Thomas handed the maitre'd some money. He requested a bottle of their best wine be brought to our table. Everything was so beautiful and romantic. The waiter pulled the chair out for me and then Thomas. The maitre'd brought the wine and poured each of us a glass. Thomas handed me the white carnation.

"What a nice surprise. A white carnation, wine, you really outdid yourself." How did you know I liked carnations?"

"George told me." Thomas wanted so hard to make the evening a pleasant one. "Good food, good company. I meant to say earlier that you looked lovely." He was searching for the right words.

I was wearing a flowered tropical sundress with white sandals. When he said I looked lovely, I must have turned four shades of red.

"For five months you haven't seen me in anything but scrubs. Anything would be better," I giggled.

"You didn't have to wear a dress for the occasion. It's beautiful. You're beautiful."

I felt my face turning a deeper red as I said, "Thank you."

The waiter came with water and Italian bread with butter and took our order. I had eggplant and Thomas ordered the Pasta Alfredo.

We felt like two fish out of water not knowing what to say to the other.

The salads arrived.

I sipped my wine looking at Thomas. "You said you wanted to talk."

"I do about a lot of things but I'm not good at opening up."

"Why not start off with something else and then lead into what you really want to say," I said fumbling around with the Italian bread.

Thomas took a couple of bites of his salad and looked at me. "I know that you want me to open up since that night a few weeks ago. You know, when I lost control… I really don't know what to say. Since I've come here to recuperate, I've been psychologically depressed over my condition. I knew that I looked like something from the Holocaust. I saw how you tried to keep mirrors away from me but I knew what I looked like. I could see the flesh hanging from my bones. In the day, you kept me busy with therapy. Chaplain Cook stopped by to play chess. General Sherman and Admiral Lewis met with me and kept my mind active with military intelligence briefings. Even after my information became outdated, they still kept me in the loop. They valued my opinion and that help to boost my self-worth but at night, I had too much time to think. I thought about the beatings, the bug-infested food and water, watching my men die on the mission and in the prison camp and other things that I just can't talk about due to the nature of the mission. The NVA tried to break me but they couldn't. They only succeeded in making me more hard headed – more determined."

Thomas made a fist and started to hit the table. I grabbed his hand.

The main course came. I let go of Thomas' hand. I asked the waiter to refill the wine.

Thomas continued, "You showed me kindness, tenderness. You took care of me. Before you say anything, like it was my job, I have seen other people do their job and then I've seen how you do your job. This was a case of you going beyond the call of duty. You showed your compassion when my physical condition was revolting to everyone including me. The embarrassment I felt at not being able to wash myself or go to the bathroom… you did your best to ease those feelings. What I feel now, I am having trouble putting into words….

"Thomas," I said, "You don't have to say anything…."

"Yes I do." Thomas took my hand and kissed it. "I care for you deeply, Marla. As we have gotten to know each other, I see how much we have in common and how we could have a life together."

I was blown away by what I heard. I sat there for a moment

absorbing all that he said and finally replied, "Thomas, you are right that I am the kind of person that gives 100%. It's never been just a job to me. You are an incredible man; the kind of man I haven't met in my 8 years in nursing. I knew early on that I had feelings for you but…." I looked down for a moment and then continued, "We have our duty to our country. An involvement isn't possible."

"Are you worried about what Admiral Lewis or General Sherman would think?"

"No, but given our current situation there are certain rules that need to be followed. When you are better and if we still feel the same way, then we could pursue those feelings if that is where you are going with this." I looked at the tablecloth not wanting to look in those deep blue all consuming eyes of his.

"That wasn't what I wanted to hear."

"I wish I could give you a different answer but I can't. You are my patient and when the time comes that you are no longer my patient then it would be appropriate to see one another, if that is what we both want."

I was dying inside. I didn't want to say any of this. I had such feelings of love for him but I still had my job to do. I knew that if I declared my love for him, Admiral Lewis would find another nurse to finish the rehab and I didn't want that.

It was relatively quiet through the rest of dinner. When we finished, the staff car took us back to Oahu General.

I could see the disappointment in his face but Thomas didn't know the meaning of the word "no."

Maybe that was to my advantage given my love for him.

Chapter 18

The next day while I was in my going over some reports, Thomas called Dr. Fong and George and asked them to come to the therapy room and informed them what happened the night before. He asked Dr. Fong what were the rules of involvement between a nurse and a patient. Dr. Fong said that while there was an unwritten rule not to get involved, he wouldn't do anything about a patient and nurse becoming involved with one another. As far as the Navy was concerned, someone needed to ask Admiral Lewis. Thomas asked for help in planning another evening together. George had an idea but said to give him a few days to get everything he needed. After some cajoling, Peter agreed that he would talk to Admiral Lewis.

Admiral Lewis wasn't thrilled when he heard of what Thomas was planning but wasn't opposed to it either because both he and General Sherman could see a tremendous change in Thomas psychologically. Being romantic with me could be just what the military ordered.

Thomas' therapy was progressing well. Since Thomas was in Intelligence and his specialty was Planning, his plot to change my mind was about to be implemented.

It was Saturday night around 7:00 p.m. I had just finished

my paperwork for the day when George came to my office with some clothes.

"Marla, Thomas is waiting for you in the therapy room and requested that you put on these clothes." It was a pair of black pants and a sweater top.

"George, what's up?" I asked.

"I don't know. I'm just the messenger."

"Like hell you are. You're just not telling me," I responded.

The hospital was quiet. On Saturday, everyone left early so there was no one around when I went to the PT room.

The PT room was shaped like a large rectangle. Along the back wall were the stationary bikes, leg curling machines, free weights, chest machines; the left wall had the parallel bars; the right wall was the shower area. In front of the shower area was the massage tables. The whirlpool was to right as I entered the room; straight ahead was a large open area with mats on the floor for exercises like sit-ups, push-ups, jump rope, yoga, stretching and other physical therapies as assigned by the doctor. In the left corner, on a pedestal, was a television set that was occasionally turned on when things were slow. Most of the time the patients and therapists liked to listen to music so a record player with records and a radio were kept underneath the TV.

I walked into the therapy room. In the open area, I saw the flickering lights of two candles. There was a blanket spread across the mat with a large wicker picnic basket on it. As I walked slowly across the room, I saw Thomas standing to the left walking toward me, leaning on his cane.

"Glad you could make it," he said cheerfully.

"Me too. I didn't know what to expect when George came by."

"How about a picnic? We can pretend we are outside under a tree..."

"Sounds great."

Thomas took my arm.

"You need help sitting down?" I inquired.

"Yes," replied Thomas.

I helped him get comfortable on the mat. I sat down across from him as he opened the picnic basket and handed me a white carnation in a small vase.

"Pretty flower for a pretty lady," he said.

"Isn't that romantic? Thank you for the flower." I took a long whiff. Now I eagerly waited for what was next. At that moment, I felt like a little kid waiting for my mother to hand me the next present from under the tree on Christmas morning.

Thomas pulled out two plates, two sandwiches – one ham and one turkey, assorted fruit and a bottle of champagne. We each took a half of the other's sandwich. Then he pulled out silverware, champagne glasses, potato salad and two pickles. We ate in silence enjoying the food and the atmosphere. I was curious whose idea this was so I spoke first.

"So who dreamed up this little get together? George?"

"George. He helped me plan all of this."

"Good guy, George is."

"He told me you've known him 6 years?"

"Yes, and we've been though a lot of interesting times. Remind me to tell you some of them sometime."

We continued to eat. When we finished the sandwiches and potato salad, Thomas said, "I asked George to get us an assortment of fruit. He went all out." Thomas pulled out what had to be some of the biggest strawberries I had ever seen. They must have come from California and cost a fortune.

"OOO strawberries. I love strawberries," I exclaimed.

"I know he told me. I have a surprise. He told me you liked this also. I hope this works."

Thomas pulled out a little pot and inside was hot melted

chocolate. George had already melted the chocolate and dropped off the pot to Thomas earlier. Thomas dipped a strawberry in the chocolate and fed it to me.

I took a bite. I felt my eyes rolling back in sheer delight.

"Delicious," I responded.

"Wonderful," exclaimed Thomas. He took a piece of cantaloupe and ate it. The juice dribbled down the corner of his mouth. I instinctively took my napkin and began to wipe his mouth. Thomas grabbed my hand and looked deeply into my eyes. Those ocean blue eyes were the most enchanting mesmerizing eyes I ever gazed into.

Our eyes were locked together for what seemed an eternity. I finally turned away.

"Would you like some champagne?" asked Thomas.

"Love some," I replied.

As Thomas worked the cork out of the bottle, I could see his rippled arm muscles bulge. I tried not to feel turned on but all I wanted was to have him take me in those big strong arms. The cork popped and the bubbly spilled over. I picked up the two glasses. He filled each glass half way and put the bottle back in the basket. I handed Thomas his glass.

"What should we toast to?" asked Thomas.

"How about to your recovery?" I replied with a smile.

"How about to my recovery with the help of a great nurse?" Thomas said with a bigger smile.

With that we clanged our glasses and drank. Thomas asked me if I wanted a refill on my champagne. I said great and he refilled both glasses.

The champagne started to hit us. Our feelings for each other became harder to control.

I spoke first. "So Thomas, what shall we talk about tonight?"

"Oh, I don't know. How about relationships? I spoke to Dr. Fong. While relationships aren't exactly encouraged, they aren't exactly prohibited. Admiral Lewis didn't seem to have a problem with it either. Why didn't you tell the truth last week?"

I avoided answering the question. Instead I responded, "It's perfectly normal for a patient to have feelings for his nurse."

"Is that what you think this is, just a patient having some grateful feelings?" I could see Thomas was getting angry. "It's far more than that. You told me you had feelings for me too or is it common for you to have feelings for all your male patients."

"Touché." I replied. "I didn't mean it that way. Out of all the soldiers passing through here, I never had feelings for anyone the way I have feelings for you…"

"Then why not act on your feelings," said Thomas rather strongly.

"Because I was afraid if anyone knew I had feelings for you, they would pull me from your case. More importantly, in a short time you will be well and leave for Vietnam. The hole in my heart will be a lot bigger if I get involved than if I don't." I could feel tears welling up in my eyes but I fought to hold them back.

"How do you know I'm going back?" Thomas snapped. "I don't even know that. I do know what I feel right here and now. I can only live one day… one moment at a time and at this moment, I'm here sharing a picnic with a beautiful woman. We have champagne, good food, candlelight… what else could we want."

"Thomas…"

Thomas stopped me. He leaned over and kissed me slowly. When I responded, he pulled me to him more aggressively.

I stopped suddenly.

"What's wrong?" Thomas asked.

"I can't," I replied as I stood up.

"Why?"

"I just can't."

"Whatever it is tell me, let me help you," he pleaded.

"I can't be with you because you will leave me through no fault of your own. I can't handle going through a loss of that magnitude." The tears came.

"Come here," he said gently.

I bent down and looked at him face to face. Thomas gently wiped the tears away with his hand.

"I'm not going anywhere – not tonight or anytime soon. We can just hold each other if that is all you can handle. This night is ours."

He reached down, took my hand and kissed it. I reached over and kissed him on the cheek and gave him a big hug. Then I reached into the picnic basket and poured us another glass of champagne. We sipped it and sat without speaking for a few minutes. The silence was deafening.

I was thinking, oh Thomas, please hold me, kiss me, make love to me like no man has ever made love to me before.

I put my glass down and without saying a word I brushed my lips lightly against his. I raised my hands and ran them through his hair. Thomas responded gently by rubbing my back. He allowed me to call the shots. It was my decision how far I wanted to go.

Thomas wanted me badly from the first day he woke up in the hospital. I had months of pent up feelings for him and these feelings were bubbling to the surface. I hadn't felt this way about a man in many years.

Thomas has been focused on his duties as a Special Forces Officer working in Intelligence. He hadn't had anytime to devote to finding the love of his life. He wasn't into one night stands. When many of the men went to Saigon or Da Nang on three day passes, Thomas stayed behind reviewing reports or reading.

It felt good to have a woman in his arms again. A woman he cared for; a woman he loved.

I was so devoted to duty that except for the monthly get together with the other PT nurses; I was studying new PT techniques, going to Karate classes or reading books. I wasn't into one night stands either. I was now able to enjoy the love of a man. It had been so long. I loved Major Thomas Smith with all my heart and that scared the hell out of me. The champagne had relaxed me. I felt my guard coming down. I began unbuttoning Thomas' shirt.

"Are you sure you want to do this and this isn't the champagne talking?" Thomas said with concern.

"I'm sure. I've wanted you for a long time. I just needed to relax a little."

"I've wanted you too," he said as he pushed back my long hair and kissed my neck.

I finished unbuttoning his shirt and with an uncontrolled passion that I had never felt for any man, started running my hands though the hair on his chest.

What wonderful chest hair. I loved a man with a hairy chest. It was such a turn on. I began nibbling his neck eventually working my way down to kissing his chest."

Thomas kissed the top of my head and rubbed my shoulders. He was still unsure of how far I wanted to go and decided to take his cues from my movements.

I came up to Thomas' mouth and kissed him gently at first, then longer and harder.

I pulled back for a moment and told him to wait. I went to the linen closet. I pulled out some sheets and towels. I laid them on the mat next to the picnic basket. I blew out the candles and turned on Frank Sinatra's "It was a Very Good Year." I asked Thomas how much pressure he could put on his leg.

"About 75%," he replied.

I told him to stand up using his cane as support. Thomas complied.

I opened Thomas' belt. Then I got down on my knees and opened his shoe laces. He stepped out of them. I stood up. He put his arms under my sweater massaging my lower back. My skin tingled as he made his way up to my bra.

I zipped down his fly. Thomas was extremely aroused.

He whispered in my ear. "You know how much I want you but I need you to want this for yourself too with no regrets."

I put my finger to Thomas' lips.

"I want you as much if not more than you want me," I said as I reached down and tugged at Thomas' trousers until they dropped down. Then I helped him out of them. I removed his shirt so he was standing there in his briefs. I whispered that he should sit down and I helped him sit down on the mat. I took off his socks. I got on my knees opposite Thomas. He took me in his arms and we kissed. He pulled my sweater over my head. Facing him on my knees, he opened the top of my pants and slowly pulled down my fly. I stood up and pulled my pants off for him. I had only my bra and panties on. It was almost too much for Thomas to endure.

I said, "Thomas, I'm going to sit on your left leg. Keep the right one out straight and let me know when you need to move."

"Always the nurse," Thomas mused.

I gently sat down and started kissing him, my hands moving from his chest area to his crotch. Thomas was aroused and responded by reaching behind me and unhooking my bra. He ran his hand up to the bra straps and gently pushed them down. Thomas turned me on my right side facing him and kissed each breast as he ran his hand across my stomach. He surprised me by rolling me on my back and now he was on top. He admired how firm my body was as he moved his hands downward, caressing my back.

Thomas looked at me and asked one last time if this is what I wanted and I said yes. He moved his hand toward my inner thigh and then removed my panties. I gasped slightly. I put my hands around Thomas' briefs and pulled them down. We both ran our hands over each other's bodies exploring as much as we could as we kissed and touched for what seemed an eternity. Thomas mounted me in the missionary position. He was gentle as he inserted himself into me. He began slowly but sped up quickly all the while being attentive to my needs. I felt myself coming and screamed out, "Faster, oh God, faster." Thomas obliged. All the pent up emotion we felt for each other poured out. When we finished, I rolled out from under Thomas to catch my breath. I grabbed a sheet and pulled it over both of us.

I curled up under Thomas's arm and the two of us remained silent for a couple of minutes. Then Thomas spoke,

"You were incredible."

"So were you," I replied.

Thomas reached over and pulled a cigarette from his shirt pocket.

"Can I have one?" I asked as I wrapped the sheet around my chest and sat cross-legged on the mat. Thomas was leaning on his right side with his right hand supporting his head and his left hand holding the cigarette pack out to me. I took a cigarette from the pack, held it between my fingers and waited for a light.

"I have never seen you smoke," he said with a high degree of surprise.

"I only smoke after I make love," I said unemotionally.

"Should I ask when your last cigarette was?" said Thomas curiously.

"You really want to know?" I said as I watched his eyes peak with interest.

"Of course I do," Thomas replied emphatically.

"About 8 years ago," I stated with a straight face.

"Please tell me you're kidding," replied Thomas stifling a smile.

"I'm not," I said indignantly.

Thomas sat up and lit his cigarette. I took his lighter and lit mine.

Thomas stared at me. I could tell he was wondering why I was celibate for so long. I paused as I inhaled deeply and exhaled smoke rings all the while staring back into his mesmerizing blue eyes.

"You are wondering why I have been celibate for so long. For one thing, I haven't met a man I wanted to become involved with. I'm also a workaholic. I've been one for years. It's easier to bury yourself in your work than get involved with someone."

"Care to elaborate. I want to know more about you, Marla." Thomas took a long drag from his cigarette. He watched every move I made.

I took a drag from my cigarette. I averted my eyes from his but I could feel him starring at me. I had to look up and when I did, I confronted those deep blue eyes that melted my heart and soul.

"Begin with when you decided to join the Navy?"

"My father was the reason I decided to become a nurse and join the service. He was a medic in WWII. He left when I was two. When he came back four years later, he told stories about how he helped people but not about the horrors of war. From then on, I knew I wanted to help people too.

While my father was overseas, my dad's brother, Michael brought mom and me out from Pennsylvania to California. He owned three gas stations in Los Angeles. He was married and had one daughter who was four years older than me. Uncle Michael treated me like I was his own daughter. He placed me in private school while mom worked at a defense plant.

Dad wrote every week. Mom replied to every letter. I remember running out the mailbox looking for letters from Dad. When Dad returned, he tried to go back to school at night but it became too difficult while supporting a family. He found a job at a produce and flower mart and worked at this until the early '50s. When television was in its infancy, Dad borrowed some money and opened up a store with another guy selling TVs and used appliances. It was successful for about 9 years but as TVs got cheaper and cheaper to make, Dad couldn't make a profit so he sold the TV business and just concentrated on used appliances. Meanwhile Uncle Michael sold one of the three gas stations and was planning to sell one more. He was getting older and wasn't able to manage three anymore. Dad didn't know enough about fixing cars or he could have managed one of the stations for Uncle Michael.

I graduated high school at the age of 16 in 1955. The Korean War had been over for two years. Nursing school was expensive and Dad could not afford the four years of tuition at USC. The Navy would not take me until I was 20 so I was forced to apply for loans and grants. I was approved for a one year grant, one year loan and Dad would pay for a year. I was left with one year and no money. I figured if I worked summers and school breaks I might come up with enough to pay for tuition only. The month before I completed my junior year, I was up in my room studying for final exams when I got a call from the dorm lobby. The dorm mistress told me to come down – that I had a visitor. It was Uncle Michael.

He said, "I heard you are having problems coming up with the money for your senior year. Don't worry, I'll cover the expense but you have to promise not to tell your father because it would make him feel bad that he couldn't pay for it himself."

"Uncle Michael, I won't tell him. Oh thank you. Thank you so much."

I kissed and hugged him. Tears were streaming down my face and he had tears in his eyes.

"Make me proud, Marla in whatever you do whether it is the Navy or nursing or anything else you do in your life," he said.

"I will," I replied.

"During my senior year, I ran into some problems with keeping my grades up. I didn't party like some of the other girls but the long clinical hours combined with class time, labs, and studying caused me to suffer severe sleep depravation. Other students had the same problem. Some handled it well. Others like me went to the campus doctor for the little red pick me up pills. Before I knew it I was hooked on amphetamines. I knew I had a problem but I also knew I needed those damn pills to get my degree. Things had gotten out of hand. At first I didn't know what to do but then I did what I always did when I had a problem: I called my father and explained the situation.

Graduation was two weeks away. Dad found a doctor and arranged to have the situation handled after graduation. To this day only a handful of people know what happened. The day after graduation Dad drove me to the hospital for the three weeks of in patient rehabilitation. The official records say undisclosed medical problem. The Navy was informed of the truth and they were not surprised. This was common problem among nursing school seniors. My delay in entering the Navy was not significant enough to cause a problem but then terrible news struck. The day I got out of the hospital I got a call from Dad telling me that Uncle Michael had a heart attack and died en route to the hospital. I couldn't contain myself. I just started bawling.

Upon being informed of the death in the family, the Navy postponed my orders to report and I was able to attend the funeral. It was only the beginning of many such losses in my life.

I finally arrived at boot camp and spent the next 9 weeks learning everything I could about the Navy. Since I was a nurse, I entered as an officer with the rank of Ensign. I was originally assigned to the Hospital Ship 'Mercy' stationed in the Pacific. I could have been assigned to a base hospital in Japan or Guam but as it turned out the Navy had just instituted a new requirement in which they wanted new nurses to do their first year on a hospital ship. I immediately applied for reassignment because I wanted to pursue my first Masters degree in Nursing and a second Masters degree in Physical Therapy. After the appeal went up the chain of command, I had my first encounter with Admiral James Lewis, who for the next 8 years would become my indirect Commanding Officer and friend.

The Navy granted an indefinite stay of ship duty. I attended the University of Hawaii while assigned to work at Oahu General Hospital. Oahu General had a contract with the military to take care of their servicemen and women. I received my first Master's degree in 1962 and my second Master's degree in 1965. With a degree in Physical Therapy nursing, I worked with the physical therapists, doctors, nutritionist, and of course nurses – bringing to the table many of the new concepts being taught in school – to construct a state of the art physical therapy program. I wanted a model for the rest of the country and as time went on, my dream became a reality. My motto was, 'If it's physical, it's therapy.' I needed to get in better shape. I began with yoga and meditation, in addition to riding a stationary bike three days a week. I found a Karate studio close to the hospital and enrolled.

I met someone when I first arrived in Hawaii that I thought I was in love with. He was a pilot stationed at Hickam Air Force Base. One of his buddies was slightly injured in a test run and was at the hospital receiving therapy. That's how we met. He said all the right things and soon we became involved. About 6 months later, he was transferred to the mainland. He left without saying good-bye. His friend felt sorry for me and broke the news of his departure. I was heartbroken. To this day I don't know what happened to him nor do I care. He didn't even have the common decency to tell me he was leaving. He was probably seeing multiple women and didn't want a scene. I put him out of my mind and moved on.

I extended my work hours to 12 hours a day 6 days a week. I loved the challenge. I submitted new and innovative physical therapy ideas to the Navy. I was all gung-ho in promoting them. The Navy took the ideas seriously and decided to give me a chance to put them into action. It was 1965. The United States had escalated the war in Vietnam. Wounded men were coming to Hawaii for treatment – rehabilitation. The Navy saw my program as a possible way to rehabilitate the men and either send them back to the mainland or reunite them with their units.

My program worked well and I was happy in my job. Things were going great until I received that horrible phone call saying my father had a heart attack and was gone. I was grief-stricken. My mother had collapsed and was in the hospital. I was granted funeral leave and returned to Los Angeles immediately. With the help of my cousin, I made the final arrangements. After the service, I had a week to decide what to do with mom. I couldn't leave her in Los Angeles by herself. I called a real estate broker and listed the house. I took her back to Hawaii to live with me. She could live in my condo until she was well enough. Then I would help her find an apartment. My mother was like a fish out of water – no husband, no friends, nothing to occupy her time. Eventually she just willed herself to die. Six months later, I was on a plane back to Los Angeles with mom's body so she could be buried next to dad in the military cemetery.

I immersed myself in my work. Had I not had my career at that time, I don't know what I would have done.

With regards to the rehabilitation of injured servicemen, the military set up a system that any man that could return to his unit within 30 days would stay at a field hospital in NAM; those with more severe injuries were shipped home for evaluation and if they were able to return to their units later would be reunited, and if the injury was too severe, they would be discharged. I was given the green light to establish a physical therapy nursing program in one hospital on each of the other islands and train their staff. The Navy contracted these services with the hospitals as they did with Oahu General. I received a promotion to Lt. Junior Grade. Eventually, the Navy had me expand the program to five major cities on the mainland.

Wounded and severely maimed soldiers returned in high numbers. Their injuries were foreign to our doctors. Thomas, I'm sure you know all their weaponry but we didn't know how to treat the injuries. Our doctors consulted with French doctors who had experience with these types of injuries. Without the French, we wouldn't have been able to treat these injuries appropriately. The Vietnamese used weapons called the punji sticks which as you know are sticks of bamboo whittled at one end to a point. Human excrement is smeared on the pointed end. They dig holes in the ground and plant the punji sticks. Then they cover the hole with dirt and leaves. When a soldier stepped on the covered area, the stick would penetrate his boot. This caused immense pain and infection. The soldier couldn't walk therefore requiring two other soldiers to carry him out. This effectively cut down the odds for the Vietcong and North Vietnamese Army. Sometimes the soldier would have to have his foot amputated because gangrene would set in from infection.

These traps would be planted by unexpected Vietnamese people like an elderly woman or a small boy. Other traps were set at groin level to take out a man's genitals. Recently, I have been seeing self-inflicted injuries. Soldiers intentionally shooting themselves in the foot so they wouldn't have to go back and fight. Then there were "frag" bombings. I know you have seen these. This was when a member of the soldier's unit, usually a disgruntled sergeant or lieutenant, would roll a fragment grenade underneath their superior's canvas bunk. Many officers died. No branch of service was immune to fragging but it was worse in the Army. To make matters worse, the fraggers were seldom found.

The Navy was pleased with the established physical therapy programs. Congress and the Pentagon discussed expanding it as more troops were headed to Vietnam and more returned injured. So there's my life. My entire family is gone except for one cousin on the mainland."

I took another drag. "Work has become my life. I never stop learning because I take classes in everything. I push the envelope constantly. I am permanently stationed at Oahu General by the Navy and became their Nursing PT Manager and am the State of Hawaii's Physical Therapy Nursing Director. There is talk of forming a National PT Nursing Directorship. If that happens, the Navy wants me to run for it. I don't know if I want it or if I can even take on the additional duties. Of course I am subject to relocation or reassignment at any time which is how you became my patient. Now you know my entire life except I live in a one bedroom condo near the hospital and have two fish named Mango and Orange." I paused and continued to gaze into Thomas' eyes. I took my final drag on the cigarette.

"For better or worse this is my path," I said with a sigh. "I love my job but there has always been something missing which was the love of a good man. But I was afraid to let someone in because I didn't want that person to leave me the way I had been left by everyone I have ever loved in the past. Can you understand how I feel? Everybody I have ever loved has left or died." Tears ran down my face. I did the best I could to brush them away with my hand.

Thomas took my hand. "I can't say why the pilot left without even saying good-bye. I do know he's an idiot and you are better off without him. As far as your parents and uncle are concerned, rationally you know they didn't leave of their own free will." Thomas paused and took a drag from his cigarette. "What about Peter, George, and your other friends?"

"Friends are not the same thing, even the best of friends. With regards to my parents, I realize my father didn't have a choice but my mother built her world around my father. Instead of a world with someone, all I built was a wall. Well, the wall just came down because I just let you into my heart." I turned my head away and crushed out my cigarette on the empty dinner plate.

"You asked me some time ago if I wanted to talk," said Thomas seriously. "I wasn't ready to share intimate details of my life with you or anyone else. I had just been to hell and back and saw the Devil. Talking about it only caused me to relive painful memories but now I want you to know my background," said Thomas apprehensively.

Thomas crushed out one cigarette, picked up another cigarette and lit it. He offered one to me. I took it, lit it and listened intensely to what he was about to say.

"I was born into a military family in 1932. My father was a

career officer. He retired as a Full Bird Colonel. My mother stayed at home and raised me. I don't have any brothers and sisters. I graduated three days before the Korean War started. Since I was ten, I wanted to follow in my father's footsteps and join the military. Being 6'1" and weighing 185 pounds, I knew I would be accepted into the Marine Corp. and hopefully Special Forces. I worked out with weights and jogged every day. I wanted to be in the best possible condition when I entered basic training. I was accepted into the Marines on my 18th birthday. My mother found out at my graduation party. She wasn't pleased but she understood. I received orders to ship out the following week.

I went through basic training and passed with flying colors. I was shipped to Korea after a one week leave with my parents.

I landed in Korea in early October 1950. I was with the Marines 10th Corp. In the Home by Christmas Offensive, our soldiers encountered a surprising reality when we ran up against 300,000 Chinese troops. General MacArthur had done a dumb thing by splitting our forces and sending the 8th Army up the east side of Korea and the 10th Corp. up the west side. The Chinese infiltrated on all sides. We retreated after a fierce fight at the Chosin Reservoir. I was one of only 1,000 guys to make it to the Marine stronghold at Hagaru on the reservoir's southern tip. From Hagaru, we started down the long mountain road to Hungnam. The weather conditions were beyond terrible. The roads were icy and narrow not to mention at each bend was an ambush waiting to happen. The cold was the worst. At night, the temperatures dropped to 20° below zero. Rations and water had to be thawed over open fires. We took turns thawing out in a warming tent before going back to our foxholes. Frostbite was a huge problem. I think it was the 2nd week of December that we made it to Hungnam. During the fight at Chosin, I won a bronze star for heroism.

After Korea, I stayed in the military. My goal was to become a career officer like my father. I went to officer's training school, then back to college to get my Bachelor's degree. I graduated in 1958 with a Bachelor's degree in Physics. I went on to get my Master's degree in Mathematics.

After I completed school, I went into Special Forces. I received specialized training and was assigned to Intelligence. The United States started sending advisors to Vietnam. I wanted to be an advisor. My hope turned to reality when I was sent on my 1st Tour of Duty to Vietnam in 1962."

Thomas stopped for a moment to collect his thoughts. He took a couple drags on his cigarette. I sat there completely enthralled with his story. I had no idea he had been through so much but I knew there was much more to come. I couldn't wait to hear it.

Thomas continued, "I was recalled to the Pentagon in 1964 for new orders when troops were beginning to be sent to NAM. I was a Lieutenant at this time. I spent a year learning new techniques of interrogation, covert operations and other secret plans our government had for Vietnam. There was a top secret special forces group called SOG (Studies and Observation Group) which was the largest and most complex covert operation initiated by the United States since the days of the OSS which was the Office of Strategic Services. SOG began waging war against Hanoi in 1964.

The mission was complex. It included fighting the VC and NVA in neutral Laos and Cambodia. This could mean blowing up bridges on the Ho Chi Minh Trail to keep supplies coming from the north. The Ho Chi Minh Trail including the 29 side trails connected to it is approximately 12,000 miles long and about 20 feet wide. The estimate is that at least a million people will move up or down the Trail during the war along with trucks, bicycles and elephants. SOG was also responsible for going in and rescuing downed pilots with their "Operation Bright Lights" program. This unadvertised service was secret. Our Special Forces men risked their lives to save downed pilots near or on the Trail. Many SOG men never returned either being listed as KIA or MIA. It was an Operation Bright Lights mission that caused me and my men to end up as POWs for six months in Laos. SOG included psychological warfare and sabotage raids against military and civilian coastal installations. We did everything and anything we could think of to rattle the enemy's cage."

Thomas paused and took another drag on his cigarette. He looked at me for a moment. His eyes were narrowly focused, his voice detached like a man telling someone else's life story, not his.

"After briefings at the Pentagon, I returned for my 2nd Tour of Duty in mid 1965. I was stationed at Khe Sanh which was located near the Laotian border. Two months after I arrived, I was temporarily reassigned to Da Nang to set up an interrogation unit for captured VC. After I set up this unit, I returned to Khe Sanh as part of the SOG Operation Bright Lights team. In December of 1965, during the rescue of a downed pilot, I got hit in the shoulder. The injury was not life threatening but I would not see any action for awhile. I went to Japan to recuperate. It was at this time I received the Purple Heart, another Bronze Star and a promotion to Captain.

I went home to see my parents after my shoulder healed. They greeted me warmly but they had just received terrible news. My dad had been diagnosed with terminal cancer and didn't have long to live. My father, Colonel William Smith was very proud of me. He said, "Son, I don't want you to grieve for me when I die. Promise me, you will move forward with your military career.""

Less than a week later, my father passed away. I made all the arrangements. He was buried with full military honors at Arlington National Cemetery. Mother handled dad's death well but the true test would be when I shipped out a week later.

Mother cried when I shipped out the following week. I promised I would write and I kept my word. Mother busied herself with the auxiliary woman's group at the military base and was soon chairwoman of fundraising events.

Chapter 19

"I returned to Vietnam for a 3rd tour of duty July 13th, 1966. By July 26th, I had been out on 9 missions when SOG had expanded its' recon teams from 5 to 20. I wasn't even back two weeks when my recon team was ambushed while trying to rescue a downed pilot. One squad member was killed instantly. The rest of us were taken prisoner by the NVA. The NVA felt they had hit the jackpot. They took us to a primitive make-shift prison deep in the Laotian jungle. Not seen from the air, the prison was a holding area for Americans and South Vietnamese until we could be sent to Hanoi. We suspected these camps existed but intelligence was scarce on the particulars. When we arrived, we saw people shuttled in and out. Later we estimated the average stay was two weeks; however, captives stayed longer if the NVA thought they had someone special that could give them American intelligence information. One of the guys in our squad was a cocky Lieutenant who had limited field experience. Everyone viewed him as untrustworthy."

Thomas finished his cigarette and took another from his shirt pocket. He asked me if I wanted another one.

"No thank you," I replied as I watched every move he made. He lit up and continued with as much disassociation as I had ever seen when telling a story.

"The NVA took each of us to their special interrogation rooms and began their persuasion process.

The Lieutenant was a pompous ass and I knew he would be trouble. I told him to keep quiet. Because I was the senior officer, I also knew I would see the brunt of the interrogation. I ordered my Sergeant nicknamed 'Big Papa' to keep an eye on the Lieutenant when I wasn't around. The 4th captured member was a Corporal nicknamed 'Joker.'

The NVA took me down to the first interrogation room. The Colonel strolled in and slammed the door. I was fluent in Korean and Vietnamese so I knew what was coming. He shouted to the guards in Vietnamese to hit me with their rifles butts. My only offense was my stubborn will to resist and my only defense was my wits. The Colonel wanted me to call out to the others but I refused to do so. They kept kicking and hitting me until the Colonel ordered them to stop.

He said to me in Vietnamese "It is better to cooperate than to die."

Thomas said it in English first and repeated it in Vietnamese imitating what I imagined was the Colonel's voice. A chill ran down my spine. I sat riveted waiting for what was next.

Thomas continued, "I acted as if I didn't understand what the Colonel said."

"How many men are in the area and how many airplanes are at the bases?" the Colonel said in English.

I replied in English, "I don't know what you are talking about."

This angered the Colonel. He told the guards to tie me to the chair so I couldn't move and give me some time to think about my confession. The Colonel left the room and went to the area where the Lieutenant, Big Papa, and Joker were being held. Big Papa had already told the Lieutenant to say nothing during the interrogation but the Lieutenant was petrified.

I knew that I and I alone had the exact intelligence information that the NVA wanted. Big Papa knew part of it; so did Joker, but the Lieutenant was briefed with false information. I knew the Lieutenant didn't know the truth. I heard the Lieutenant scream to the NVA that he would fully cooperate with them so long as they agreed not to hurt him. The NVA Colonel promised. The Lieutenant was taken to a room where he wrote down all the information he knew. According to the Colonel's promise, the Lieutenant would be taken to another area to receive a good meal and a shower.

Big Papa and Joker looked out their small window and saw the Lieutenant walk from the building into the courtyard. A NVA soldier walking behind the Lieutenant pulled a handgun from his waist and shot him in the back of the head. As he stood over his dead body, the NVA soldier spat on him and said 'traitor' in Vietnamese."

Thomas stopped for a minute to collect his thoughts. He took a couple of drags on his cigarette.

"Thomas, you don't have to say any more. It's ok," I said as I reached for his hand.

"No, my love, I want you to hear this. You asked me throughout my recovery if I wanted to talk. I didn't want to. I didn't think I could but it is better I get this all out once and for all unless you don't want to hear it," Thomas said pensively.

"Of course I do. I just don't want you to relive something so painful…."

"After all these months of pent up emotions, it feels good to tell you."

"I'm listening," I said thinking, oh God, what kind of Pandora's Box did I just open up? I reached for a cigarette from Thomas' shirt pocket, lit it and moved closer to him as he spoke.

Thomas continued, "The Colonel returned to me. My body was sore from the beatings. I had been sitting in the same position for hours. I told the Colonel I had to go to the bathroom. A guard brought a rusted can which I used as my toilet throughout my captivity. After I used the can, the Colonel asked in Vietnamese if I was ready to talk. I didn't answer; I didn't want the Colonel to know I was fluent in Vietnamese. The Colonel nodded to the guards and they shoved me against the wall and pelted me with their fists. They continued to hit me until I nearly passed out. The Colonel said 'enough' and I was dragged back to my cell. I peered out my window and learned the fate of the traitorous Lieutenant. The NVA hung his body from a tree in the courtyard for all to see. They left it there for days which provided food for the vultures.

We each endured our share of beatings but I was their favorite target because the NVA believed I was the senior officer – no man in SOG had any identification on them – so they had no way of knowing who was in command and what information we possessed.

The Vietnamese were excellent at torturing their prisoners. One particularly brutal round of torture involved them tying my hands and feet together at the ankles in front of me. It was their favorite form of getting someone to talk. The guards tightened the ropes until I was folded in half at the waist and unable to breathe. Then bent in half, I was hoisted up onto the hook to hang by ropes, letting the weight of my body pull the ropes even tighter, cutting off circulation to my arms and legs. Still I didn't talk. I was lucky I didn't suffer permanent nerve damage as I know many men did, because of this kind of torture.

After 6 months of captivity and a starvation diet with

beatings almost every day, it looked like we were going to die when I heard a guard say that we were going to be moved to Hanoi. It was time for someone else to try to get the information out of us. We were each kept in separate cells, chained to the wall. I used my drinking cup to tap a message on the wall using a form of Morse code to communicate to Big Papa and Joker. I devised an escape plan. Joker had contracted some kind of breathing problem, possibly pneumonia. He didn't want to be a hindrance to the escape and asked to be left behind. I told him that we would all get out together.

I can't talk about the escape because it is classified but after we got out of that hellhole, we traveled what we believed was southwest. We were hoping to run into a recon team. Because of all the time we spent in captivity and a MIA classification, I now believed the upper brass had written us off as KIA.

Each of us had lost over 50 pounds of our body weight. Of the three, Big Papa was in the best shape as he was 50 pounds overweight to begin with but we were all malnourished. We had three problems: avoid the NVA and VC, find water and food, and signal a recon party when we found one which could take a day or a week or never."

Throughout my listening to Thomas' horrific ordeal, I had been puffing on my cigarette. I crushed out the butt on the plate. Thomas took a final drag and crushed his cigarette next to mine.

As I sat across from him, I couldn't help but stare into his eyes and feel his pain. He continued, "We wandered for 13 days. During the last day, we heard helicopters circling the area. I went to check it out while Big Papa looked after Joker. There was a recon team about 100 meters from us. Big Papa helped carry Joker while I stayed a few paces ahead. With extreme caution, we approached a clearing. I left a three letter message in the dirt. It said 'MIA.' We went into the brush to wait. A recon team was bringing out a downed pilot. One helicopter took off taking gunfire all the way. The pilot must have radioed that they were taking heavy NVA fire. The pilot ascended quickly which meant that there would be an aerial assault of some kind, maybe napalm. Then I saw it pause; the helicopter was hovering. It looked like the pilot saw our MIA message in the clearing and called it in to headquarters. They didn't leave but they had to keep their distance to avoid being shot down by the NVA. They <u>had</u> seen our message.

Joker yelled that NVA were bearing down on us. The three of us ran from the bushes. The helicopter saw our predicament and instituted landing procedures. The blast of machine guns and mortars filled the air. Big Papa and Joker climbed into the helicopter. I grabbed a CAR-15 from one of the guys and provided cover. The pilot screamed for me to get into the helicopter now. I wrapped my arm around the bottom of the helicopter as it began to ascend. I continued to shoot at the NVA coming at us but I ran out of ammunition. One of the guys in the copter handed me a side arm and the two of us kept shooting. We were about 100 feet off the ground when I was shot in the leg. I yelled out as I was being pulled in. A medic applied pressure to control the bleeding. I saw Big Papa come over to hold pressure while the medic prepared some kind of inflatable suit. The recon men in the helicopter dropped grenades as we flew off. The medic did as much as he could to stop the hemorrhaging and the copter flew me to Khe Sanh for medical treatment. I remember arriving at the base and being transported by stretcher. The medic had pumped me full of morphine so things got a little fuzzy after that. You know the rest."

Thomas finished speaking and looked up at me. Nothing was said for a minute. I didn't know what to say after a story like that so I changed the subject when I broke the silence.

"I'm going to take a shower. If you would like to join me…"
I didn't finish the sentence. I got up, put a towel around
me, picked up two additional towels and walked across the
physical therapy room.

I could feel Thomas watching me. The smell of smoke
lingered in the air as I stepped into the shower. I turned on
the water and began soaping up. I had given Thomas much
to think about and he had given me more than enough
to absorb. I was in the shower about three minutes when I
heard him coming across the mat.

He stopped at the entrance to the shower. I didn't know
why. I went on doing what I was doing. If he wanted to come
in, the invitation was there.

I was washing my hair when Thomas joined me. I felt a
soft hand on my shoulder and I turned around. He placed
his strong hands gently around my waist. I had soap in my
eyes and couldn't see him but I could feel his breath on my
cheek. I moved forward and found his soft lips. We kissed.
He helped me rinse the soap out of my hair and off my face.
Then he pulled me to him and kissed me again on the lips.
The kiss became more passionate. I backed off for a moment
to adjust the shower head to a fine spray, picked up a bar
of soap and a washcloth and began to wash him. I started
with his neck and moved toward his shoulders and chest.
As I washed his magnificent hairy chest, I could feel myself
become aroused again. Thomas reached for my hand and
grabbed the cloth to wash my neck, arms, back, with him
gently caressing my breasts.

I grabbed the removable shower head and rinsed the soap
from both our upper bodies. I began to soap up the rest
of Thomas and he did likewise. Both of us began exploring
each other's bodies. He brushed my crotch and I nearly went
crazy with excitement. We rinsed again. Thomas became
stimulated and wanted to make love. I guided him to the

oversized ledge at the back of the shower. I had him sit back. I mounted him this time. The water made things a little slippery at first but once I was in position, I held on to Thomas for dear life. The intense passion that came over us was as if the two of us became one at climax. I felt a complete sense of peace and love that I had never known. Thomas was all I needed or wanted. Now I was scared to death. In four weeks, his therapy would be over and after that, what happened was anyone's guess. I tried not to think about that and just enjoy the moment but a sick feeling formed in the pit of my stomach. I just wanted to hold on to him forever never letting him go.

Thomas told me he never felt better. He made love to me with the gentleness of a lamb yet the dominance of a lion. He, too, was thinking that in four weeks his therapy would be over and most likely be asked to return to Vietnam but he didn't want to dwell on that. He wanted to enjoy this moment and plan for more of these moments with the love of his life. He held me with the same kind of feeling I had for him. I sensed that.

We finished showering. Both of us grabbed towels and dried off. I grabbed another one for my hair.

I asked Thomas for a cigarette. He said he left them by the picnic basket. I walked over, took one and lit it. I gave him one and lit his.

I took a drag and gazed at Thomas for a long time. Thomas spoke. "You're ok with what we did?"

"I'm better than ok, and you?" I responded inquisitively.

"I'm great." Thomas paused to get his thoughts together.

"You don't have to say anything…" I said.

"No, I need to." Thomas walked over. I looked at him. Before I could say a word he said, "Marla, I love you, more than I have ever loved anyone in my entire life. Where things go from here is anyone's guess but I do love you."

"Oh, I love you too, Thomas. I wanted to say something earlier but I was afraid."

"I knew by the way we made love that you felt the same way. Never be afraid, my love. Promise me."

"I promise." I grabbed him and hugged him. I didn't want the evening to end but I said, "We need to get going."

"So soon?" replied Thomas like a kid who was just told he had to stop playing and come in to eat supper.

"We need to get dressed and get you back to your room before it gets too late."

We walked across the room and got dressed. I picked up the picnic basket and we left the PT room.

As I closed the door, I looked back and I thought to myself I would never look at this room the same way ever again.

Chapter 20

The next four weeks passed by quickly. Thomas walked with just the slightest limp. It wasn't noticeable to an untrained eye and it certainly was not a hindrance when he walked. Two weeks prior to the end of his therapy, Thomas decided to ask me to marry him.

He went to George and Peter for help. The only time that Thomas was alone was when he was showering so he called each of them and asked them to meet him in the shower area.

"So we're here. What's up?" said Peter.

"I want to propose to Marla. I need a ring," said Thomas.

"That's something you need to pick out for yourself," stated Peter.

Thomas replied in a perturbed tone, "And how am I able to do that being cooped up here?"

"I've got an idea," said George. "My cousin owns a jewelry business in town. Let me make a call. I'll see if he makes house calls." Everybody chuckled.

The next day Thomas went to shower as usual but was met by George's cousin. There on a black velvet skirt were 15 rings, 5 across by 3 down. Thomas looked at the various diamonds but didn't see anything he liked. George's cousin pulled out a box from his pocket. He opened it. There sat a beautiful two carat diamond ring. One carat in the middle with two - one quarter carats on either side set in platinum.

Thomas said, "I'll take it! I also need two wedding bands."

"I'll need Marla's ring size," replied George's cousin.

George spoke up. "I'll see if Maria can find out Marla's ring size. Ok?"

"Great," Thomas replied.

Thomas jumped into the shower. No time to lose. By the time I got down to the PT room, he was ready to begin therapy and I never suspected a thing.

Around 4:00 p.m., I received a call from Admiral Lewis. He asked me to meet him that evening. I suggested the Tiki Bar at 11:30 p.m. I waited until Thomas had gone to bed and took a cab to the bar. Arriving before Admiral Lewis, I ordered my usual 7 and 7. Admiral Lewis arrived five minutes later and he ordered a Jack Daniels on the rocks.

"Good evening Admiral. You wanted to see me?" I said as I took a sip of my drink.

The bartender returned with the Admiral's drink, put it on the bar and left. Admiral Lewis nodded.

"Yes Marla, I wanted you to hear it from me first. We need Thomas to return to his position in Intelligence as soon as possible. He's vital to the war effort. I can't discuss the details here because it's classified but I would debrief you if you desire. We can't make him do another tour. He has been involved in Vietnam since the early days and he's already done 3 tours. If he told General Sherman that he would not return, we would have no choice but to respect his decision. We will meet with him this week to ask him if he would return to NAM as soon as his therapy is completed. I'm sorry, Marla. There was no other way to break it to you." Admiral Lewis sounded almost apologetic.

I sat there for a moment and drank my drink without

responding. Admiral Lewis downed his drink, paid for both and left without saying another word.

Staring straight ahead for a few moments, I let the bad news settle in. I knew this would happen and now that it did, all I felt was numb. I downed the rest of my drink. No surprise in asking him to return to NAM, but I hoped against hope that they would send Thomas elsewhere. I thought about having another drink but decided against it so I called a cab and returned to the hospital.

The next morning, Thomas called Admiral Lewis from the shower area phone to inform the Admiral that he was going to ask me to marry him. Talk about timing. That was probably the last thing Admiral Lewis expected or was it?

"I need your help," Thomas said to Admiral Lewis.

"What would you like me to do?" Admiral Lewis replied.

"I'd like you to arrange a dinner or something at the Officer's Club. I'd prefer a quiet dinner for two with dancing. Can you book this?"

"Of course, when do you want to do this?"

"As soon as possible. I already picked out the ring," Thomas said excitedly.

"Is tomorrow too soon?" inquired Admiral Lewis.

"No, that's perfect."

"Consider it done."

About 2:00 p.m., General Sherman showed up at the PT room to talk to Thomas. I was disinfecting the whirlpool machine when he walked in.

General Sherman and Thomas were across the room by the parallel bars. I couldn't hear anything they said but I watched their body language closely.

"I know you are going to ask Marla to marry you tomorrow." General Sherman said unemotionally.

"News travels fast but why do I sense you didn't come

here to congratulate me?" Thomas stared into the General's steely blue eyes.

"Look, Marla is across the room and can see we are having this conversation so I might as well be up front with you and tell you that last night Admiral Lewis met with her after you went to bed to let her know we would ask you to return to NAM upon completion of your therapy."

"He what?" yelled Thomas.

I could see by Thomas' body movements that he heard the news.

"Permission to speak freely, sir?" Thomas replied.

"Permission granted."

"I've had more than my share of time over there. I've been shot three times courtesy of Charlie and one of those bullets nearly cost me a leg…"

"Thomas, before you continue, you know as well as I do that Military Intelligence is in your blood. You have been doing it for years." General Sherman started raising his voice and a few of the patients in the physical area looked over. He lowered his voice to a whisper. "Because of you, we gathered key points of information against the NVA in Laos. Even the men believe you are returning."

"So who told the men that? I spent several months in a NVA prison camp and nearly died between the disease, lack of food and water, the beatings and the torture. I was almost crippled for life from a bullet that shattered my leg. I have a metal rod for a femur. I finally found someone I want to spend the rest of my life with, someone I love, and you want me to go back to that shithole. Begging the General's pardon but you must think I'm nuts if I agreed to this."

"I would never think you are nuts because you are a career military man just like I am. I'm not asking you to do it for me; I'm asking you to do it for your country," replied General Sherman stoically.

"That's a low blow," Thomas said. "I'm pissed off that you would use my patriotism to get me to return to NAM for a 4th tour. I've given the last 17 years of my life for my country. My father served in the military until his death and my grandfather before him. I don't know what more you want or expect from me."

"I want you to think about it. I NEED you to think about it. You've done 3 tours. I can't order you back but please give it serious thought. The Government needs your expertise in the war effort."

General Sherman was about to leave when Thomas asked him to arrange a briefing on why he should return and why someone else isn't as qualified to take his place. General Sherman said he would be in touch. They saluted each another and General Sherman left.

General Sherman and Admiral Lewis called Thomas and me requesting us to put on our dress uniforms and join them at the officer's club the following evening.

I asked Admiral Lewis what the occasion was. He was rather vague. He told me he needed me to meet some very important people. I didn't give it too much thought because I had so much on my mind that I figured this was a standard 'dog and pony show' that the Admiral would have me attend on occasion to talk to people about my PT program.

The General sent a car for Thomas and the Admiral sent a car for me. They were pretty deceptive in keeping me in the dark about what was about to happen.

When I arrived, there were several high ranking military people in the room. Thomas arrived about five minutes after me. I was escorted on stage by Admiral Lewis. Thomas was seated next to me. I asked him what this was all about and he said he didn't know. That part was true because he didn't know we were both about to be decorated.

General Sherman stood up at the podium tapping his water glass.

"Thank you for coming," he said clearing his throat. "It is my great honor to present the official recognition of the rank of Major to Captain Thomas Harrison Smith known as "Bear" to all his friends. I am also here to present him with his POW medal, his Purple Heart and his Silver Star medal for heroism in the face of the enemy." Major Smith rose and shook hands with General Sherman. Thomas was presented with his medals. The official military photographer for Stars and Stripes snapped General Sherman and Thomas shaking hands. Everyone clapped.

General Sherman sat down and Admiral Lewis stood up.

"It is my proud and distinguished honor to introduce Lt. Marla Bristol, Registered Nurse. Her degrees include Bachelor of Science, Nursing, Masters of Science, Nursing, and Rehabilitation Specialist Physical Therapy Nursing. Lt. Bristol exceeded the expectations of her superior officers by tending to the wounds of Major Thomas Smith, 24 four hours a day, 7 days a week for the past six months. For this exemplary action, the Navy has raised her rank to Lt. Commander. I stood up to receive my increase in rank. Stars and Stripes snapped a picture of Admiral Lewis and me. The audience clapped.

"This concludes our brief ceremony. Appetizers and drinks will now be served," said Admiral Lewis.

General Sherman whispered to Thomas, "The next room has been set up for you and Marla."

I had taken my seat when Thomas walked over to me. "Come on," he said. He escorted me off the stage to the private dining room. I looked at him and said,

"You set me up."

"I swear I knew nothing about the ceremony."

I paused for a moment and said, "Ok, I believe you. I saw

the look on your face but you knew something was going to happen tonight."

"I knew we were going to have dinner." Thomas pulled my chair out for me to sit down. He was always such a gentleman.

"Shall we order?" said Thomas.

I nodded.

"Waiter!" shouted Thomas.

The waiter came right over and we placed our order for two filet mignons medium rare, baked potatoes, salad, vegetables and rolls with butter. I had a glass of red wine and Thomas ordered a Crown Royal. Dinner was delicious. I had no room for dessert but Thomas insisted we order some. I ordered a scoop of chocolate ice-cream and Thomas ordered a slice of apple pie. He left the table pretending to use the bathroom asking the waiter to delay dessert by a few minutes.

He returned to the table with a white carnation. He took my hand and kissed it. Then he bent down the best he could on one knee and uttered the words I had waited my entire life to hear, "Will you marry me?" he asked.

He reached into his pocket and pulled out a ring box. It was the most beautiful diamond I had ever seen. I was overcome with emotion. Tears welled up in my eyes. Thomas got up from the floor, sat down on the chair next to me, looked into my eyes and said,

"Well?"

"Of course I'll marry you. I'm so happy I can hardly speak."

Thomas slipped the ring on my finger and gently kissed my lips. The waiter appeared with dessert. We ate without speaking. After we finished, the waiter turned up the music and left. Thomas took my hand and led me to the dance floor. He held me close to his body but I trembled with fear.

I remember thinking that I fell in love with a wonderful man but a Special Forces Major who would soon leave for Southeast Asia. This amazing man has asked me to be his wife. I knew Thomas felt me shake so I spoke before he could ask what was wrong.

"I love you so much I can't even put it into words. You have made this one of the greatest nights of my life; one I'll cherish forever. But I'm scared, Thomas. I'm scared of losing you because I know that as much as you love me, you're going back to NAM. Don't say anything now. Just hold me."

Thomas didn't respond. He held me close.

We danced quietly for a while. We spoke little the rest of the evening. NAM was on both our minds. After an hour of dancing to Frank Sinatra, Dean Martin, Sammy Davis Jr., and Tony Bennett, we returned to Oahu General. When Thomas entered the room, he asked me to sleep next to him. He didn't have to ask twice.

I smiled, didn't say a word, undressed, crawled into bed and fell asleep.

Chapter 21

The next morning I awoke first. I was lying next to the man I loved, afraid to make any noise at all. My mind ran through all the events of last night: the promotion, the engagement, and knowing Thomas has been asked to return to NAM. Fear consumed me. He hadn't told me he was going but I knew with every fiber of my being that he would leave me for Vietnam.

Thomas started to stir. He looked over at me and began stroking my hair. He said in his Boggie voice, "A penny for your thoughts, kid." I thought back to the first day we met.

I was on my left side and brought my right hand up so I could play with his chest hair.

"Oh nothing," I said as coy as possible.

"I don't buy that for a second. You didn't sleep well last night. Please tell me what's wrong," Thomas said caringly.

"I'm sorry. I didn't mean to keep you awake."

"You didn't. I loved having you beside me. What's upsetting you? Talk to me." Thomas began stroking my cheek.

"Nothing's wrong. I love you. The most wonderful man in the world just asked me to marry him. I'm happier than I have ever been."

"But?" he said knowing there was something else I wanted to say.

"No buts. I've got a wedding to plan and there's so much to do," I said excitedly.

"And you need to know if I'm going back to NAM. General Sherman is pressuring me. I must give him an answer, either yes or no, but before I do I need to be briefed on the current situation."

I turned on my right side. I couldn't bear to look at him right now.

"Darling, I'm sorry. I have to hear what the military has to say. I am caught between a rock and a hard place," he said as he brushed my hair back and gently stroked my shoulder.

I couldn't contain my anger. I got out of bed, put on my robe, faced Thomas and said, "Sure...you want me to say I understand but I don't. God, how I love you Thomas. I knew you were a career military man when I met you just as you knew I was a career military woman but in my case I'm not being shot at. You know I will support your decision 100% whatever it may be. When we take our vows for better or worse, in good times and in bad, there won't be two people anywhere who will take those words more seriously than us."

Before Thomas could respond, I ran out of the room and cried.

Later that day, General Sherman came to the therapy room. I saw Thomas and General Sherman walk toward the conference room.

"Have you decided what you are going to do?" asked General Sherman.

"I told you I need more information before I make a decision," Thomas replied firmly.

"I have five hours of information compiled for your review. If you decide to go, then we will continue the briefing."

I saw Thomas later that day.

"Well?" I said knowing he knew what I was thinking.

"Plan the wedding," he said. "I want to marry you as quickly as possible."

I didn't know whether to jump for joy or worry that our time together was growing short.

I enlisted the help of Maria who would be my Maid of Honor. I wanted a beach wedding. Maria went to the Hilton and asked permission for Thomas and I to have our wedding on their beach front property with them catering the affair. They said fine.

I called Admiral Lewis and asked if him if he would give me away. He replied, "It would be an honor."

I had to pick the flowers. I went to the florist that the hospital dealt with and picked out my bouquet plus the boutonnières. White carnations, of course.

Selecting the right dress was the hardest part of all. With so little time, I was afraid that I would have a problem finding what I wanted. I went to three dress shops. The final one had it. I found my dress, veil and garter. Alterations would only take five days.

The last item on my list was to contact the person who would marry Thomas and me. Since neither one of us was religious, Thomas and I agreed that Chaplain Cook should officiate so I left a message for Chaplain Cook to call.

It was late when I arrived at the hospital. Thomas was getting ready for bed when I walked in. "Long day for both of us," he said.

"Long day," I said exhaling.

"Well?" he said anxiously.

"All the arrangements are made except confirming that Chaplain Cook will marry us. Have you called your mother?" I asked.

"I will tomorrow. When are we getting married?" replied Thomas.

"The day after you are released from the hospital which is a week from Sunday at 5:00 p.m."

Chapter 22

The days leading up to the wedding flew by. Thomas' last day of therapy had arrived. The girls threw me a wedding shower in the large conference room. They decorated it with hula dolls, piñatas and balloons.

I tried to do my work but the constant interruptions made it impossible to think and my mind wasn't on a party but on Thomas and Vietnam. Meanwhile Thomas' buddies were getting ready for his bachelor party. At 5:00 p.m. he was officially discharged from Oahu General, a place that had been his home for 7 months.

Thomas saw me walking down the hall toward the conference room. He went over to me and we kissed. He whispered, "See you soon."

I whispered back, "Tomorrow I will be your wife."

The bachelor party was pretty standard with beer, hors d'oeuvres, and female dancers none of which interested Thomas. His mind wasn't on a party.

After the party, Thomas needed a place to stay. Admiral Lewis offered him his guest house. I went back to my condo.

I didn't sleep at all. I don't know if was the excitement I felt about becoming Mrs. Thomas Smith or the worry I felt that after the wedding, Thomas would be returning to

NAM. After staring at the ceiling for two hours, I finally got up at 7:00 a.m., called Maria and asked her to come over. The wedding was at 5:00 p.m. With such short notice, only 125 people from Oahu General, the Marines and the Navy showed up. Had there been more time to get the word out, at least 250 people would have attended.

It was a perfect day for a wedding. Not a cloud in the sky; the ocean was clear and the sand, pure white.

The canopy was adorned with white carnations.

My dress was white with a scoop neck. Tiny beads were sewed into the bodice. It glistened like abalone shells in the sunlight. The train stretched three feet but would be fastened to my waist after the ceremony.

I wore a small pearl necklace that had been my mothers. Pinned to the inside of my dress was a white embossed handkerchief with the initials SB. It had been my father's. My hair was styled into a bun to accommodate the veil which tied under my hair and covered my face. Around my right leg was a blue satin garter that Thomas would throw after I threw the bouquet.

Before the ceremony, Thomas' mother came to the bride's room.

"Knock, knock, can I come in?" she said.

"Yes of course, please," I replied.

"Are you ready?" she asked with nervousness in her voice.

"I've been waiting for this moment all my life," I said happily.

"Marla, I know you will make Thomas a wonderful wife." Patricia went over to her purse and took something from it. "I want you to borrow something from me to complete the something new, something old, something borrowed, something blue. It was my mother's at her wedding and I wore it at my wedding."

I looked down and saw this lovely gold bracelet, so delicate and fine. Patricia fastened it around my wrist and said, "Welcome to the family. I've always wanted a daughter. I couldn't have had a better one than you. I love you Marla."

I hugged her and said, "I love you too mother."

Time was growing short. Patricia and Maria helped me with my veil and train.

Thomas was waiting for me at the altar, dressed in his military uniform.

Chaplain Cook arrived. He took his place in the middle of the canopy with best man Peter Fong, in a black tux next to Thomas. George ushered the people to their seats.

Maria wore a light pink flowered Hawaiian dress.

Patricia wore a cream colored suit with matching hat. General Sherman was her escort. He was in full dress military regalia.

Admiral Lewis arrived in his dress whites.

The naval quartet began playing background music at 4:45 p.m. while everyone was being seated.

Chapter 23

At 5:02 p.m., the ceremony began. Patricia was escorted down the aisle. Maria followed alone. When she reached the end, she turned to face Peter. There was silence as I appeared holding Admiral Lewis' arm. Everyone rose as "Here Comes the Bride" was played. I couldn't stop smiling. I looked from side to side as we approached the end of the aisle. When we got to the first row, Admiral Lewis picked up my veil, kissed me on the cheek, looked at Thomas and said, "May you both always be as happy as you are at this moment. Take care of her, Thomas."

Thomas looked at Admiral Lewis and replied, "I will, sir"

Admiral Lewis took my hand and placed it on top of Thomas'. Thomas took my hand and we walked to the canopy. Chaplain Cook began:

"One of the greatest joys of my life has the ability to join two people who love each other in the bonds of matrimony. Throughout the ages, couples have pledged themselves to one another forsaking all others. I have performed many ceremonies over the years and in all that time I have never seen two people so in love with the other as I have with Marla and Thomas. While I have known Marla since she entered the Navy 8 years ago, I met Thomas during his recuperation at Oahu General. We talked about many topics including sports and chess. Ah, chess. I finally found a worthy opponent after all these years. I enjoyed myself immensely engaging in such a brain stimulating activity. I was not surprised that Marla and Thomas fell in love. However, I usually have reservations with marriages under the circumstances in which they met but after spending time with both of them; I could see they were destined to be together. It is a personal honor that they called me to officiate."

Chaplain Cook continued, "Let us pray. Great and Glorious God, bless these two people who are about to be joined in your covenant known as marriage. Amen.

Before reciting the vows, it is customary to read a poem or Bible passage. Marla and Thomas left it to my discretion to select something that would fit this moment. I selected my favorite passage, 1 Corinthians 13:1-8, 13 (GNT).

'I may be able to speak the languages of human beings and even of angels, but if I have no love, my speech is no more than a noisy gong or clanging bell. I may have the gift of inspired preaching; I may have all knowledge and understand all secrets; I may have all the faith needed to move mountains – but if I have no love, I am nothing. I may give away everything I have, and even give up my body to be burned – but if I have not love, this does me no good.

Love is patient and kind; it is not jealous or conceited or proud; love is not ill-mannered or selfish or irritable; love does not keep a record of wrongs; love is not happy with evil but is happy with the truth. Love never gives up; and its faith, hope and patience never fail. Love is eternal. There are inspired messages, but they are temporary; there are gifts of speaking in strange tongues, but they will cease; there is knowledge, but it will pass. Meanwhile these three remain: faith, hope, and love; and the greatest of these is love.' Amen.

Do you Thomas take Marla to be your wife, to love and

cherish, through better or worse, through sickness and in health, for richer or poorer, for all the days of your life?"

"I do," replied Thomas.

"Do you Marla take Thomas to be your husband, to love and cherish, through better or worse, through sickness and in health, for richer or poorer, for all the days of your life?"

"I do," I replied.

"The rings."

Peter handed Thomas Marla's ring and Maria handed me Thomas' ring.

Chaplain Cook continued, "A ring is a circle with no beginning or ending as is your love for one another. Thomas, repeat after me, as a symbol of my love for you Marla, I give you this ring, to wear all the days that we both shall live as a reminder of my love for you and the vows we have taken today."

Thomas repeated the vow.

"Marla repeat after me, as a symbol of my love for you Thomas, I give you this ring, to wear all the days that we both shall live as a reminder of my love for you and the vows we have taken today."

I repeated the vow.

"I now pronounce you husband and wife. Thomas, you may kiss your bride."

Thomas lifted my veil and kissed me. A cheer arose from guests.

The guests were ushered to the buffet area located 50 feet away. We had a small head table: Thomas, me, Admiral Lewis, Patricia, Peter, Maria, General Sherman, and George. There were ten circular tables set up for the guests. The centerpieces were little Hawaiian hula dancers.

The buffet consisted of roast beef, ham, chicken, mashed potatoes, rice, green beans, carrots, fresh pineapple, mixed green salad with a choice of four dressings and a beautiful three tier wedding cake for dessert.

A special surprise of native dancers and fire eaters were the entertainment.

The band played and announced the first dance.

Thomas took my hand and led me to the make shift wooden dance floor set over the sand. The band played, "Moonriver" from the movie "Breakfast at Tiffanys." Thomas ran his hand against my cheek and said, "You are so incredibly beautiful."

My blood froze as I realized at that moment he had made his decision. He was going back to Vietnam. I had to confront him. I looked at him with tears in my eyes.

"You made your decision. You're going back to NAM," I said restraining my voice to a whisper.

Thomas looked away not wanting to confirm my feeling.

"I'm right aren't I?" I said again pressing for the answer I didn't want to hear.

"Yes."

"When do you leave?"

"I'm not sure. I haven't received my orders yet. I have to go back and do some basic training. We'll have time together, I promise. Admiral Lewis may know more."

I stopped dancing with Thomas and walked over to Admiral Lewis.

"Would you like to dance, sir?" I said all militarily.

Admiral Lewis replied, "I would be honored."

Patricia sensed something was wrong and walked over to Thomas.

"Thomas, did you two have a fight on your wedding day?"

"No, mother. Marla received news she was hoping she wouldn't hear. I might as well tell you now. I'm going back to Vietnam within the next two months."

Patricia looked at Thomas in disbelief. She couldn't utter a sound.

Before Admiral Lewis could speak, I said, "You win. He's yours. When does he leave?" Admiral Lewis was taken aback by my attitude.

"His orders haven't come through yet. You're taking this better than I thought," he replied in surprise.

"What did you expect? A temper tantrum? Thomas is grown man with a mind of his own. I can't stop him nor would I even want to try. I can only love him and support whatever decision he makes. I don't want him to go. I'm dying inside that he decided to go back to that God-forsaken place. This rotten war brought us together. I pray to God that it doesn't tear us apart."

I looked at Admiral Lewis for a minute. I decided to ask the question that had been eating at me for all these months.

"Admiral."

"Yes Marla?

"Did you and General Sherman really pick me because I was the best at nursing care or was there another reason?"

"Marla, you are the best rehab nurse around; anyone who knows your track record can't argue with that. I've known you for 8 years. I knew if anyone could bring a man back, you could. That's all there was to it."

I suspected he was lying but didn't want to press the issue.

I walked away and announced it was time to throw the bouquet. All the women gathered on the dance floor. I threw it and one of my nurses from Maui caught it. Thomas pulled off the garter while all the guys whistled loudly. He threw it. Peter caught it and turned four shades of red. He didn't mean to catch it. Thomas had thrown it so far back that it hit Peter in the head.

A rickshaw carriage drew closer. It was Thomas' special surprise. We got in and drove off. I waived to everyone as we pulled away. The rickshaw took us to a limo which was waiting for us at the front of the Hilton.

"Driver, take us to Hickam Air Force Base," said Thomas.

"My pleasure, sir," replied the driver.

Chapter 24

For the next 10 days, we were both on leave. Thomas had arranged to spend the entire time seeing and experiencing as much as possible starting with the island of Maui. He coordinated it with Maria. We rented a condo there for 3 nights. Waiting for us when we arrived from Maria and George was a bottle of chilled champagne, a vegetable and fruit basket and a basket of bagels with cream cheese and lox. There were two boxes on the sofa. One was from me to Thomas and the other was from Thomas to me. We opened our packages. My gift was a beautiful black negligee with matching panties. Thomas' gift was sexy red underwear with a matching silk robe. He dropped the present on the sofa. He opened the top button of his dress uniform and walked over to me and took me in his arms and kissed me as passionately as he had the night we made love in the therapy room.

I told him he needed to wait while I changed out of my wedding dress. I took my present and went into the bedroom. Thomas undressed in the living room. I took a little longer than normal to get ready because I found out quickly it was easier to put on a wedding dress than to take it off, especially when you have a zillion buttons to unbutton down the back and no Maid of Honor to help out. When I appeared, I was a little out of breath. Thomas stood there staring at me like

he had in the PT room. We went over to the food and champagne. He had already uncorked the bottle and poured each
of us a glass of bubbly. I walked over to the record player and
put on some Dean Martin.

We began to eat some of the fruit when the door bell
rang. I ran into the bedroom. Thomas went to the door and
called out, "Who is it?"

The voice responded, "Special Delivery."

Thomas opened the door and there were 5 cartons of
Chinese food from the best Chinese place on Maui, "Yong
Fu", with a note saying, "From your friends at Oahu General."
Thomas looked for some money to tip the driver but the
driver replied it was already taken care of.

Thomas brought the food over to the table. It was all of
my favorite dishes. Mu Shu Chicken, Sweet and Sour Pork,
Scallops with Vegetables, Vegetable Chow Mein and Egg Foo
Young, plus a large Won Ton Soup, huge box of rice and
assorted appetizer tray.

"I guess the gang thought that we wouldn't want to leave
the condo for a while so they made sure we had enough food
and boy do we have enough food," I said with a laugh.

Thomas laughed too as he bent over to kiss me on the
cheek.

After we ate, I changed the music. We danced to a little
Frank Sinatra. Gently, Thomas took me into his arms as he
had in the PT room and made passionate love to me on the
sofa. We whispered to each other how much we loved the
other. I never felt as happy as I did that night.

The next 10 days we lived as much as most people do in
10 years.

Maui was known for a beautiful waterfall and shimmering
blue pool. Thomas picked up a rental car and a map and
drove to Ulaino Road beyond Kahanu Garden. We sat on the
rocks while the water splashed us in the face. Because the

waterfall is only 20 yards from the sea, we left to walk along the beach.

The next day Thomas decided to teach me to snorkel. We went to local dive shop and rented equipment. At first, it was strange breathing out of a tube in my mouth but I eventually got the hang of it. We explored the fish close to the cove because I was a little squeamish about going too far from shore. I loved the fish. To see them in their natural habitat was a treat. After I mastered snorkeling, the next day Thomas took me back to the dive shop for scuba lessons. This was a little trickier. I was scared and thrilled at the same time. I didn't scuba on Maui; I just had lessons. Thomas saved the scuba diving for one of the three days we spent on Kauai. He took me to Po'ipu to see the coral. This was a place where novice divers went. We also visited the north shore sites of the Tunnels Reef and the Kele Lagoon. The reef and fish were colorful. I felt safer diving there because it wasn't an ocean dive.

After three days in Kauai, we went back to Oahu. I borrowed Peter's '65 Mustang Convertible so Thomas and I could drive to Diamond Head. We had a picnic lunch and hiked the half hour trail up to the rim to see the incredible panoramic view of the southern coast of the island.

One day we visited Chinatown and ate lunch at Wo Fats, Chinatown's longest standing restaurant.

Another day we visited the Byodoin Temple. It was a traditional Japanese Buddhist temple and had just been completed when we visited. The design of the temple was based on the famous 900 year old Phoenix Hall of Byodo-In at Uji Japan. The temple was surrounded by gardens and carp guarded by pecking peacocks.

On the 10th day of our honeymoon, Thomas received a call. He would be receiving his exact orders within the next 72 hours. Soon he would be returning to active duty.

The orders said Thomas needed some basic training and he would ship out in approximately two months.

It was then that the nightmares returned. I begged Thomas to talk to a military psychologist. Reluctantly he did, but this did not stop him from receiving a clean bill of health psychologically and returning to NAM.

Because of his rank, he was allowed to live off base with me until he shipped out with the exception of a two week training period when he was on field maneuvers. I went back to work but cut my hours to 10 hours a day, 5 days a week. I wanted to be there when he got home so we could have dinner and spend as much time together as possible. We made the most of the weekends but time passed quickly. Thomas was scheduled to leave two weeks before Christmas 1967. I asked Thomas where he was being stationed. He said it was classified. I spoke to Admiral Lewis. I pleaded with him to tell me where Thomas would be. Admiral Lewis told me his final destination was Khe Sanh.

The night before he shipped out, Thomas was restless. I could feel the unrelenting terror. I knew he was dreaming about those terrible days in Laos.

Thomas tossed and turned the entire night. He awoke at 6:30 a.m. The staff car was due at 9:00 a.m. He stared at the ceiling holding me tightly against his body. It was the best feeling in the world. He didn't know that I was awake almost the entire night trying to enjoy the last moments of him being next to me until he had to leave. Thomas wanted to make love one more time.

"Marla, are you awake," he whispered.

"Yes, sweetheart," I replied.

"I love you," he said as he kissed the top of my head.

"I love you too."

"I want to make love one last time."

"I want you to make love to me but please don't say one last time. Just say for now."

We made love. When we finished, Thomas pulled me close to him and held me until he had to get ready to leave. I begged him to hold me for just a few minutes more. The time had finally come that he had to get up and shower or he wouldn't be ready when the staff car came. He asked me to join him in the shower which I eagerly obliged.

I watched him shave and comb his hair. I remembered when I was a kid how my father used to wash his face and shave in the bathroom sink. I would sit on the toilet with the lid down and watch him. That was our time for us to talk about things like school or my plans to go into the Navy. Even when I was a kid, I knew this was the path I would take.

The staff car was due in 5 minutes to take Thomas to the plane. I was standing in my robe, my hair in a towel, smoking a cigarette watching Thomas adjust his tie. Thomas took a drag from my cigarette. Then he took me in his arms and kissed me.

"Be safe. Come back to me," I said.

"Marla, my plane doesn't leave for two hours. Please come down to see me off."

"I can't. I hate good-byes. It's better if we just do it here."

There was a knock at the door. I cringed. I pulled Thomas against my body and kissed him passionately.

There was another rap at the door.

Thomas yelled, "Just a minute." He kissed me one last time.

"Are you all right?" he asked.

"I will be. You better go. I don't want you to be late."

"I'll write you. You'll write me. Before we know it, we'll be together." Thomas was desperately trying to reassure me and in some way himself that he would return.

"I love you so much. Please come back to me Thomas. We have a lot of living to do."

"I love you too. I'll come back. I promise."

Thomas opened the door, picked up his duffle bag and walked out.

I puffed on my cigarette staring at the closed door. It took all my strength not to run after him and scream, "Don't go."

After I heard the jeep pull away, I went to the phone and called Chaplain Cook. It was 9:02 a.m. I knew he was in every morning by 8:00 a.m.

"Chaplain Cook?"

"Marla, what do I own this pleasant phone call?" he said in his usual cheery voice.

"Thomas just left for the airport. He's returning to NAM. I guess I just needed to someone to talk to," I said feeling knots in my stomach.

"I'll pray for him as I pray for everyone else over there."

"I appreciate that Chaplain Cook. I better get dressed and go to work or I will go nuts thinking about this."

"Marla, remember you can call me anytime you need to."

"Thanks, Chaplain Cook. I'm sure I will take you up on that offer while Thomas is gone."

As I hung up the phone, a wave of reality hit me. All I could do was sit on the bed and weep.

Chapter 25

Chaplain Cook drove to Hickam Air Force Base. He inquired as to which flight Major Thomas Smith was on and preceded to the plane. Thomas was drinking a cup of coffee, talking with some of the guys he was flying out with when Chaplain Cook approached.

"Chaplain Cook, what are you doing here? This is a pleasant but unexpected surprise," said Thomas.

"Marla called and told me you were leaving this morning. I had been meaning to see you before now to see if you wanted to read another book that I had in my collection but with the wedding, honeymoon, and training I never had the chance to see you until now."

"Sure, what is it?"

Chaplain Cook pulled a small black leather-bound book out of his jacket. It was the Bible. "Thomas, I know you aren't religious but you told me in the hospital that the Book of Psalms was helpful to you. I remember your exact words were, 'David really went through some tough experiences and wrote so expressively.' There are many stories in the Bible that are equally tough: the Book of Job, the story of Moses, and the Gospels of Matthew, Mark, Luke and John which chronicled the life and ministry of Jesus just to name a few. Are you interested?"

"Chaplain Cook, of course I'll take the book. I don't know how much time I'll have with all the assignments that are on my plate but I like to read before going to bed so I'll plan to read a little each evening until I finish it. Thanks for thinking of me," Thomas said.

The two men shook hands.

Chaplain Cook said, "I'll be praying for you, Thomas."

"Thanks, Chaplain Cook but please pray for Marla too. I think she's going to need it more than me."

"I'll pray for both of you."

With that, Chaplain Cook got into his jeep and left. Thomas turned around and walked toward the plane. As he thumbed through the Bible, he found a note.

It read, "Thomas, I will be praying Psalm 91 for you every day until you come back, your friend, Chaplain Cook."

Thomas went to Psalm 91 (GNT) and reread it.

'Whoever goes to the Lord for safety, whoever remains under the protection of the Almighty can say to him,

"You are my defender and protector.

You are my God; in you I trust."

He will keep you safe from all hidden dangers and from all deadly diseases.

He will cover you with his wings; you will be safe in his care; his faithfulness will protect and defend you.

You need not fear any dangers at night or sudden attacks during the day or the plagues that strike in the dark or the evils that kill in daylight.

A thousand may fall dead beside you, ten thousand all around you, but you will not be harmed.

You will look and see how the wicked are punished.

You have made the Lord your defender, the Most High your protector, and so no disaster will strike you, no violence will come near your home.

God will put his angels in charge of you to protect you wherever you go.

They will hold you up with their hands to keep you from hurting your feet on the stones.

You will trample down lions and snakes, fierce lions and poisonous snakes.

God says, "I will save those who love me and protect those who acknowledge me as Lord.

When they call to me, I will answer them; when they are in trouble, I will be with them.

I will rescue them and honor them.

I will reward them with long life; I will save them.'"

Thomas closed the book. He said to himself, "I hope for Marla and my sake that this Psalm comes true."

Chapter 26

With Thomas gone, I went back to working 12 hours a day, 6 days a week. I hoped the long hours would help fill some of the emptiness in my life but I found nothing could compensate for the loneliness I felt. I wrote Thomas at least three times a week while I constantly worried about him. Since Thomas was in Intelligence, he could not talk about his assignment so we wrote about how much we missed each other and how we looked forward to seeing each other soon. I wrote him weekly updates of what happened on "Bonanza." Part of me found this a crazy thing to do but "Bonanza" was a deep connection for us.

It was early 1968. A ceasefire was declared between the United States and North Vietnam during the Vietnamese holiday of Tet. Intelligence had some unconfirmed sources that said the ceasefire would be broken. Thomas was supposed to be in Saigon for a high level meeting but his flight was delayed when the NVA attacked Khe Sanh. Khe Sanh was under siege from mid January through April 1968.

When I heard the news, my heart sank. On the 2nd day of the attack, a rocket hit a bunker at the eastern end of the base detonating 1,500 tons of ammunition stored there. The explosion knocked over helicopters, perforated tents, sending shrapnel into buildings and igniting jet fuel.

Another round hit a tear gas cache which sent a cloud of the stuff over the base for several hours. The battle was just getting started. By February, the NVA had inflicted a 50% casualty rate. There were other problems like nauseating odors from piles of garbage and excrement burning in oil drums. Rats infested the base forcing everyone to wrap themselves tight when they went to sleep. Still the NVA continued to bomb Khe Sanh.

The big C-130 cargo planes were unable to land because part of the runway was knocked out. Only the smaller C-123s landed to bring supplies. Unfortunately they could only carry a third of what the C-130s could carry.

We saw many casualties from there yet intelligence was scarce. I called Admiral Lewis. He told me that Thomas hadn't made it out of Khe Sanh despite two attempts but didn't have any updated information. I asked Admiral Lewis to find out through one of the cargo pilots if Thomas was alright. He called in a favor from an Air force Colonel who contacted a base commander sending planes into Khe Sanh. One of the C-123 pilots telegraphed a message to Admiral Lewis which said Thomas was ok. I was so relieved.

Khe Sanh was saved but was eventually abandoned in June of 1968. Why? Who knows? The military does things that the common person doesn't understand. I have tried to believe that they have some grand picture that nobody else knows so when something seems dumb to the rest of us, it must have been the correct course of action to pursue. As I went along in my naval career, I began to see that the higher ups had no clue what was going on in the day to day operations.

Thomas eventually went to Saigon for his briefing. A couple of guys had come up with some new interrogation techniques and they wanted Thomas to be part of that program. Thomas agreed but he went back to SOG as soon as his work there was completed.

During this time, the amount of wounded men over-whelmed the hospitals. Servicemen were being saved with the latest medical techniques but the injuries were crippling. Psychological wounds accompanied these horrific injuries. The boys were young, some only 18, now crippled for life missing an arm or a leg or more. It was heartbreaking. It made me think more and more about Thomas coming backing with one of these horrible injuries or God-forbid not coming back at all.

Chapter 27

Eight months into his tour, Thomas finagled a 10 day leave to Hawaii. In case things fell through he didn't tell me he was coming and have me be disappointed, so he decided to surprise me. He hitched a ride on a helicopter to Japan and then on a cargo plane which took him into Hawaii. From the airbase, he borrowed an army jeep and drove to the hospital.

Thomas dropped in on Peter first and together, they went to the therapy area. I was working with a patient but had he arrived in another hour, I would have been in my office doing paperwork and then I would have seen him through my office window.

Thomas appeared at the door watching me give therapy to a GI whose had lost a leg and had been fitted with prosthesis. I was giving directions, spotting the soldier on one side when I caught a glimpse of Thomas through the mirror. I couldn't believe what I had seen so I asked my patient to stop for a moment so I could look across the room. My patient did as he was instructed.

There was Thomas! My heart leaped with joy. Calmly, I asked the patient to sit down for a minute. I walked over to the therapy phone to page Maria to the PT room. It seemed like forever before she appeared. Once she did, I hurried to

Thomas almost stumbling, tears streaming down my face. He dropped his duffle bag taking me in his big, strong arms.

I composed myself and asked him to wait in my office. I would be there as soon as I gave Maria instructions.

Thomas waited 15 minutes when I walked in with two sheets, two towels, two paper cups and a bottle of wine. I closed and locked the door. He pulled the window shades down. I called my secretary and said, "No interruptions until I call again." I put one sheet over the sofa. I opened the wine and poured us each a cup. We took a sip but drinking wasn't on either one of our minds. He pulled me close. I could feel his breath on my neck nibbling it as he made his way to my lips. He kissed me long and hard. He put his arms around me and worked his hands up my back rubbing my shoulders and then down to my lower back. I returned his long, hard, wet kiss. Thomas said, "Let's go home and do this right."

I replied, "I don't think either one of us could make it that far."

"I've just come a long way without a shower. I smell like sweat. At least let me go up to Peter's office and clean up," said Thomas.

"I don't care how long it's been since your last shower. It's been longer since you've held me in your arms. We've both waited a long time." I held him as tight as I could against me all the while feeling his manliness growing. He knew I was right. It was here and now. His uniform was difficult for me to unbutton in haste. He grabbed my hands and said, "Slow down, I'm not going anywhere." A big smile crossed his face. He kissed the side of my neck working his way to my cheek. His tongue lightly licked it. My body was pulsating. I felt lightheaded from all the sensations.

I tugged at the back of his T-shirt pulling it over his head. Rubbing my hands all over his chest, I laughed and pulled him close to me to kiss his soft lips.

Thomas needed to take off his boots to remove his pants. He sat down on the sofa and plop went the boots on the floor. I jumped on his lap and unzipped his pants. I stood up; then Thomas stood up and I pulled his pants off. Thomas pulled my green top over my head. He then tugged at the bow that kept my green pants up. They fell to the floor.

We gazed lustfully at the other. It reminded me how just two weeks before, I was out to dinner with George and Maria, and I lusted after a piece of chocolate cake. I couldn't think of anything else until I had it. On one level, it was the same feeling but on another level this was much more intense. After we undressed, we began to make love and it was like the first time in the therapy room. It had been only 8 months but it might well have been 8 years. Thomas was gentle. He knew all my hot buttons and pressed everyone. I knew what he liked and went for them all. Oh, how I wanted to please him. I pulled off his shorts. He did likewise with my panties. Thomas started slowly at first getting into the rhythm but I couldn't hold back any more. I begged him for more. Faster, oh please faster. I need you; I want you. Thomas sped up and we both came together.

It was splendid. I never thought in my entire life I would make love somewhere other than my home or a hotel room, but surprise, we did it right there in my office.

After we finished, I hoped I didn't yell out too loud. Everybody from my department knew what was going on my office. I started to feel a little embarrassed but then I thought the door was locked, the window shades were drawn, we hadn't seen each other in months. He was my husband; I was his wife and we loved each other. What should I be embarrassed about? Nothing!

We snuggled on the sofa for a long time. Whenever we made love, no matter what was going on around us, we felt only peace and calm. I broke the silence as I reached over trying to grab a cigarette from his shirt.

"Why didn't you let me know you coming to Hawaii on leave?" I asked curiously.

"It had been canceled three times prior to today. I didn't want to disappoint you if I told you I would be here and then had to cancel. Surprises are better, don't you think? Here let me get that," Thomas said as he took two cigarettes from the pack, and handed one to me.

"Absolutely! I love good surprises and there isn't a better surprise in the world than you being here with me," I said. I paused for a moment, took a drag and asked with trepidation, "How long is your leave?"

"Ten days," Thomas said without emotion. "I leave for DC then I return to NAM."

We both knew that in the military you took what you could and lived with the outcome.

During those 10 days, we did as much as we could but eventually it was time for Thomas to leave for DC and then return to NAM. His tour would be over in 5 months or so we thought.

Things had a way of changing.

Chapter 28

In November of 1968, one month before Thomas was to leave NAM permanently, he was asked to go to Da Nang for a high level briefing. The military asked him to extend his stay until May of 1969. He would definitely return home at that time. There were changes coming in the new administration. Richard Nixon had been elected President and he had a secret way to end the war in Vietnam. The military needed Thomas to continue his present duties to keep things on an even keel. He agreed on the condition he was granted another leave to see me.

Thomas called and told me the news. I was disappointed but tried not to show it. I told him I understood. What else could I say? It would be all the sweeter once he came home for good. He told me he had a 10 day leave scheduled for March. I arranged time off. This time no surprise visits.

Thomas arrived as scheduled March 13th, 2 years and 10 days to the day he was first wheeled into Oahu General. There was no itinerary for us to follow, just spend as much time as possible together. On our 3rd night together, we were sitting on the sofa watching TV with me nestled under his arm. Out of the blue Thomas asked me,

"Marla, honey, I never asked you how you felt about having

children. I know that you are as career military as I am but I would like to start a family. Do you want children?"

I was taken aback. Collecting my thoughts, I replied, "To be honest, Thomas, I never gave it much thought. I guess my life has always revolved around work so having a family has been the farthest thing from my mind. I guess if the circumstances were right, I would want to have a child."

"What circumstances are those?"

"Well, for starters, I would want you to be here, not in NAM or DC. If you relocated, I would have to seek a transfer and visa versa. A child needs both parents."

"I agree. What else?"

"That's basically it. I need to feel secure. It's a big step having a baby."

"I agree with you. Marla, sweetheart, I want you to have my baby."

"When?"

"When I get back from NAM, I want to start a family. I will be retiring next year when I get my 20. I want to get my teaching credential and teach either elementary school or high school math. I assume you want to stay in for your 20. Find out how the Navy feels about having a baby while in the service." He kissed me on the forehead and told me how I was everything to him.

I replied, "I love you so much."

Nothing more was spoken about this.

A week later, it was time for Thomas to leave for NAM. I don't know why but I drove him out to the airfield. I stood there and watched the C-130 take-off, all the while waiving and feeling like I would never see him again.

Chapter 29

Two and a half weeks before Thomas was due home, I became ill with what I thought was the flu. I couldn't keep anything down and was nauseated all the time. After three days of this, I called in sick and asked Peter to come over to the house with his medical bag in tow. I was in bed when he knocked at the door.

"Use the spare key," I screamed.

Peter came in. I was throwing up in a paper bag.

"Peter, I can't remember the year I have been this sick," I said between heaves.

"Let me check you out."

Peter took my vitals and informed me he didn't believe it was the flu.

"What do you think it is?" I asked.

"I think you're pregnant."

"Can't be, Thomas and I use protection. We never make love without it."

"Condoms aren't 100%. You know that," he said in a superior tone of voice.

"Yes I know that," I said as I grabbed another bag to puke in.

"Marla, I want you take a pregnancy test to confirm my suspicion. You have all the symptoms of morning sickness."

I still was mumbling about condoms. "If I am pregnant, I need to call Admiral Lewis."

"If you are pregnant, you don't have to do anything right away. First things first. Let's get the test results. In the meantime, you are dehydrated. I am putting you on IV fluids. I'll have some chicken broth sent over from the deli."

"Peter, whatever the outcome, I need the strictest confidence in this matter."

"As your doctor, that goes without saying. I'll be back later to change the IV bag and check on you. For now, the diagnosis is the flu."

The test results came back positive. No mistake. He ran them twice. I was pregnant. Since I was having trouble keeping anything down, Peter put together a bland diet and gave me a bottle of prenatal vitamins. He continued the IVs. Based on the time table I gave him, I was about 5 weeks along.

"Peter, I don't want to tell Thomas or the Navy just yet."

"This isn't a secret you can keep forever," Peter said in his normal factual tone of voice.

"True but I want to tell Thomas in person. Then we can go to Admiral Lewis together and see what the fallout would be. I figured two weeks give or take a couple of days wouldn't be a problem."

"It's your decision whatever you want to do," Peter replied.

I started to feel more nervous as time moved closer to Thomas' homecoming. Six days before Thomas was to return home, I wrote an emotional letter which wasn't my normal tone.

It said, "To the love of my life, my dear Thomas, I am counting the minutes until we will be together again. I close my eyes and I can feel your strong arms around me. When I take a breath, I can smell your manliness and I smile knowing that I am the luckiest woman in the world to have you in my life.

I have a few surprises for you one of which is a brand new console color TV with an AM/FM radio, and phonograph. I went out and bought the newest Frank Sinatra album. On your first night home, my love, I want you to think about what you want to do. We could listen to Frank and cook steaks. Or we could watch 'Bonanza' on the new TV and order pizza in. Or we could go to the 'Villa Sorrento,' eat, and enjoy the sunset. You don't have to answer now. Just think about it. Well, I'm at work and I've got to run off to a meeting. Write soon. I love you. – Marla."

Thomas stared at the letter for a while not knowing what to say. He picked up a pen wrote the following letter:

"My darling, sweet Marla, I too am counting the minutes until I am home holding you in my arms. I think about the fragrance of your body and it stimulates me beyond words. I miss your silky smooth skin touching mine at night. Whatever you want to do when I return home is fine as long as it includes you wearing that black sexy negligee I like so much. I was surprised but pleased that you purchased a console color TV for the condo. I look forward to watching 'Bonanza' in living color. Maybe I'll finally see the NBC peacock in all its glory. I can't image what other surprises you have in store but I know they will be pleasant ones.

Bob Hope came to entertain the troops not far from here a few days ago. I was unable to go but most of guys in camp went and said he was very funny.

I have to go now. A big hug and kiss, Love always, Thomas."

It was now a short 36 hours before Thomas was to leave Vietnam. He was excited as were all the other 'short timers' to finish their tour of duty. There were about 15 guys sitting around having a beer, smoking – some playing cards and the rest just talking or reading.

Thomas finished an entry in his diary. He crushed out his cigarette just as the loud speaker announced that he was needed in the Colonel's office immediately.

This couldn't be good news.

Chapter 30

"Major Smith reporting to the Colonel, sir."

"Major, I need you to lead a recon team. Headquarters received a distress call that two SOG recon teams are under attack by the NVA in Laos. They were sent to rescue a downed pilot."

"Begging the Colonel's pardon but isn't there anyone else that can lead this recon effort. I leave for Hawaii in 36 hours."

"I thought about this before I asked you to come to my office. I am aware you are about to leave for Hawaii after 4 tours of duty. However, there is no one more qualified to lead the mission. Our best intelligence states that this area is near the spot where you were picked up after your escape from the POW camp."

"Yes, sir. I will assemble the team and be ready to leave in 10 minutes."

Thomas saluted the Colonel and left his office.

Thomas left with 5 men. The helicopter dropped the group one kilometer east of the NVA stronghold. The SOG men quietly maneuvered into position; Thomas was point man leading the others through the thick brush. Thomas' group came upon the 1st and 2nd recon team. Of the 1st recon team, two were dead, two wounded and one was unhurt and that was the infamous Lt. Anthony Lambello. Of the 2nd team, four were dead and two were badly wounded. Thomas ordered air cover with an additional helicopter to fly the wounded men out. He then directed two bomb runs in attempts to clean out the pockets of NVA soldiers that were sniping at them. The downed pilot had already been rescued by the 2nd recon team. He was unharmed. Thomas' team helped the wounded and the pilot to the pick up area. Another helicopter was sent in to extract the dead. There was an unwritten creed to never leave a brother behind.

Lt. Lambello was frozen stiff with fear. He was of no use to anyone. Thomas put him on the copter with the wounded men. Thomas and his recon team provided cover as the dead and wounded were loaded into the helicopters.

As the last helicopter was loading, Thomas ran out of ammunition. Another CAR-15 was thrown to him. The pilot was screaming he needed to take off.

Thomas screamed, "Take off, damn it, take off!"

The 3rd recon team was there backing up Thomas. After the copters with the dead and wounded took off, another helicopter landed to extract the 3rd team. Thomas yelled at his guys to get into the copter. He was low on ammo but provided cover as his guys got in. Thomas finished the second CAR-15. He was thrown a third CAR-15. As the helicopter was taking off, an NVA soldier waited until Thomas was pulling himself in. A single shot rang out. The bullet went in at a side angle under Thomas' flack jacket hitting him in the abdomen. Thomas yelled, "I'm hit," and started to fall out of the copter but two guys grabbed him and held on. One guy dropped a couple of grenades just as the pilot took off. After they left the area, the two guys struggled to pull Thomas into the helicopter. The medic attended to Thomas but he was bleeding profusely. The pilot radioed that they had another seriously wounded soldier.

Thomas' last words on the helicopter were, "Tell my wife that I love her."

He lost consciousness. The doctors at the evacuation hospital evaluated Thomas and operated immediately. The internal damage was extensive. They needed to stabilize him and fly him to the hospital ship where they had better surgical equipment and a more modern operating room. General Sherman was notified of the situation and he called Admiral Lewis. When Admiral Lewis received word he screamed, "How could this have happened," over and over slamming his fist on the table.

Chapter 31

Thomas was supposed to call to let me know what time his plane was due at Hickam. I didn't hear from him but I rationalized that he was busy and would call when he could. I tried to feel like everything was ok but as more time passed, I became increasingly worried.

Upon receiving news that Thomas was wounded, Admiral Lewis called for a staff car to pick up Chaplain Cook. Admiral Lewis wanted Chaplain Cook there when he told me the news. Chaplain Cook was visibly shaken. He pulled himself together knowing he had to be there for me. He felt like someone had hit him in the gut with a 2x4. It was 8:30 a.m. Admiral Lewis already booked me on a cargo plane to Wake Island. From there, he arranged to have a helicopter drop me on board the hospital ship. Finally, Admiral Lewis called Peter.

"Is Marla in?"

"Yes. Would you like to talk to her?"

"Not over the phone. I'll be over shortly."

Peter got an uneasy feeling. "Is everything alright?"

"No," replied Admiral Lewis trying to keep his emotions in check.

"Did something happen to Thomas? Is he dead?" Peter asked. For the first time, genuine emotion came over him.

There was no answer on the other end of the phone.

"When you arrive at the hospital, come to my office first," Peter said anxiously.

Twenty minutes later Admiral Lewis arrived with Chaplain Cook and two Marine escorts.

I was sitting in my office like I always do going through the last of my paperwork for the morning therapy sessions. I still had not heard from Thomas. Even Peter hadn't dropped in with my morning coffee which was fine with me because I had to stop drinking it due to the constant nausea. I decided that I was being entirely too pessimistic. I had received Thomas' letter yesterday and was excited that he would be coming home late tonight or early tomorrow.

I needed to reschedule a meeting. I picked up the phone to dial when I looked out my window and saw the Admiral's entourage coming up the hospital steps. I dropped the phone and gasped, "Oh God, please don't let Thomas be dead."

I ran out of my office to the entrance of the hospital. Peter saw the four men from his 2nd floor window. He ran down the steps.

I screamed, "My God, please tell me Thomas isn't dead."

Admiral Lewis began to speak but Chaplain Cook cut him off.

"He isn't dead but he's been badly wounded. Our last report is that he was in surgery," replied Chaplain Cook trying to keep his voice from cracking.

"We're flying you out to be with him now. You will be briefed on the way to the airport," said Admiral Lewis.

The Admiral's staff car took me to a cargo plane. The helicopter was waiting at Wake Island which brought me to the hospital ship, "Mercy."

When I arrived, Thomas was out of surgery. The prognosis was grim.

Dr. Clarke approached me. "I'm sorry. We tried our best but there was just too much internal damage."

I tried to contain myself.

"How much time does he have?"

"I can't say. It's a miracle he's hung on this long. I think the reason he's still alive is he has some things he has to say to you. He also has a last request only you can fulfill."

"Is he in a lot of pain?"

"Some, but he won't let us give him any more morphine until he sees you. Go to him now. You will have complete privacy. Call me if you need me." Dr. Clarke put his hand on my shoulder.

I stood in the doorway. Thomas looked exactly like the day the first day I met him with an IV of normal saline, a unit of blood, a heart monitor, and Foley all attached to his frail body. He looked pale and in pain. Tears welled up in my eyes but I fought them back with all my might. Pity was not on the agenda. I walked over and touched his hand. Thomas' eyes flickered open. He turned his head slightly.

"It's not just a dream. You really are here," he said with a raspy tone in his voice.

"Yes sweetheart, I'm here." I kissed his hand.

"I screwed up. I'm sorry."

"Sorry for what?"

"For not fulfilling my promise to you."

"Who said you haven't fulfilled your promise. You have been the best husband a girl could have ever wanted. I love you so much."

"I love you too. I need to tell you what happened."

"I already know. I was briefed by Admiral Lewis."

"But he doesn't know everything."

"But he does. I know all about the recon and how you saved those guys. General Sherman promoted you to Lt. Colonel. You will receive the Distinguished Service Cross."

"Great, another medal for the box," said Thomas wincing in pain. "Darling, there isn't much time. I need to say a few things to you. Please tell my mother that I loved her. I wished I could have seen her one last time. Second, more than anything else, I wanted to come back and have a life with you but I couldn't ignore my brother's call for help. Tell Chaplain Cook I read the book he gave me. The military must have based it's creed on John 15:13. I did what I had to do, Marla. I was the only one with the most experience who knew the terrain so I was tapped to lead the 3rd recon team.

Sweetheart, there was a guy who survived the 1st mission, a Lt. Anthony Lambello. He was the source of all the problems. Pursue this for me, please. He must be brought to justice for all the pain he caused. If it wasn't for him, I wouldn't have had to lead the 3rd recon team. I needed to come in and rescue our guys after their mission went bust because of that bastard.

I didn't see the NVA soldier who shot me. He shot me as the helicopter was taking off. Can you forgive me?"

"I'll say it again. There isn't anything to forgive."

I took his hand, put it up to my face and whispered, "It's ok. I love you. I have always loved you and always will."

"And I you, remember that. Wherever you are, whatever you do, I will be watching over you. Try to believe that. I know there isn't much time." Thomas writhed in pain. "I have three requests. Please take all these tubes out of me. I can't die hooked up to these machines. I thought that when I died years from now, it would be at home in bed next to you." Thomas' pain increased. "After you take this stuff off me, please give me a shot of morphine to take the edge off the pain. Please get in bed and hold me until I go."

I looked at Thomas and nodded. I unhooked the monitors, the IVs, the Foley, and gave him a morphine shot. I took off my clothes and curled up next to my dying husband.

"I know this must be difficult for you," said Thomas.

"I would walk through hot coals if you asked. If I could change places with you, I would," I said. I put my hand on his chest like I always did rubbing his chest hair.

"I know you would. Lay with me. Hold me," Thomas said quietly.

I laid there and held him.

Nothing more was said but each of us had tears in our eyes.

Thomas' breathing slowed. The end was near. I reached for his hand and squeezed it gently. He squeezed back a little. It wasn't long after that that he was gone. I continued to lie next to him for a few minutes. Reality set in. Thomas was dead. I began to sob. Then I screamed, "Damn war, Damn war!"

Chapter 32

I arose 15 minutes later, dressed and called Dr. Clarke. He was in the next room so it only took a moment for him to arrive. He put his arm around me in an attempt to console me but I was beyond consolation. I felt as if my whole world had ended. If I started to cry again, I knew I wouldn't be able to stop. I asked Dr. Clarke if I could go to the radio room to call my mother-in-law. I requested that the burial detail be delayed until I returned. Dr. Clarke said he would leave everything as it was. He escorted me to the Communication's section of the ship. Captain Richards had been notified of Lt. Colonel Smith's passing. He was waiting for me in Communications.

"My condolences, Lt. Commander Bristol. I avail my services to you in whatever capacity you need until your departure."

"Thank you, Captain. I need to place a call to Albany, NY. Here is the number. It is my mother-in-law's residence. Once someone answers, please let me talk first," I said brushing the tears off my face.

"Yes, Lt. Commander."

I stood there watching the Communication's office place the call. It took 5 minutes for the call to connect to Patricia's house.

"Hello Anna, it's Marla. Esta Patricia en casa? (Is Patricia home?) No? Donde esta Patricia? (Where is Patricia?) Fort Bragg? Gracias. (Thank you.) Adios. (Good- bye)."

"I need you to place a call to Fort Bragg. I need to speak to the Commanding Officer," I said in a more urgent tone of voice.

The Communications Officer replied that this could take a moment. I looked at him and said, "Take all the time you need. I am not looking forward to this call."

The Communications Officer on base picked up the phone.

"Hello, my name is Lt. Commander Marla Bristol Smith. I am looking for Mrs. Patricia Smith. I was told she was a guest on base."

"Yes, she is the guest of General Butterfield and his wife. They are in the officer's club. Would you like to be transferred to her?" asked the Communications Officer.

"Please transfer me to General Butterfield, sir," I replied.

"One moment please." It felt like eternity but it was only a few seconds before General Butterfield came on the phone."

"General Butterfield speaking."

"General Butterfield, sir. My name is Lt. Commander Marla Bristol Smith. I am Patricia's daughter-in-law."

"Oh, how good of you to call. Patricia has spoken highly of you."

"General, unfortunately this is not a social call. I need to relay some bad news to Patricia about Thomas."

The General's voice dropped to a whisper.

"How badly is he wounded?" he asked.

"He passed less than an hour ago." Tears streamed down my face. My nose started to run. "I didn't want her to receive the official Marine notification." The Communications

Officer handed me his handkerchief. I whispered, "Thank you."

"Where are you?" said General Butterfield.

"Aboard 'Mercy,' outside the Philippines. I was with Thomas when he died. The Navy flew me in from my base in Oahu. I made it with a few minutes to spare. Can you please call Patricia to the phone?"

"Would you like me to tell her?" replied General Butterfield.

"General, thank you. I appreciate the offer but I feel it's my responsibility. I need you to be there for her. It is necessary for her to catch the next flight to Hawaii either by commercial or military plane. Ask Admiral Lewis if he can arrange a military flight."

"I'll make some calls. Either way she will be there."

"Thank you sir."

I could hear General Butterfield calling Patricia to the phone.

"Patricia, can you come here for a minute? Your daughter-in-law Marla is on the phone." His voice never gave away that bad news was waiting for her.

Patricia got up from the chair. She smiled as she walked to the phone but the smile suddenly changed to panic. She knew before anyone said anything that something happened to Thomas."

"Hello?" said Patricia.

"Hello, mother – it's Marla." I tried to keep a steady tone to my voice.

"Marla, honey, it's so good to hear your voice. Today is May 8th isn't it? If I am not mistaken Thomas is returning home today. Is that why you are calling? To tell me Thomas is there and wants to say hello."

"No mother, that's not the reason. I'm calling to tell you…

Oh God…mother…Thomas is gone, he died less than an hour ago." I started crying again.

Patricia screamed, "No, it can't be," and dropped the phone. General Butterfield helped Patricia to a chair while his wife Joyce held her hand. The General picked up the phone.

"I will call you back and let you know when Patricia will be in Hawaii."

"General, will you be accompanying her?"

"Yes, Mrs. Butterfield and I will be there."

"I will be leaving 'Mercy' within a few hours with a short stop at Wake Island. You can always leave a message for me at Oahu General."

"Acknowledged. Lt. Commander… Marla, I…I am very sorry for your loss."

Barely keeping my composure I replied, "Thank you sir."

Chapter 33

I was escorted back to Thomas' room. I cried so hard I got the hiccups. Dr. Clarke came in. He said it was time to prepare Thomas for transport to Hickam Air Force Base.

Normally soldiers who died were sent to the Philippines to have their body prepared for return to the United States. I asked that Thomas and I fly directly to Hawaii and my request was accepted. Thomas had the right to be buried in Arlington National Cemetery because of his medals and rank but I wanted him buried in Hawaii. Captain Richards came to his room to escort me to the guest quarters while the burial detail performed their ritual. We entered the room. Captain Richards spoke,

"Can I get you anything to eat or drink? I'm sure you must be a little thirsty."

"No thank you Captain. I appreciate the offer."

"Lt. Commander Bristol…"

"Call me Marla."

"Marla, I know I said earlier how sorry I am for your loss but you don't realize that I am very affected by the death of your husband."

"I'm not sure I follow you."

"My son, John is an Air Force pilot based in Saigon. He flew secret bombing missions over Laos and Cambodia. He knew your husband very well. Three months ago, John flew a mission over the Ho Chi Minh Trail and was shot down along with two other pilots. The situation was bleak. You probably know what your husband did in NAM, rescuing pilots. Many recon guys lost their lives going into the jungle after our airmen. Your husband led the recon team that saved my son. He was responsible for saving many servicemen as part of his normal everyday job never giving a second thought to his own personal safety on the many missions he personally led. John wasn't supposed to tell me the details of his mission but he needed to talk to someone. Your husband was 100% Special Forces. He knew his job and was good at it."

"Captain, were you aware my husband was due to come home in less than two days when he was killed."

"No I didn't. I am even sorrier to hear that. John had nothing but high praise for Lt. Colonel Smith. I do know he loved you very much. John told me that at the officer's club the men would talk about their girlfriends or wives. Many cheated. Lt. Colonel Smith showed your picture all around. He was faithful. All he talked about was how he couldn't wait to come back and start a family with you."

I broke down and cried.

"I'm sorry. I didn't want to make you feel worse. I just wanted you to know that you are not the only one feeling a tremendous loss. He touched the lives of so many and saved many of our servicemen. I don't know what happened on that last recon mission. You may never find out because as you know Major Smith's work was top secret. If it were me, I wouldn't give up until I found out the truth."

"Thank you Captain."

There was a knock at the door. It was Dr. Clarke. Captain Richards left and Dr. Clarke entered.

"I wanted to let you know that your husband will be ready

to leave in 90 minutes. I came to check on you. Can I get you anything? A sedative perhaps?"

"No, thank you Dr. Clarke. I'm fine."

"I suspect you aren't. You need to take care of yourself Marla. If you want to talk to someone I'm here or I'll call the ship's Chaplain."

"If I need to talk, I'll come to the infirmary, Dr. Clarke."

"I'll leave you to get a little rest. I will be back in an hour and a half."

Dr. Clarke left. I sat on the floor with my back against the bunk staring at the wall. I couldn't get out of my head what Captain Richards told me about Thomas. I thought when he went back he was going back to Intelligence and limiting his field work. I knew better than anyone about the nightmares and the restlessness but somehow he must have found a way to live with it. He must have had a hell of an iron constitution to go out into the jungle to rescue his brothers all the while keeping his own emotions in check. What happened on that final mission?

Oh, dear God, did he know how much I loved him and supported him even though I was scared to death that things would end the way they did. My stomach felt like a giant rock had taken up residence. I kept mulling this over and over in my mind. Before I knew it, there was a knock at the door. It was the Captain.

"Marla, it's time to leave. A helicopter has landed on deck to take you and Lt. Colonel Smith to a connecting flight at Wake Island From there, the transport plane will fly both of you directly to Hawaii. You will be met by a full military escort once the plane lands at Hickam."

"Thank you for making all the arrangements, Captain." We saluted one another. I followed the Captain upstairs on to the deck. To my amazement, the entire ship's personnel had assembled, down to the last midshipman, cook's helper and engineer. As I walked to where my husband's casket lay ready for transport, each of the ship's personnel stood at attention, saluting us. I could see tears in their eyes. I saluted back trying to make as little eye contact as possible. I had to hold on to what composure I had otherwise I knew I wouldn't be able to make the long journey home. Captain Richards escorted me to the helicopter. As six sailors were loading the flag draped coffin on the helicopter, Dr. Clarke walked over to me and put his hand on my shoulder.

"Please take care of yourself. You need all your strength now."

It was if he knew I was pregnant but maybe I looked so bad that he just wanted to give me words of encouragement. Either way, I was leaving. It was best to keep the conversation to a minimum.

As the helicopter departed, I looked down and saw the crew continuing to salute.

Chapter 34

We landed at Wake Island. During the transfer, the pilot asked me if I wanted something to eat or drink. My nausea was a 24 hour a day, 7 day a week affair. I thanked the pilot and asked him to bring me a Coke. I had no idea what time it was or even what day it was. Everything had become a blur. The pilot returned with my soda. I never left the casket of my dear Thomas, not for one minute. After we were airborne for Hawaii, I slept beside the coffin for a couple of hours.

On final approach, I asked the pilot to contact Hickam to see if my mother-in-law had arrived. Patricia was there with General and Mrs. Butterfield. She had landed only 30 minutes before. I was informed that Peter and George were at the airport waiting for the transport plane to land. Once we landed, the military honor guard approached. The flag draped plain pine casket which held my dear sweet husband was about to leave the plane.

Six Green Berets entered the cargo plane to escort Lt. Colonel Thomas Harrison Smith to the military mortuary located behind the hanger. A 7th Green Beret was assigned to be my personal escort. I wanted to walk behind the coffin alone but protocol called for an escort. I mustn't break protocol. I felt like my whole life was protocol. My husband was dead. Now comes the "dog and pony" show. I didn't know if

I could stand it. Furthermore, if anyone needed an escort, it was my mother-in-law. Later, I had a conversation with General Sherman and she received one.

As I was walking down the ramp behind the casket, I heard a scream from the tarmac. It was Patricia. She broke free from General Butterfield and ran toward the procession. The MPs caught her and restrained her long enough for Peter to administer a sedative.

The Special Forces men never stopped. They continued to carry the casket to the temporary mortuary. I stayed with Thomas, part of me wanting to help Patricia and part of me not wanting to let Thomas out of my sight. Time was moving slowly one moment and quickly the next.

Admiral Lewis entered the hanger.

"Marla, why don't you leave and get some rest. Thomas will be in the hands of military personnel until the funeral," he said in a concerned tone of voice.

"Yes, I know. I simply can't find the energy to leave him. Perhaps you could call Dr. Fong."

Admiral Lewis left and told Peter I needed him.

"Admiral Lewis said you wanted me, what's wrong?"

"I'm nauseated, dizzy and afraid to stand up."

"I'll get a wheelchair."

"Don't you dare! I will walk out of here. I just need someone to lean on so I won't fall down. I'm sure once I get something to eat and drink I will be fine."

"When was the last time you had something to eat or drink?"

"I had a Coke during change of aircraft at Wake Island," I replied waiting for the fallout.

"What? That's it?" Peter replied in a stunned tone of voice.

"Uh, huh."

"Here take my arm."

I took Peter's arm and we walked to the Admiral's staff car which took us back to my condo.

"Marla, you are not taking care of yourself. It's not just you that you need to think of," said Peter in his righteous tone of voice.

"Don't you think I'm well aware of that? The nausea is a constant reminder," I yelled back.

"I'll have some bland food sent over. I'll be back to check on you in an hour."

"Forget the food. Bring an IV." I paused for a moment to catch my breath. "Peter," I yelled. "Please find out how Patricia is doing. I'm extremely worried about her."

"I'll find out but you need to rest right now."

Right after Peter left, I crawled to the bathroom and threw up in the toilet. When Peter came back an hour later, I was asleep on the bathroom floor.

Peter woke me and asked, "What happened?"

"I threw up. I don't remember much after that. I must have passed out. I just can't deal with the nausea," I said while I was trying to catch my breath. "I'm sorry, Peter, I didn't mean to snap at you."

"Come on, I'll help you back to bed."

After I got into bed, Peter hooked me up to an IV.

"Did you see Patricia?" I asked with great consternation.

Peter didn't answer.

I repeated my question. "Peter, did you see Patricia?

"Yes, I did. She's not doing very well. The fact is the base doctor has her heavily sedated. While I was finding out how she was, Admiral Lewis asked me if you wanted him to take care of the arrangements. I told him to call you. I was under the impression you wanted to do it personally. Was I right?"

"Peter, you know that I want to take care of it. Why didn't you just tell him that?" I said angrily.

"I wanted to convince you not to. Marla, you are under an

inordinate amount of stress. That's not something you need in your condition. It would be best if the arrangements were handled by someone else," Peter said in his usual unemotional way.

"No way. This is the last thing I can give Thomas and it will be done my way. Give me the phone."

Peter knew better to argue with me when I was in this kind of mood. He handed me the phone. I called Admiral Lewis. I told him everything I wanted from the kind of casket, time of funeral, chapel, who would perform the service, which dress uniform would be worn – even down to what music would be played. Then I asked him to send over Chaplin Cook.

Chaplin Cook came over to the condo later that evening. I was in bed with my IV as my companion. I could see he wanted to say something but decided against it. I began with the funeral arrangements. Then I discussed my health. Because Chaplain Cook was bound by the same confidential person to person ethics that I am bound by as a professional in the medical field, I knew he could not reveal my pregnancy to anyone so I confided to him I was about seven weeks pregnant. I felt relieved to talk to someone other than Peter but I still felt so alone.

The phone rang. It was General Sherman.

He began without a hello, "Five high ranking people who worked with Thomas at the Pentagon want to attend the funeral but they need it postponed a day because they are unable to be there by the scheduled time."

"Absolutely not, sir," I said firmly. "I will not postpone the funeral. There are other people's feelings I have to think about, mainly Patricia. She's close to having a breakdown. She needs closure and so do I."

"I would like you to reconsider," General Sherman said firmly.

"Is that a request, General or do you plan to get Admiral Lewis involved and make it an order?"

"Marla, I would never do such a thing."

General Sherman seemed miffed by the accusation but I knew him as a ruthless man who got what he wanted and if anything or anybody got in his way, he would pulverize his opponent. Thomas told me he had many knock down drag outs with him but they always stayed on the same page. I needed to test that.

"Begging the General's pardon but how would I know that? My husband is barely dead 24 hours and you are making what I feel is an unreasonable request. I have already planned Thomas' burial. I don't want this turned into a circus or some event to highlight someone's political career. I won't let it. Either they can make it at the scheduled time or not."

I slammed the phone down. I didn't receive a return call. I had gotten my point across.

Thomas' funeral was the worst day of my life. It was May 11th, 1969. I received a call from Admiral Lewis that his staff car would pick me up at 11:00 a.m. for a private viewing, with the funeral beginning at 2:00 p.m. He told me in confidence that a very intense battle had started near the place where Thomas was killed. It was on Dong Ap Bia also known as Ap Bia Mountain in the rugged, jungle-shrouded mountains along the Laotian border of South Vietnam (now known as Hamburger Hill).

"Admiral Lewis, I don't want to hear about the war today. I'm burying my husband. Can you please respect that?" I said wearily.

"I'm sorry Marla. I was being insensitive. After the reception, I will have to leave with General Sherman to deal with this. I felt I owed you an explanation," he said apologetically.

"You don't owe me anything Admiral Lewis, except to pay your respects to Thomas at the funeral."

"Of course," he replied in a low voice.

I arrived at the mortuary. Patricia arrived shortly before me. Peter and George had arrived a half hour after.

The four of us were the only ones to see Thomas. Even Admiral Lewis and General Sherman were excluded which didn't sit well with either one of them. Too bad. Maybe I should have extended the offer but I just didn't feel right about allowing those two men to see Thomas. They were the two men who asked him to return to NAM and caused his death. It was an NVA bullet that took Thomas' life but Admiral Lewis and General Sherman were the ones who ordered him into battle. They were the ones responsible for his death. Worse yet, the politicians we voted for were the ones who decided where we send troops, why we go to far off lands, and why thousands of men and women come back in pine boxes and tens of thousands of wounded service personnel have their lives changed forever.

Peter and George felt helpless and uncomfortable. They didn't stay long. Patricia cried uncontrollably and had to be escorted out by General and Mrs. Butterfield.

I was alone. My military escort stayed six feet back at full attention. I touched Thomas' cheek with my hand and kissed his forehead with my lips. "Oh, Thomas, I love you so much. There was so much we were going to do together. This stupid war! What's it all about? All this human suffering and wasted lives. Why, Oh God, did you take my husband from me?"

The tears started to flow; they wouldn't stop. A tear drop fell on his cheek. I brushed it away. My escort came forward. He handed me his personal handkerchief. I could see tears in his eyes. I said, "Thank you."

He saluted and went back to his post. I stood there a long time. Chaplain Cook came in. He said it was time to begin the service. I didn't want to say good-bye, to close the coffin forever and never see him again but I had to. I bent down and kissed Thomas one last time on the lips. The casket was closed. I was ushered away from Thomas by my escort.

General Sherman and General Butterfield accompanied a heavily medicated Patricia to the front row where I sat with Admiral Lewis and Dr. Fong. My nausea was so bad I didn't know how I was going to make it through the service. I asked for a cola and crackers prior to the start of the service but nothing helped. My guts were turning inside out. I was burying my husband today. I wanted to scream out in anger but I knew for everybody's sake I had to keep my composure.

The mortuary was unable to accommodate the number of people who wanted to attend so the service was moved outdoors. I was asked numerous times about eulogies. There were several people who wanted to speak. I didn't think my mother-in-law could stand a long service so I limited it to just General Sherman and myself.

Chaplain Cook began with the Psalm 23 (GNT).

"The Lord is my shepherd; I have everything I need.

He lets me rest in fields of green grass and leads me to
      quiet pools of fresh water.

He gives me new strength.

He guides me in the right paths, as he has promised.

Even if I go through the deepest darkness,

I will not be afraid, Lord, for you are with me.

Your shepherd's rod and staff protect me.

You prepare a banquet for me, where all my enemies can
      see me;

You welcome me as an honored guest and fill my cup to
      the brim.

I know that your goodness and love will be with me all

my life; and your house will be my home as long as I live. Amen."

He continued with a letter from the men who served with Thomas that were still stationed in NAM.

It stated, "We are extremely sorry that we are unable to attend today's funeral of our brother, Lt. Colonel Thomas Harrison Smith known to all of us as "Bear." Bear was a mentor; a friend to everyone who knew him. He found his faith in Hawaii while recuperating from a leg injury two years ago. The person responsible was Chaplain Benjamin Cook. From Chaplain Cook, he learned two Bible lessons. Psalm 91 and John 15:13. To his wife and mother, may you both find these Bible passages a comfort today and in the days ahead. We know this is tremendous loss. We want you to know you are in our thoughts and prayers. Please remember that Lt Colonel Smith was an American Special Forces Soldier and as a Special Forces Soldier he lived and died by our creed.

'I am an American Special Forces soldier. A professional, I will do all that my nation requires of me.

I am a volunteer, knowing well the hazards of my profession.

I serve with the memory of those who have gone before me:

Roger's Rangers, Francis Marion, Mosby's Rangers, the first Special Service Forces and Ranger Battalions of WWII, the Airborne Ranger Companies of Korea. I pledge to uphold the honor and integrity of all I am – in all I do.

I am a professional soldier. I will teach and fight wherever my nation requires. I will strive always, to excel in every art and artifice of war.

I know that I will be called upon to perform tasks in isolation, far from familiar faces and voices, with the help and guidance of my God.

I will keep my mind and body clean, alert and strong, for this is my debt to those who depend upon me.

I will not fail those with whom I serve. I will not bring shame upon myself or the forces.

I will maintain myself, my arms, and my equipment in an immaculate state as befits a Special Forces soldier.

I will never surrender though I be the last. If I am taken, I pray that I may have the strength to spit upon my enemy.

My goal is to succeed in any mission – and live to succeed again.

I am a member of my nations' chosen soldiery. God grant that I may not be found wanting, that I will not fail this sacred trust.'"

Chaplain Cook finished reading the letter. Tears were running down his face. He reached up with his prayer stole and wiped them away. He announced that I wanted to say a few words.

The nausea returned like a tidal wave. Peter helped me to the podium. "Thank you for coming," I began. "Today we are remembering a wonderful man, Lt. Colonel Thomas Harrison Smith whom most of you knew on a professional level as a leader, a mentor and a friend. However, I knew him on another level. I met him at his lowest point. He had been wounded in NAM. He came to Oahu General to recover from his time in a POW camp and two gun shot wounds to his leg. Over his 7 month recovery, we fell in love. Thomas asked me to marry him. The happiest day of my life was when I became his wife.

I knew that it was possible that he would return to Vietnam. He did not have to return for a 4th tour. He was torn between his duty to the country he loved and the love he had for his new wife. I told him that he had to do what made him happy. What made him happy was serving his country but at the same time he looked forward to next year when he would have his 20 years in the military. He wanted to retire, go back to school, get his teaching credential and teach high school math. He asked me what I thought of that. I said if that's what made him happy that was fine with me. He also wanted to start a family once he got out of the service because that would also make him happy. I wanted what he wanted.

Unfortunately in life things don't always have a way of working out the way you plan. My father who should rest in peace always had a saying, 'Men make plans and God laughs.' Thomas and I made our plans but God had other plans for us. Thomas was my best friend, my lover, my husband and my world. He was my soulmate. Even though our time together was short, I will always be thankful I had him in my life."

I left the podium. General Sherman went up to speak.

His eulogy was short. He talked about what a fine officer and friend Thomas was to everybody who knew him.

Before Chaplain Cook finished the service, he spoke on his friendship with Thomas. Then he concluded with a reading from Ecclesiastes 3:1-8, 19-20 (GNT) and touched on John 15:13 (GNT).

"Thomas and I met while he was recuperating at Oahu General. He was having a particularly bad day when I showed up. We would engage in a game of chess when we could. I gave him the Book of Psalms to read at that time. I pray Psalm 91 for every soldier in harms way. When Thomas was leaving for his last tour of duty, I gave him the Bible. He said he didn't know how much time he would have to read it but he promised to read a little each night. I never had a chance to ask him what he thought of the various stories in there but it was apparent that he lived John 15:13 (GNT) which states, 'The greatest love you can have for your friends is to give your life for them.' In my time as a military chaplain, I have found that so many men disregard their own safety for the life of their brothers. Thomas was no exception. I will now conclude the service with Ecclesiastes 3:1-8, 19-20 (GNT):

'Everything that happens in this world happens at the
     time God chooses.
He sets the time for birth and the time for death,
the time for planting and the time for pulling up,
the time for killing and the time for healing,
the time for tearing down and the time for building.
He sets the time for sorrow and the time for joy,
the time for mourning and the time for dancing,
the time for making love and the time for not
     making love,
the time for kissing and time for not kissing.
He sets the time for finding and the time for losing,
the time for saving and the time for throwing away,
the time for tearing and the time for mending,
the time for silence and the time for talk.
He sets the time for love and the time for hate,
the time for war and the time for peace.
…the same fate awaits human beings and animals alike.
One dies just like the other. They are the same kind of
     creature.
…They are both going to the same place – the dust.
They both came from it; they both go back to it. Amen.'
This completes the memorial service."

It was time to go to the graveside for internment. Thomas' casket was loaded on a horse-drawn carriage. I walked behind; my head bowed; my mind in a fog. Peter tried in vain to convince me to ride in the limo but gave up after the first no.

A white horse without a rider marched next to me with the boots facing the opposite way in the stirrups. This riderless horse dates back before the Civil War which meant the officer was killed in battle.

Patricia rode in the limo behind me with General

Butterfield and his wife accompanying her. When we arrived at the graveside, Thomas was honored with the missing man flyover and taps.

One of the honor guards presented the American flag to Patricia and me. She was inconsolable. General Butterfield and his wife each grabbed a hand and led her to the limo. I went over to Thomas' casket, knelt down, kissed it, and placed a white carnation on the top of it. I walked toward my seat. My military escort was waiting to lead me back to the limo. I had the flag under my left arm.

I saw Peter sitting in the back when Chaplain Cook approached and said, "Marla, nothing I say could possibly make you feel better right now."

"You're right, Chaplain Cook. I'm angry. I'm angry at everybody and everything."

"And you have a right to feel that way. I don't have any magical words of comfort. I know you are hurting. Everybody who knew Thomas is hurting too but if you let me, I want to read you something that might give you some comfort."

"More words from the Bible?" I said sarcastically.

"Yes, but only if you want to hear them."

"Ok," I thought what the heck; maybe I could find some peace in what Chaplain Cook was going to say.

"Marla, this was one of Thomas' favorite psalms: Psalm 121 (GNT)

'I look to the mountains;

where will my help come from?

My help comes from the Lord, who made

heaven and earth.

He will not let you fall; your protector is always awake.

The protector of Israel never dozes or sleeps.

The Lord will guard you; he is by your side

to protect you.

The sun will not hurt you during the day, nor the
    moon during the night.
The Lord will protect you from all danger;
    he will keep you safe.
He will protect you as you come and go now
    and forever.'
Marla, if you need anything, you know where to reach
me."

Before I could react, Chaplain Cook walked away and
Peter came over and sat down.

"How are you feeling? Are you still nauseated?" he
asked.

I wanted to say something like well, those are two stupid
questions but I realized he was just being concerned. My
face must have been pale. I hadn't been able to keep any
food down. I had just buried my husband. Emotionally I was
a wreck but I kept myself composed and replied, "Worse now
than ever."

"Come, let me take you home," he said.

"I can't go home yet. There is a reception at the base I
must attend."

"Marla, you need to go home and rest."

"I'll go home after the reception," I repeated.

High ranking dignitaries from the mainland had attended
the funeral after all. They expressed their sorrow to me. For
the first time I saw men who really meant what they said.
They knew Thomas in D.C.; they worked side by side with
him in person and by radio; they genuinely respected him;
and they were sorry for his loss. My hope was that these men
would help me uncover whatever it was Thomas wanted me
to find out. I couldn't think past the moment but I knew that
I would be calling on them some day.

I also had the opportunity to corner Admiral Lewis and

General Sherman. I had a question to ask them that had been on my mind since I was assigned to care for Thomas.

"Admiral, General, please excuse my bluntness but why did you select me to care for Thomas when he came in from Japan two and a half years ago and please don't give me some happy horse-shit that I was the only person for the job. All of us know this isn't true. There is always someone else just like there was someone else that could have led the mission that killed Thomas."

Both Admiral Lewis and General Sherman were taken aback by my attitude but dismissed it and answered the question.

"We consulted," said Admiral Lewis, "after we got word that Thomas was seriously injured and we knew he needed 'round the clock care. I knew that you were a rehab nurse but I also knew that you had other qualifications that made you right for the assignment. Early in your career, you worked with men 12 hours a day 6 days a week to get them on their feet, or to teach them how to use an artificial arm or to teach a blind man to maneuver in a sighted world. Just because you went into administration and didn't work as much with disabled veterans didn't make you less valuable. It made you more valuable because you still oversaw the hard cases. We knew Thomas would be a hard case. We needed a hard nurse. Not an unfeeling one but one who would get him back on his feet and give him the will to live in the event he lost his leg."

I stood there a moment trying to absorb everything Admiral Lewis said.

"But you knew there was a chance that so much togetherness would cause an attraction between us didn't you?" I replied.

"We thought their might be that chance but then again we both knew that you and Thomas were career military people. If something more came between the two of you, so much the better because a man has multiple needs – physical, mental, and emotional. I knew you would be the one to help him in all three areas. The two of you were intensely devoted to your country and to your work. We knew that despite anything personal between the two of you, the military would come out on top."

I was stunned. I looked at the two of them and blurted, "To hell with both of you and the military." I ran to Peter. I told him to take me home immediately.

I cried for two straight days. Everyone called to see how I was. I had to take the phone off the hook. Peter came over but I told him to go away. I wanted to be left alone. I didn't realize a person could cry so much. I felt my heart had been ripped from my chest. My Thomas was gone and I had to face life without him.

It didn't take long for my emotions to affect the baby. I began spotting. I called Peter. He came to the condo and took me to St. Francis. Peter called his friend, an OB/GYN specialist to check me but it was too late. I was losing the baby and needed a D & C. I requested Peter called Chaplain Cook before surgery. The only question I could ask was why. He said he didn't have an answer. Bad things happen to good people. No one, not even the most righteous person can escape it. It wasn't much of a consolation but Chaplain Cook knew I didn't want to hear a sermon so he didn't deliver one. After the D & C, I gave Peter permission to call Admiral Lewis to inform him I would be off work for a week and the reason why.

I never told Patricia. What was the point? She just lost her only son. How would she handle the loss of her only grandchild? After I came home from the hospital, Patricia came to live with me. I predicted she would go down hill fast and she did. I hired a private duty nurse to care for her in the day and I took care for her at night but her depression deepened and I was forced to put her in a nursing home near Oahu General.

I visited Patricia three times a week but the last time I was there she was heavily sedated because she would cry for hours on end to the point that she gasped for breath. The meds would calm her down but the tears still came. When I visited, I wasn't sure if I made things worse or not. After our visits, I went home and sobbed for an hour. I knew this wasn't healthy but Patricia had no family except me. I had to visit to let her know someone cared. We shared a bond, the loss of Thomas, but she felt she had nothing to live for and willed herself to die. I saw it with my own mother. It was just a matter of time.

I was in my office when I got an urgent phone call that Patricia had taken a turn for the worse. She had contracted pneumonia which was not an uncommon condition in nursing home patients. I rushed over and found her in soft restraints. I asked the attending physician why. I was told she tried to pull out the IVs. She screamed her deceased husband's name constantly and that she was coming to join him. The attending gave her 2 milligrams of Ativan intravenously. The sedative had already taken affect by the time I arrived. I asked that the restraints be removed and her doctor agreed.

"Marla, my dear, you came," said Patricia as if she were looking through me, not at me.

"Yes, mother I'm here," I replied as I took her hand in mine.

"I saw William this morning. He was standing by the window talking to me," she said pointing to the spot on the floor.

"Yes, mother," I said agreeing the best way I could.

"It's my time to join him, Marla. He has come to take me home. It's my time." She repeated it over and over.

"Please don't say that, mother. I need you here."

"No," she said with her old strong voice. "I've made peace with everything. I'm going to see Thomas too."

I tried not to cry.

"Mother, please don't leave me," I begged.

"You'll be fine. You have your Navy career and your friends. Someday you will meet a man to keep company with," she said confidently.

Patricia reached up and started stroking my hair gently.

Tears flowed down my face.

"Mother, being with another man is not what I want," I said sternly.

"I know. Thomas knows but you need to have a life. You are young. Remember that I love you and I will see you again." Patricia stopped talking. She turned her head toward the window.

"William, honey, I'm ready to go."

"Mother, wait – mother," I yelled.

I saw the smile on Patricia's face fade.

The machine flatlined; she was gone. I heard the overhead speaker say "Code Blue to Room 9 Stat." The crash team worked on her for 15 minutes before the time of death was called.

I sat by her bed and cried. When I finished, I picked up the phone and called the mortuary. They made the arrangements to ship Patricia back east to be buried next to Colonel Smith. All the top brass were in attendance. It was hard for me to look at them again so short a time after burying Thomas.

Chapter 35

Patricia's funeral presented me the opportunity to ask about the classified material I requested. At the reception, I approached Admiral Lewis and General Sherman.

"I'm sorry for your loss Marla. I know how close you and Patricia were," said Admiral Lewis.

"My deepest condolences," responded General Sherman.

All I could mutter was thank you Admiral, General. My anger was white hot. I looked them both in the face and replied, "So, while I have you both together, when will I get my clearance to find out about what happened to Thomas on that last mission?"

Admiral Lewis looked at General Sherman and replied, "Maybe never. We are being stonewalled."

"Who's doing the stonewalling?" I inquired.

"We aren't sure but we have an idea General Lambello is behind it. Marla, we think it is best you leave this alone," said Admiral Lewis shooting a glance at General Sherman.

"Admiral Lewis, I deserve some answers. Not just because I was his wife but as a Naval Officer, I smell a massive cover up here. It was Thomas' last request that I look into this. I will pursue this until I have an answer or die, whichever comes first."

General Sherman was about to speak when Admiral Lewis cut him off. "We agree with your assessment that someone is covering up for someone or something however there is nothing we can do right now. Everything is classified."

"Begging the Admiral and General's pardon but you leave me no choice but to take this to a higher level," I said knowing this would aggravate both of them.

"Marla, don't do anything you will regret later," said Admiral Lewis sternly.

"Admiral Lewis, General Sherman, permission to speak openly."

"Permission granted."

"Aren't you pissed off that a high level military person is probably covering up a major screw-up which cost the lives of many good service personnel? Don't let this be another My Lai. I seek the truth and only the truth despite whose ass may get fried on this one. If you and General Sherman want to disavow any knowledge of what happened, then speak now…."

"Marla, it would be disrespectful to Thomas' memory for us to remain silent during this probe but we can't speak until certain information becomes declassified."

"Then I guess I will be the one to light the fire under the military to declassify the mission."

I walked away without saying another word to either one.

Five years later, Admiral Hargrove succeeded Admiral Lewis upon the Admiral's retirement. We developed a good working relationship. It was my hope that Admiral Hargrove would help me move things along. Only time would tell.

Chapter 36

I felt my whole persona change during this time. I was angry against the military and the Government. Hundreds of thousands of soldiers came back physically and psychologically injured. Tens of thousands returned in body bags.

I felt pity, a feeling I never had for my patients who would have to live with their injuries the rest of their lives.

I also felt empty; my heart and soul had been ripped from me. I couldn't work enough hours to fill my day. The nights were torture. Everywhere I looked I saw Thomas: the condo, the hospital, the PT room, the beach. I couldn't get away from it. I thought about a transfer but Hawaii had been my home for so long that I decided against requesting one. Counseling didn't help. This was one problem I had to deal with alone. I had to make some changes. I sold the console TV and bought a small TV for the bedroom. I took all the Rat Pack albums, put them in a box and stored them in the garage. I tried to change the condo around but it didn't matter what I did, everything reminded me of my husband.

I returned to meditation, took new classes, read, but insomnia took its toll. When I would fall asleep, I would relive my final moments with Thomas dying in my arms, his funeral, the miscarriage and Patricia's death. I awoke every night in a cold sweat. The stress overwhelmed me. I found a

Navy doctor to prescribe a low dose of Valium which I took throughout the rest of my career. The nightmares dissipated; I finally rested at night. My attitude against the military never softened but I was able to return to my job and my life with a positive attitude.

Patricia's final words haunted me. William was there. She wasn't afraid to die because she didn't want to live in a world without her husband and son. I obsessed with the thought: Is Thomas waiting for me?

I went to Chaplain Cook for answers. What I didn't know is that Chaplain Cook was struggling with his own feelings from a letter he received from the Chaplain of Thomas' unit a few days after Thomas' funeral.

The letter began:

Dear Chaplain Cook:

My name is Chaplain Timothy Karlsson. I was Thomas' Chaplain in Vietnam. I am writing to you because I think he would have wanted you to know the impact you had on his life. Before this tour of duty, I had met Thomas on his numerous trips to Saigon and later Da Nang. He was respectful but did not have an interest in God or religion. After he returned to NAM fully recovered from his injuries, it was like I was talking to a different man. He would come to see me when he could and ask questions about different Bible stories he read. He attended worship when he could and even showed up at Bible study when he wasn't out on a rescue or flying to a briefing or knee deep in paperwork.

It didn't surprise me when Thomas asked me if I knew someone who could make him a cross to wear. Not one of gold or silver but one of wood with nails across the wood of the cross. When I asked him why he wanted this type of cross, he replied that while Jesus had risen and was no longer on the cross, the nails signified his suffering. Thomas explained that he saw so much suffering and experienced some himself, the nails were his way of remembering Jesus' suffering before he died. Maybe a part of him needed the constant reminder of his own suffering too. I don't know because we weren't able to talk about it before he was called out on the final mission that took his life.

Thomas was wearing the cross when he was brought to 'Mercy' for surgery. It was removed and put with his personal effects. When I heard he passed, I called the ship and asked for the cross while Marla was to receive the rest of Thomas' personal items.

Chaplain Cook, you know Marla better than I do. From what Thomas told me, she is still seeking her faith and struggling with the mysteries of why God does what he does. This is why I asked for the cross. And now, this is why I am sending the cross to you. I hope that you will find the right time and place to give this letter and the cross to her. Let her know that Thomas loved her, loved God, and loved his brothers-in-arms. He did the only thing he could do, according to John 15:13. That didn't mean he loved her less than the military. In fact, for the first time in years, I saw Thomas love something other than military and that was God and Marla.

Blessings in Christ,

Chaplain Karlsson.

Chaplain Cook folded the letter, returned it to the envelope with the cross and put it in the lower left hand drawer of his desk. With everything that was going on, he lowered his head into his hands to think. What was the right time? Thomas was gone; Patricia was gone; the baby was gone. Thomas believed but Marla…she was still doubting… questioning.

Chaplain Cook was in his office when I knocked. "Come in," he yelled. The Sunday sermon was on his desk, a red pen next to it ready to do its duty to make changes.

"Is this a bad time to see you, Chaplain Cook?" I said pensively.

"There is a never a bad time for you to visit, Marla. So what do I owe the pleasure of your company? Not that you need a reason to see me," he said cordially. "Please, sit down."

I felt uncomfortable. Why? I don't know. I sat down and blurted out, "I am struggling with something Patricia said to me before she died and I don't know if you can help me sort it out or not." I didn't want to put him on the spot but I knew I just did.

"I've known you a long time, Marla, so just say whatever it is that is bothering you."

"Patricia said that William was there, in the room and she was going to be with him. She said Thomas was there too. Chaplain Cook, will I be reunited with my husband?"

"You have never wanted the sermonized version of any situation. I have seen you through the best of times and the worst of times. That is what life is: a series of seasons like what I read at Thomas' funeral in Ecclesiastes."

"You are evading a straight answer," I said firmly.

"Not everything is black and white like it is in the military. Religion and beliefs are gray areas. I can only tell you what different religions believe. What you end up believing is up to you." Chaplain Cook paused for a moment and looked me straight in the eye and said,

"Is what you want to know is, if there is life after death? Is there a heaven? Is there a God?" said Chaplain Cook inquisitively.

I nodded.

He proceeded, "What you've asked are some heavy questions but I will do my best to explain what some of the religions of the world believe. Then you can make up your own mind.

Regarding God, does he exist? As a Christian Chaplain, I

believe in God, that He exists, and that He suffers with us. Because we have free will, we can't hold God responsible for the evil that men do. Even God's own Son, who was without sin, went to the cross and died for the sins of the world. Other religions such as Judaism and Islam believe in God. However the Buddhists do not believe in God. The Hindus have different beliefs from believing in one God to the belief in multiple Gods to not believing in any Gods. The Hindu religion can be somewhat complicated to explain.

You asked if there is life after death. This varies widely on which religion you are talking about. The Hindus believe in reincarnation and in order to find salvation, a Hindu must engage in certain rituals, come to the realization of reality and self-reflection and devote oneself to the God or Gods he/she choose to follow. Eventually the Hindu will reach Nirvana which is the peaceful escape from the cycle of reincarnation. That's the best I can do in explaining the Hindu religion.

The Buddhists believe that people should do good, avoid evil and purify the mind. They also believe in reincarnation and Kamma. Kamma is similar to Karma and the saying that what goes around comes around. The Buddhists believe that positive actions will elicit positive consequences and negative actions will elicit negative consequences. Since Buddhists do not pray to God, when they need to ask for forgiveness of a wrong doing, they believe that they go to the person they have wronged and say they are sorry. If that is not possible, then they let the matter go and forgive themselves.

Judaism believes in life after death. Their belief is that there is little meaning to life, to God, to man's constant strivings and achievements unless there is a world beyond the grave. They believe in a soul and death is not the final chapter. It is the beginning to a new world or world to come. Three of Judaism's basic tenants of faith are God exists, God will reward the good and punish the wicked, and the dead will be resurrected. Immortality is a major part of the Jewish faith. Jews believe that the body returns to the earth but the soul returns to God who gave it. They also believe in the eventual resurrection of the body which will be reunited with the soul at a later time. An example of bodily resurrection can be found in Ezekiel 37, also known as the 'Valley of the Dry Bones' prophesy.

You asked when you lost your baby why was all of this happening? The Jews believe that there are good people who suffer and bad people who prosper. Life is unfair but for the Jews they believe there will be spiritual punishment and rewards. God balances the scales because he is a just and righteous God.

Christians also believe in judgment, reincarnation and life after death. In 2 Corinthians 5:10 (GNT) Paul discusses judgment, 'For all of us must appear before Christ, to be judged by him. We will each receive what we deserve, according to everything we have done, good or bad in our bodily life.' For Christians, in the New Testament, it is always the resurrection of Jesus that is presented as the guarantee of the believer. In 1 Thessalonians 4:14 (GNT), it states, 'We believe that Jesus died and rose again and so we believe that God will take back with Jesus those who have died believing in him.' For the Christian, it is the death and resurrection of Jesus that guarantees the forgiveness and future resurrection of all who choose to unite with Christ and his cause. 1 Corinthians 15:20 states, 'But the truth is that Christ has been raised from death, as the guarantee that those who sleep in death will also be raised.' and 1 Peter 1:3 states, 'Let us give thanks to the God and Father of our Lord Jesus Christ! Because of his great mercy he gave us new life by raising Jesus Christ from death.' Christians claim that Christ not only died for man's sins but also rose physically from death as proof that God had truly accepted His sacrifice. According to Christian teaching, man will rise from death one day – some to life everlasting and others to everlasting shame and contempt.

Marla, there are other Bible quotes which point to eternal life and the resurrection and judgment but I don't want to go on and on quoting scripture. I know you want a simple answer but all I can do is tell you what different people believe.

You asked about heaven. Most religions mention heaven or a word with a similar meaning. Buddhists, as I stated earlier, do not believe in God but they believe in heaven. Their motto is, 'Anyone can go to Heaven if they so wish. They just need to be good.' Common translation is: 'Thus as you sow, you shall reap.'

Finally, I come to Islam. The Muslims adhere to an absolute submission and adherence to the commands of Allah without objection. He who chooses the path of guidance of his own free will, fulfills the duties and refrains from the prohibitions, he is a legitimate Muslim. If he deviates, neglects worship and commits an act that is prohibited, then he is an unbeliever. Muslims do believe in resurrection. They believe Islam is the only religion acceptable to Allah. So if you are a Jew, Christian, Buddhist, etc., you are a loser. Muslims believe in angels to keep count of man's deeds which will be shown to man on the day of resurrection. They believe in heaven and hell. A large tenant of faith is if you obey Allah you will be rewarded. Disobey him and you will be punished.

Now after all that you want to know my personal beliefs. As a Christian Minister, who has studied the Bible and other religions, have counseled service personnel and their families for the past 16 years, I believe in the Trinity – God, Jesus and the Holy Spirit – and that at the end of my life, I will be judged. It is my hope that I will be worthy to enter the

Kingdom of Heaven. I have learned over my career that there are many similarities in religions. I encounter them on a daily basis. I see people practice their faith so I believe there are many paths to God. It is not my place to tell someone if you don't believe X, you will go to hell. All I can do is answer your questions to the best of my ability and let you make up your own mind.

Now going back to the first question, do I believe that Patricia saw William? Maybe she thought she did because she was pumped full of medication which could have caused hallucinations or maybe he was really there. It doesn't matter. What does matter is she thought she saw him and she's at peace," Chaplain Cook said.

"It matters to me," I said disappointedly.

"If it matters that much to you, then you need to believe that Thomas will be there when your time is up here on earth. Keep that thought alive. Have faith that you will see your beloved husband at the end of your life. That will be the fire that burns within you. Let nothing come between you and that belief."

"Thanks Chaplain Cook. I appreciate your time," I said feeling better.

"You're welcome as always," he replied.

Chapter 37

A month after Thomas died, I received a large package without a return address.

I opened it.

It was Thomas' personal diaries dating back to when he first joined the military. There were 11 books, organized by date. Thomas must have told someone he trusted that if anything happened to him, to send the books to me. The person knew the intimate details of Thomas' death because there was a printed note in the box which read, "Get the bastard and get him good!"

I thumbed through the books one by one till I got to the one from the time that Thomas was a POW. I could make out the date that he wrote these entries from the hospital during his recovery but the book wasn't in English. I wasn't sure what language it was but I knew that if Thomas was writing in a foreign language he didn't want the books easily read by anyone who might happen to come upon them.

I sat there numb by the realization that I might have something tangible in my pursuit of Lt. Lambello but I couldn't read the diaries.

I pondered my options. This needed to be kept as quiet as possible. I couldn't go to Admiral Lewis or any military person for help.

It dawned on me that someone at the University of Hawaii, Linguistics Department could look at the diaries and hopefully translate them.

I made an appointment to meet with the Dean of Linguistics.

The next day, I called in sick and left for the University.

"Dean Berger, thank you for seeing me on such short notice," I said cordially.

"My pleasure, Lt. Commander. Your problem intrigued me. You mentioned you received some of your husband's diaries but they were written in a foreign language. What languages did your husband speak fluently?"

"Only Korean and Vietnamese that I know of but this was neither."

"Let me see," he replied. These older diaries are in Korean but you are right, these new diaries appear to be written in German. I need to confirm this with a colleague of mine. Could I keep them and get back to you?"

"Yes, Dean by all means."

As I left Dean Berger's office, I was completely baffled that as much as I knew about Thomas was as little as I knew about him. Where did he learn German?

The next day Dean Berger called me at work.

I shut the door.

"Yes, Dean, what did you find out?" I said anxiously.

"Lt. Commander Bristol, it is German and Korean. I will find a couple of students who will discretely translate these diaries. Only the two we discussed, correct? From March 1967 through the final entry of May, 1969.

"Yes, thank you. I will pay whatever it costs.

"I know two highly qualified students but I have to contact them and ask them if they want to become involved in this project. I'll get back to you."

Two days later Dean Berger called.

"The two qualified students I spoke of are available. One speaks German fluently, born in Germany, of German parents and immigrated to the United States at the age of 14. His name is Hans. The other student is a Korean-American born here in Hawaii. He reads and writes Korean flawlessly. His name is Truc. I can send them over to see you at your convenience."

"Can you send them to my home this Sunday at 4:00 p.m.?"

"I'll set it up. Consider it a meeting unless I call you to change it."

I couldn't wait for Sunday. Was I ready for what I would hear? I felt apprehension yet I could hear Thomas' voice pushing me on.

Finally it was Sunday. Precisely at 4:00 p.m., Hans and Truc arrived. I invited them in. I offered both a cold glass of lemonade and some cookies.

"Hans, Truc, Dean Berger told you why I asked you here," I said. "I need to have these diaries translated. They were my late husband's and are very important because it could contain information that a certain person in his unit caused many men to be wounded or die, including my husband. I will pay you for your efforts. I know you are both full-time students but if you could work on it as much as possible, I would be grateful."

"It's summertime. Neither one of us are taking full loads. We would be honored to help. Don't worry, Lt. Commander Bristol. We will figure them out and get back to you shortly," said Hans.

Truc bowed.

Hans shook my hand and they both left.

I heard from Hans over the next three months at least once a week. The positive things were Thomas' handwriting was legible and the books were preserved in plastic so they were in good condition. The negative thing was because Thomas spoke German fluently, he didn't write it well in the beginning so to compensate, he went back and forth between English, German and Korean. Truc was invaluable in translating this portion of the diaries. I went to work every day but my mind was on the diaries. I prayed they would finish the translation before the fall semester began. Labor Day was next week. I was at work when the phone rang.

"Lt. Commander Bristol, it's Hans. I have some good news. Truc and I have finished the translations."

"Oh, thank God."

"I have to warn you what we translated wasn't pretty. It got to me and it really got to Truc," said Hans.

"I know, I know."

"I hope you really do. I'll come by to drop off the diaries and the translation at your convenience."

"Hans, can you and Truc meet me tonight after I get off work? I'll pick up some take out Chinese and pay you for your time. About 8:00 p.m.?"

"Ok," he replied.

Hans came by right on time.

"Where's Truc?"

"He couldn't make it but sends his regards."

"How much do I owe you each of you?"

"Nothing," he said as he picked up a plate. He put some Chicken with Pea Pods and rice on his plate.

"Nothing!? Oh I'm sorry that can't be."

"Listen, Lt. Commander Bristol, we spoke to Dean Berger about translating the diaries and about accepting payment. We cannot find it in our hearts to charge you."

"But you and Truc spent so much time?"

"Consider it helping you in furthering your effort to nail the person responsible for killing your husband," said Hans as he ate a helping of rice.

"What did my husband say?"

"If you want to know that, start half way through the second diary translation."

Hans put his plate and chopsticks down and handed me the transcript. "Thanks for dinner," he said as he picked up from the table.

"But you hardly ate."

"It's ok. I'll pick something up on the way back to the dorm. Good luck Lt. Commander."

Hans grabbed his duffle bag and left.

I was dumbfounded. What was in the diaries that caused Truc and Hans to act the way they did? What did Thomas say?

Well, it was time to find out.

I gave a cursory look at the first transcript. A date caught my eye: March 8th, 1967. That was the date Thomas woke up from his surgery at Oahu General. I read the entry.

"I'm in Oahu General Hospital. I survived six months as a POW with an additional 13 days wandering the jungles of Laos. I was shot twice in the leg, one bullet shattering my femur. I had surgery and now have a rod in my leg replacing the bone. Thank God the doctors saved my leg from amputation. As a Special Forces Officer, I couldn't handle being a cripple. It is bad enough I look like a skeleton, skin hanging from my bones, my face sunken in, tubes everywhere in my arm, neck and penis. I feel totally helpless. Yet I am happy to be alive. I survived. The enemy did not break me under torture. I also have the kindest, sweetest nurse a guy could have. When she looks at me, I don't feel that she pities me. I feel like she cares about me as a person. Her eyes show a strength of character that I can draw on."

I stopped reading. Tears rolled down my face. I now understood why Hans and Truc couldn't take any money for translating this very personal information but I decided I would go to the University tomorrow and give Dean Berger a check for both of them. I wondered if the day would come that I would meet the men that Thomas was imprisoned with in Laos.

I picked up the second transcript and turned to an entry made in December 1968 and continued reading.

December 6th, 1968. I have been in Mai Loc, in the Quang Tri province since Khe Sanh closed in June. I have had to fly back and forth between here and Da Nang for briefings but this is my home for now. We need this base because we need to be close to Laos to pick up the fly boys that are shot down while bombing the Trail. There are rumors that there are moles in some of the units. Most of us believe it is the South Vietnamese but no one is above suspicion. I have felt my unit is as trust worthy as it gets until today when a new guy, Lt. Anthony Lambello Jr. transferred in. His father is General Anthony Lambello Sr.: A two star general going on three. I and others in the outfit smell a rat. This guy looks and acts like a rat but all I have is a bad feeling. I will try to pull his records from his last outfit.

December 17th, 1968, I couldn't get Lt. Lambello's records because they are sealed. That makes me believe he is a rat but all I can do is keep an eye on him. His father is not a man to be crossed, way too powerful. A couple of my men have come to me with the same suspicion. Is he a spy? Or is he just an idiot – too stupid to know anything and the rest of us are spooked because of his father. Only time will tell.

January 12th, 1969, Today, my unit made two pick-ups on the Trail. I spent four days in Da Nang. When I got back I got an earful about Lambello from the all the guys. I heard one was thinking of fragging him. I put a stop to that immediately. The General is pressing to have his little boy go on missions. So far we've kept him pushing paper. I don't think this guy has the balls to go on a mission or worse yet, he could be so stupid as to get us all killed. My instincts about Lt. Lambello get stronger with each passing day that he could be a mole or be inadvertently passing information to the enemy but I have no concrete proof. Until I do, I am stuck.

January 29th, 1969, Lt. Lambello is in training and I'm stalling. The Colonel called me in last night and I flatly told him that Lambello is a detriment to morale and doesn't belong here. Off the record he said he agreed with me but that we had to appease the Joint Chiefs and Lambello's father.

February 8th, 1969, I'm leaving in three weeks to see my beautiful wife. I've been given orders to train Lambello for a mission but stall him from going out on one until I get back. Send him to Da Nang, make up anything that has to be done but keep him out of action.

February 27th, 1969, I leave for Hawaii in a couple of days. Lambello still can't shoot, can't hold a 50 pound pack, basically can't do anything a recruit can do in boot camp yet he is a Special Forces Officer. What a laugh! If only I had the power to transfer his ass – he is an accident waiting to happen. Yesterday, one of the guys set off a firecracker behind him. The result: he peed his pants. If he wets himself when a prank is played, how well will he react when real gun fire goes off around him? This is not a guy I want on a drop in the 1-0 or 1-1 position or any position for that matter. The feeling that we have a mole or moles in the unit has intensified. Last week classified documents were stolen from a Sergeant in Saigon. Now I know Vietnamese will steal food, watches, clothing and anything else that they can get money for but classified documents? We have no proof against this Sergeant except he was "distracted," that is he was in bed with a Vietnamese girl.

March 20th, 1969, I had a wonderful 10 day leave with my wife. After I left her, I had to go to Da Nang for some more briefings. Now I am back in the hellhole again. The politics are as bad as ever. Leaving Marla was the hardest thing I had to do but I look forward to May when I will be in her arms again. Richard Nixon is the new President. I thought we would have more support from him in bombing the Trail and rescuing our pilots but it seems our Ambassador to Laos must think we are all expendable. Everyone acts like we are. We have a job to do. Instead of getting help, boulders are put in our way, especially General Lambello. Does he want his son to die on a mission? If so, to prove him a hero? Or God forbid does he want his son to lead a mission as unqualified as he is? If that's the case, we all get to pay for that mistake with our lives. It's bad enough we are fighting the enemy but now we have to fight our own people too. I've tried to talk to General Sherman about this but he is unable or unwilling to intercede.

April 3rd, 1969. We've run five missions since I've returned. The Trail is as active as ever. We can't seem to knock the activity out – either the road itself or the people on it. The pilots are flying more runs and there are more rescues because the planes are being shot down. It seems like they know exactly when the pilots are leaving. The leak must be coming from high on the food chain but someone within the outfit is also feeding information to the enemy. I've spoken discretely to officers in other units and they tell me they believe the same thing. There is a mole in the South Vietnam Government and there are enemy agents infiltrated among the South Vietnamese Army. Some of them have persuaded Americans to help their cause. I can't say that Lambello is a mole just like that Sergeant in Saigon who happened to become "distracted" but it is very coincidental that at the exact times we are called to go out on missions, the NVA knows where we are.

April 19th, 1969, A dry run is scheduled to prepare

Lambello for a mission. The guys assigned to the detail are bitching to me; I've talked to the Colonel. I have no choice – I have to wet nurse Lambello: orders from his father.

April 22nd, 1969, The dry run took place two miles from camp. The only good thing was Lambello did what he was told. The test will be when he sent on a live mission.

April 30th, 1969. I am counting the days when I can be with Marla yet I am ill at ease with the situation here. There is little I can do. The mole is still undiscovered. Lambello hasn't been battle tested. I leave for Hawaii in a week.

May 6th, 1969, 36 hours to go. All the short timers are sitting around having a couple of beers and some smokes. I've got some last minute paperwork to complete. The overhead speaker goes off. It's the Colonel. I'm to report to his office as soon as possible. There must be a problem with the units that left for the downed pilot. I have a real bad feeling about this…. Ok, I'm not going to be negative now. If I have to go, it will be like any other mission. Then I will be off to Hawaii and in my beloved wife's arms again.

Side note: Mad Dog just came over. Bad news: Lambello is out there on the first team. This must be his screw-up. My gut turned over. I told Mad Dog to take my diaries and bury them in the safe spot. If anything happened to me, he was to ship them to my wife.

My darling Marla, if you are reading these entries, then you know everything that transpired. You also know that I love you and have always loved you very much. You were my world, my life and my soul."

I buried my head in the transcript as I cried uncontrollably.

I closed the transcript.

After a few minutes, I opened the transcript and read the final entry, "Marla, this is Mad Dog. If you read this, you found someone to decipher the diaries. We all know who and what Lambello was but we were unable to prove it. For the sake of Thomas and the rest of us, GET HIM!"

Chapter 38

For six years after Thomas' death, I had been stonewalled. I had no proof that Lambello was a mole or he caused the death of the men on the mission except Thomas dying words. I needed to talk to the survivors of the mission but as long as we fought in Vietnam, everything was classified. We were never supposed to be in Laos so any record of our soldiers being there has been denied.

Finally the war ended.

It was May 1975, the month after the fall of Saigon. Even though I had made waves in D.C., Admiral Hargrove raised my rank to Commander. I had successfully run the PT departments of the State of Hawaii and was a consultant to hospitals on the mainland.

A ray of hope shone through when I received a call from Big Papa and Joker. They wanted to visit.

I was in my office when there was a knock at my door. The two ex-Special Forces Officers walked in. It was as if I had known them all my life yet I didn't know anything about them. I only knew of their existence because of Thomas' medical records.

They heard I had been calling everyone who knew Thomas for any information on his time in Vietnam. Big Papa, Joker and Bear's mission had been declassified after the fall of Saigon so they wanted to talk to me.

I was very excited to meet them. I could hardly contain myself but it was impolite of me to jump on them the minute they entered the room.

"Thank you for coming. I am happy to have this opportunity to speak with both of you," I said as calmly as possible. "Can I get you anything? Coffee perhaps?"

"No thanks," they responded.

"Joker and I have been discharged from the service," began Big Papa. "We understand that you wanted to talk to people who knew Thomas. We know you want answers to questions you may have about the time we served with him. There are a few things we are not able to talk about such as the escape from the POW camp but everything else is on the table."

"How long did you know my husband?"

"A long time. We both met him on our 1st tour of duty. All of us were called "advisors.""

"Were you friends? I mean did you socialize together off duty?"

"Bear didn't party much but he couldn't have been a better friend to me."

"I loved him like a brother. He put his life on the line for me and for you too Big Papa," said Joker.

"Marla," began Big Papa, "All I can say is that hellhole prison camp was worse than anything you could possibly imagine. Our escape was just as hair-raising. We were under orders not to talk about it to anyone. Bear was shot providing cover for us climbing into the helicopter. Joker and I were shipped to Japan to recover because our injuries weren't severe. At least we were able to talk to each other about what happened there. We still had the nightmares but we had each other as an outlet."

"Bear had nightmares. He told me all about it in private," I replied softly.

"Then you know the Vietcong and North Vietnamese were very good at torturing people. Bear built up an incredible tolerance to pain. I don't know how he did it. Those bastards did everything they could to break him but they didn't. As you probably know by now, he possessed information they badly needed."

I felt the tears welling up and had to fight to keep them back.

"It was apparent by the injuries inflicted on him when he arrived that they worked him over severely," I replied.

"Had we not gotten out of there when we did, the three of us would have died within a few days or a week at the most. Bear listened to the guards and figured out when the right time was to go and then we got out."

"We were lucky Bear was fluent in Vietnamese," said Big Papa.

"No, Big Papa, that wasn't luck, that was our ace in the hole," replied Joker. "He kept that a secret all the time we were there."

"Big Papa, Joker, do either one of you know where Thomas learned German?

Big Papa smiled.

"While we were being held, we tried to divert our minds. Bear was very good with languages so I taught him German. He became fluent very quickly."

"Did you teach him to write it?" I asked in a hopeful voice.

"No, I'm afraid I wasn't able to do that but he could have learned it from a book or if someone gave him a few lessons. Why do you ask?"

"The diaries he kept when he went back to NAM were

partly in Korean but toward the end of his tour of duty, they were all in German."

"Marla, telling you the details of how Bear became your patient is important to you but not nearly as important as what happened the day he died. Right?" said Big Papa.

"Right."

"The problem is that mission is still classified. My suggestion is that you go to the Governor, Senator, Congressman, and any high ranking official you can in the military to have the information declassified or have your security clearance upped in order to see the files. We don't know what happened on that final mission. The men I have spoken to want to talk but all of them say they can't. Someone or some entity is stopping them."

I was crushed and was unable to hide my disappointment because I knew in my heart it was General Lambello's fault that no one could or would speak openly.

"Big Papa," I asked, "Do you personally know the guys who survived the mission?"

"Yes," he replied.

"If I can get the mission declassified, would these men testify at a hearing?" I asked anxiously.

"I know all the survivors would make a point of nailing the son of a bitch responsible. One of the mission's survivors is paralyzed but I know he would be there too. Do what you can. Let us know what happens. Here is how you can reach me," said Big Papa.

Big Papa handed me a piece of paper with his phone number on it.

"And me," said Joker also slipping me his phone number.

"Thank you for coming." I said as they got up and left my office. I watched them from my office window as they walked down hospital steps, climbed into an old Ford truck and drove away.

I didn't move for a long time all the while thinking about our conversation and then it dawned on me. There was a man who visited Thomas in the hospital during his recovery. I never knew his relationship to Thomas but he came every day while Thomas recuperated. He must have been giving Thomas German lessons. How else could Thomas have written the diaries in German?

Chapter 39

Three more years passed. It was 1978. The Government continued to ignore my requests for information. I spent every moment away from work reading and rereading the diaries looking for something – anything to further my case against now Major Anthony Lambello Jr. but his father General Anthony Lambello and the connections at the Pentagon stopped me cold.

Then Steven Roberts, Chief of Detectives of the State of Hawaii, entered my life. Because of him, I met the Governor, both United States Senators and the Hawaiian Congressman who happened to be a veteran himself. My life changed forever.

It was about 9:45 p.m. on a Friday evening. The phone rang. Whenever the phone rang at that hour, I knew it couldn't be good news but I went against my instincts and picked it up.

It was Peter. "Marla, I need you to return to the hospital this evening. Can you be there in 20 minutes?"

"Whatever it is, can't it wait until tomorrow?"

"I wish it could. I got a call from Admiral Hargrove who received a call from the Governor. There was a bomb blast in front of the Office of the Chief of Detectives of Hawaii."

"Who was hurt and how bad?"

"The Chief of Detectives, himself, Steven Roberts. He was leaving his office, some kind of party. He was getting into his car when he noticed he dropped something. When he went back to pick it up, his car blew up. He flew about 25 feet, landed on his back, arm, and head. He's in the ER right now. Dropping that package saved his life."

Not trying to sound cold I repeated, "As I said before, can't this wait until tomorrow?"

"Evidently not. Chief of Detective Steven Roberts is also known as Commander Steven Roberts in the Naval Reserve which automatically got you involved in his case. This is attempted murder. Security is going to be very tight. Admiral Hargrove wants you for two reasons: your skills as a therapist and your expertise in Karate."

"So in addition to being a nurse, I am a security agent?" I started to laugh.

"You have got to be kidding. (silence) You're not kidding. I'll be there in 15 minutes," I said as I hung up the phone.

After Vietnam, the Federal Government in its infinite wisdom decided to cut much of the defense funding. President Jimmy Carter was downsizing the military. Every dime that was allocated had to be justified and re-justified. The number of soldiers needing therapy went down to the point that my program was on the chopping block. I had to constantly lobby to save the program. I spent more time buried in paperwork than with patients. I knew that time was running out. I had cut expenditures to the bone. I was at the point of letting some of my staff go.

Commander Roberts was with Dr. Stone in ER #1 when I arrived. Peter went in. A few minutes later, Dr. Stone came out and spoke to me.

"Commander Roberts has a concussion, cuts, bruises, and possible left wrist fracture. I'm waiting for Radiology to arrive. The main problem is swelling in the occipital area of the skull. We have an Ophthalmologist and a Neurologist in with him now."

Peter came out of the room. I looked at Dr. Stone and asked, "What is his exact problem? You didn't call me here for cuts and a fractured wrist."

"He's blind," said Dr. Stone. "It could be temporary or permanent. It's too soon to know. We need to get him settled down. Then we can treat all his injuries. I have been told that Commander Roberts is a dynamic individual to say it in politically correct terms. He had to be sedated and put in soft restraints because he became combative in the ambulance. As soon as he wakes up, he is going to have a strong reaction to his circumstances. Marla, that's why I've asked you down here tonight. Admiral Hargrove has relieved you of your current duties so you can care for Commander Roberts from 8:00 a.m. to 11:00 p.m. He will be guarded 24 hours a day. The person or persons who attempted to kill him are still at large so we are screening anyone who has contact with him."

"Can I see him?" I asked so I could see who I would be nursing for the immediate future.

"Absolutely," replied Dr. Stone.

I went in. Commander Roberts was lying in bed with an IV in his arm. He had a bandage on his forehead and a larger bandage covering both eyes with gauze wrapped around his head. I thought back to all the guys who came back from NAM who couldn't see. I had to teach them how to do everything for themselves again – from dressing and showering, to eating and walking. Most thought they would never have a normal life again. Some were lucky; they regained all or part of their sight. Some were not so lucky and for those guys I was their mother, wife, priest, friend and therapist. Adjustments were hard but these men found the guts to go on with their lives. A couple kept in touch. They married, had children and went on to careers in fields where blindness wasn't a factor. They had their minds – wits – that they relied on and their will to live. I hoped that Commander Roberts would regain his sight but if not, he could be a man like those I encountered before him.

It had been a few years since I had a blind patient. I needed to go to my office and review my outline of care but I couldn't move.

I kept staring at Commander Roberts. I saw Thomas in the bed. A shiver went through me. It was all I could do not to run out of the room. My professional self kicked in. I regained control of my emotions but I felt a fearfulness I couldn't shake. I didn't want this assignment but there was no way out. Oh, God, I need to put this out of my mind. Any similarities to Thomas needed to be forgotten now.

I left the room and went to my office. My staff had long since left for the day but I shut the door so I could have complete privacy. I reviewed my outline of how to begin therapy for a blind patient. I had been in my office a half an hour when I received a call from Dr. Stone. He asked me to return to Commander Roberts' room.

"Commander Roberts has started to regain consciousness. Radiology confirmed the left wrist fracture," said Dr. Stone. "I'd like you to go to Orthopedics with him while they cast his wrist. Stay with him until he is back in a private room. I ordered a short hard cast. I know this may impede your therapy but I did not want a soft cast on the wrist in the event he falls."

Dr. Stone left. I took a deep breath and entered the room. Two orderlies and I accompanied Commander Roberts to Orthopedics.

It was after 2:00 a.m. before everything was finished. I needed to be back by 8:00 a.m. so I went up to Peter's office and sacked out on his sofa.

The next day I awoke at 7:00 a.m., showered in Peter's private bathroom, grabbed a bagel and coffee and was at Commander Roberts' room by 8:00 a.m. He was still asleep. Dr. Stone met me outside.

"He should be coming around shortly. Marla, I talked to David, Commander Roberts' right hand man. He repeated that Commander Roberts could be difficult to work with so you need to be prepared for that."

"Dr. Stone, I've been a Navy nurse for 19 years with 99% of those patients being men. One thing I've learned over the years is that men do not want to be dependent on anyone, especially a woman. I was married to a Special Forces Officer so I know that better than anyone. Commander Roberts may have a stronger personality than most of the men I have dealt with in the past but I am confident I can handle him."

"That is just what I wanted to hear," he said.

Commander Roberts awoke an hour later. I was sitting by the bed reviewing charts when he started to scream out.

I grabbed his hand and replied, "Commander Roberts, my name is Commander Marla Bristol. I am a Navy nurse assigned to help you."

This seemed to calm him down but not completely.

"I can't see," he yelled. "Where am I?"

"Oahu General Hospital."

"What happened?" he said. He stopped holding my hand. He felt his face and left hand using his right hand.

"There was an explosion. What do you remember?" I said coxing an answer.

"It was my 25th anniversary as a cop. My staff had a party for me," as he paused trying to collect his thoughts. "I was carrying the presents to the car when I dropped one. I went back to pick it up. There was an explosion. I remember lying on the ground. I could hear my number two man, David, asking me if I was alright. I remember replying I couldn't see."

"I can't see!" he repeated loudly. Commander Roberts started getting agitated. "Am I blind?"

I tried to avoid the question. "You have a fractured left wrist and a concussion. There is swelling at the base of your skull in the occipital area which is the back area of the head. This is the area that controls vision. The doctors took tests last night. The results aren't back yet. You also have some cuts and abrasions on your face and hands."

"Am I blind?" he screamed again.

"Yes, but we don't know if it is permanent or not," I tried to answer calmly. "There is a 24 hour guard on your room and I am assigned to be with you from morning until evening." Changing the subject, I said, "How does your head feel?"

"Like someone hit me with a brick."

"I'll talk to Dr. Stone and get you something for the pain. Let's get you something to eat. I'll have an orderly help you use the bathroom rather than the bedpan and urinal. I'll be back in a couple of minutes."

I went out of the room to call Dr. Stone. He ordered some Demerol for the pain. I paged George to come to Commander Roberts' room and acquaint him with the toilet facilities. I placed the order with dietary to bring a normal meal to Commander Roberts' room. George assisted him with eating, washing his face, and brushing his teeth. I decided to wait until tomorrow to have him shave. About 5:00 p.m., Dr. Stone came in. He reviewed the chart and tests. The test regarding Commander Roberts' blindness came back inconclusive."

"Marla, can I see you for a moment?" said Dr. Stone.

"How was he today?" asked Dr. Stone.

"Anxious and in pain. Do you have any news?" I said dreading what I was about to hear.

"No, and I think it will be a few days before we know anything."

"I don't think he's going to just sit around waiting for things to happen. He's a doer. He is going to be a problem," I replied with trepidation in my voice.

"You need to convince him only time will work this situation out," Dr. Stone said.

"That's a tall order, doctor," I replied.

Chapter 40

When I arrived the next morning, I found Commander Roberts already on the phone while his secretary was running around the room taking orders from him. He had turned his hospital room into his private office. I had to put a stop to this now. Things were about to get ugly. Politely but firmly, I asked his secretary to leave.

He had to want to learn. A person has to accept their circumstance in order for him or her to have a successful therapy. Whether it is adjusting to a prosthetic, or learning to speak again from a stroke, or navigating around due to blindness, a person must accept their situation. Commander Roberts did not accept that he was blind or that the blindness could be permanent. I needed to take an approach that I had never used in the past but knew other nurses who had used it. It was nicknamed, "the stick treatment" from the carrot or the stick philosophy of rewarding versus punishing certain behaviors.

I attended a rehabilitation conference in 1972, in Houston where it was demonstrated. At the time, I thought to myself, there was no way I would ever to do this to a patient but now the time has come for me to implement it.

Commander Roberts wouldn't listen to anything I said. He decided to go back to work the minute he could think.

No, he wasn't going to sit in a bed waiting around for the killer to strike. When Commander Roberts wanted to leave the hospital, Dr. Stone freaked out. I told him I would handle the situation.

"Marla, are you sure this approach will work?" Dr. Stone said in a doubting tone of voice.

"No, Dr. Stone, I'm not sure. I've never used it but I known nurses who have. We don't have any other option," I said with a tinge of sadness and frustration.

I had already refreshed my memory on what to do from the notes I took at the conference. To my advantage and dis- advantage, I saved everything. They were right where I had put them six years ago.

I walked into the room. Dr. Stone was to the right of me. Commander Roberts had taken the bandages off his eyes. Only the forehead bandage remained.

"Hand me my clothes," he barked like I was his personal slave ready to jump at his command.

"You want to be independent, get them yourself," I replied in a stern voice.

"You think you can hold me back by not giving me my clothes?" he said indignantly.

"I think nothing of the sort. Your clothes are in the closet. You might not be able to see but you aren't helpless. If you want them, get them yourself," I repeated.

Commander Roberts went toward the closet putting his arms out in front of him feeling the air for anything he might bump into along the way. He retrieved his clothes. He dressed himself even tying his tie into a perfect knot. He did a good job but received no encouragement from me.

"Would you call me a cab?" he asked half-knowing the answer.

"The phone is on the nightstand. If you want a cab, call one yourself," I replied sternly.

Pissed off, Commander Roberts went to the phone, dialed "O," spoke to the hospital operator, and asked that he be connected with a cab company. I could hear the operator say that he could dial it himself but he replied, "Would you please do it for me?" When the cab company answered, Commander Roberts instructed them to send a cab to Oahu General's main entrance.

Commander Roberts walked across the room toward the door. He hit the wall. He felt around and found the door knob, opened the door and walked into the hallway. People approached him. They wanted to help but I waived them off. It hurt me to do this but I had to show Commander Roberts' first hand that he needed to accept his situation and work on dealing with his blindness. That's why he was brought to me. I was the one everyone expected to deal with the hard cases. Frankly, I was tired of being the "go to" person – the one everyone relied on to fix situations that sometimes couldn't be fixed. This was my specialty whether I liked it or not.

Commander Roberts bumped into a medication cart but kept walking. Then he collided with a laundry cart and fell flat on his face. He got up, walked a little further bumping into two chairs in the smoking room. He fell down this time rolling under the table. Lying on the floor, Commander Roberts called out, "Commander Bristol, Commander Bristol, are you there?"

"I am here, Commander Roberts," I replied without showing any emotion all the time I felt my insides being eaten away because of what I just did to a blind man.

"Commander Bristol, I would like to go back to my room. Would you take me back there please?"

"Get up," I snapped staying as detached as possible.

Chapter 41

Commander Roberts stood up.

I said, "First take your right hand and place it here on my left elbow." I helped him find my elbow. "Now, I will walk a half step in front of you and we will return to your room."

Once we returned to the room, I led him to the bed. I pulled up a chair facing him.

"Commander Roberts, I don't know if your sight will return or not but for the time being you are blind. That's a fact. It's my job to help you function in a sighted world to the best of your ability. Being blind is only a disability if you let it be. Before you tell me I am full of crap, I have successfully worked with hundreds of veterans over the years with various kinds of injuries including blindness. I have been doing this a very long time. Admiral Hargrove would not have personally requested me if he didn't think I could help you.

We will work on the basics. Before you know it, you will do most everything that a sighted person does. You could think of a few things you normally do that you can't do, like drive a car and you would be correct. However, I can teach you to cook, clean, sew, but most importantly return to work. Your other senses don't automatically pick up the slack when one doesn't work but you can use them to your advantage by a sense of heightened awareness and practice. Are you ready to begin?"

"Do I have a choice?" he said sarcastically.

"Honestly, everyone has a choice but I know your personality type. You don't have a choice because I know you want to be independent. A good attitude is very important. We will start with lunch. Then we will learn personal hygiene. You already met George. He will be your orderly. He will instruct and assist you with showering and dressing. I firmly believe that a man is more comfortable with a man under these circumstances. I will teach you to shave, comb your hair, and brush your teeth. You are probably thinking I already know how to do all these things but it is different when you're blind. As we go along you will have a better understanding of what I mean. How about a sandwich and chips for lunch? Is turkey with everything ok?" I asked.

"Yeah, that sounds good to me," responded Commander Roberts unenthusiastically.

It was Sunday. I phoned the deli and placed an order for two sandwiches to be delivered to the Commander's room.

"Commander Roberts, I have a quick errand to run. I should be back before the food arrives. There are two police officers outside the door. Dr. Stone can be paged if you need anything. I will be back in about half an hour."

"May I ask where you are going?" Commander Roberts said inquisitively.

"I have someone I have to see and I can't break the meeting," I said without making a big deal out of it.

"I hope I wasn't too nosy?"

"Not at all."

I left.

I went to Thomas' grave. I needed a break and a good cry. I had never missed a Sunday at the cemetery since

Thomas died and I wasn't going to start now despite my new responsibilities.

I returned to Commander Roberts' room five minutes late. There was an awkward silence between us. He spoke first.

"Commander Bristol, may I call you Marla?"

"You may."

"Marla, I would like you to address me as Steven, please."

"Commander, I don't feel…"

"If I can call you by your first name, then, you need to reciprocate."

"Ok," I replied, regretting I agreed to the familiarity of a first name.

Steven blurted out, "My whole life and career depends on me regaining my sight. I will do anything and everything I can to achieve that goal."

"Please understand that it might not be possible. As far as your position as Chief of Detectives is concerned, I realize you would not be able to do field work but your mind is just as sharp as ever. Don't ever let anyone ever say that that isn't true. You can think and reason. It is important you approach therapy with a positive attitude because you need to adjust to the current situation."

I paused for a moment to make sure that what I was about to say would come across as straight a picture as I could paint it. I had never been one to mince words.

"Listen to me, Steven. Time is your enemy and your friend. Time is needed for the swelling to lessen in the occipital area of your head. As time passes, the doctors will do tests to see how the healing is progressing. There are also various degrees of vision redemption but we are jumping ahead of ourselves right now. Let's eat and focus on our therapy. I'm starved," I said as I bit into my sandwich.

"Marla, I need some assurance that I will be able to do for myself. I fear being useless and a burden to everyone."

"Steven, I don't deal well with self-pity. I have had men here worse off than you. As soon as we find ourselves sinking into the self-pity department, we need to do something to keep it at bay. There isn't time for that. You will feel frustration but we will get through it together."

After lunch we will begin with lesson one, "oral hygiene." Steven would learn to brush his teeth.

I led him to the bathroom. "Steven, your toothbrush is on the 4th shelf in the cabinet."

He opened the cabinet door and found it.

"Toothpaste is on the 3rd shelf," I said.

Steven fumbled around and found it.

"You can put your items wherever you find it more convenient. This is your bathroom, your items. You make your own road map of where they are for you to remember. After a couple of times, you will come into the bathroom, pick up the toothbrush and toothpaste just like a sighted person and brush your teeth. Ok, now take the top off the toothpaste and put it on the back of the sink. This is the tricky part. Put the end of the toothpaste next to one end of the brush and gently push paste on the brush. Good, good, you got it. Now, put the toothpaste cap back on. Turn on the water, not too much. Brush your teeth. Excellent. There are paper cups in a dispenser on the wall to your right. Pull one down and put water in it. Rinse. There is a towel behind you. You can use this to wipe around your mouth.

Congratulations – you just completed your oral hygiene lesson. Steven, you are a fast learner. At this rate, we can complete your personal hygiene early in the morning and work on familiarizing yourself with your surroundings. I am impressed with your memory. I guess being a cop has taught you to remember minute details. This will be a huge advantage over the average person."

"Thanks for the encouragement."

"I wouldn't say it if it wasn't true. Now it is time to shave." I got out the electric razor.

I was lucky. Steven was like most men. He could shave in his sleep. The only thing he would need help with was straightening his sideburns. I told him George or I would complete this task.

After shaving, it was off to the shower area. I called George for help. We gave Steven the grand tour.

"George will be right here, outside the shower door. If you have any problems at all, he will aid you. There is a place at the back of the shower for you to sit down if you need to but I prefer using a shower chair in the beginning until you become familiar with the shower. The shower head is removable. George will give you a washcloth and soap. Hair shampoo is located on the ledge to your right. I prefer to use the clock system to describe where things are. Step into the shower for a minute. The showerhead is at 12 o'clock. Reach up. Feel it? The hair shampoo is at 3 o'clock, the shower chair is behind you at 6 o'clock and the entrance to the shower is at 9 o'clock."

"That's a good system," he replied.

"I like it. I'm going to leave now. Don't forget. George is here to help you with anything you need from soaping up to rinsing off to drying off. As soon as I leave, you can disrobe. George will page me when you are finished. Ok?" I said with a slight reluctance in my voice.

"Ok," said Steven with confidence he could do this.

I looked back for moment. I saw Steven take off his suit jacket and tie. He was about to unbutton his shirt. I knew he was in good hands so I went back to my office to wait.

Chapter 42

How long have you known Marla?" inquired Steven as he started the water flowing.

"A long time. At least 15 years," replied George.

"Is she always such a take charge nurse?"

"Are you kidding? You haven't seen anything yet," exclaimed George.

"Is she married?"

"Widow."

"What happened if you don't mind me asking?"

"It's common knowledge. Her husband was killed in NAM."

"Never remarried?"

"Nope."

"She must have been young when he died."

"She was 30. That was 9 years ago. It's hard to believe it was that long ago but it was. Thomas and Marla were together only two years. The majority of the time he was in NAM but to see them together was to see a match made in heaven," George said with a reminiscent tone.

"How did she meet him?"

"He was a patient, same as you," replied George.

"Interesting," said Steven.

"What?"

"There must have been thousands of men who passed through here during Vietnam and she became involved with only one?"

"Thomas was one of a kind. I helped Marla with him just like I'm helping her with you. Same deal then as now: special orders from the military."

Steven finished his shower, turned off the water and asked for a towel to dry his hair. Then he asked for another towel for his body. The questioning continued.

"What do you mean special orders from the military?"

"Maybe I said too much," replied George hoping to change the subject. Can we talk about something else?

"No, please tell me, what special orders?"

"When you were brought in, the Governor had called the Navy to request special assistance on your case. Admiral Hargrove contacted Dr. Fong who informed Marla that she had a new patient starting immediately."

"I had no idea."

"You must be a very important man both to the Navy and the State of Hawaii."

"Interesting," Steven repeated.

At that point, the conversation ceased. George helped Steven out of the shower and into his pajamas and robe. He paged me and by the time I got back to the shower area, Steven was ready to go back to his room. It was time for his next lesson.

Chapter 43

"It is time for you to become familiar with your surroundings," I said in a reassuring voice. "In addition to the clock method, I use the pacer method. In the pacer method, you walk off the distance of the room in steps. You become familiar with each piece of furniture and every item in the room. You learn how many steps it takes to go from one item to the next. Once you learn the room you're in, whether it is this hospital room or your office at work, no one would ever know you were blind. Ready to begin?"

"Ready."

Steven was a fast learner. In two hours, he learned where everything was. It was almost time for dinner. I ordered the beginner's dinner which was a ground beef patty, mashed potatoes and green beans. While we were waiting, that uneasy silence resurfaced.

Steven finally spoke, "Are you having dinner with me?"

"Of course, I need to give you another lesson on how to eat. I want you to know that I am here for you until your sight returns or you have learned everything there is for me to teach you."

"How long am I going to have to stay in the hospital?

"That's up to Dr. Stone. Be nice to him, Steven. I realize

that this is incredibly stressful for you but he is doing all he can."

"I'll remember but it's just so damn frustrating. I can't read the paper, or reports, or watch TV."

"That's true, but you can listen to the TV, the radio, or have someone read the paper to you. Things will move faster once you become more proficient in doing your hygiene. Tomorrow we will walk down the halls and outside for some fresh air. There is a sunroom with vending machines and a smoking room with an area where some of the patients get together for conversation or bingo. I tell all my patients one day at a time."

Before Steven could respond, there was a knock at the door. Dinner had arrived. The plate had the ground beef meat patty at 6 o'clock, mashed potatoes at 10 o'clock and green beans at 2 o'clock. I guided his hand over the plate for him to get familiar with the positioning and the degree of heat emanating from the food. Steven immediately took his fork and cut the meat patty. No further guidance was needed by me. I pulled my tray to my lap and began to eat.

After dinner, I asked Steven if he wanted to listen to music or TV or have me read the paper to him. He decided to listen to the TV so he could hear the news. Some of the news dealt with him and the explosion two days ago. There were no suspects. The Hawaiian Police Department (HPD) had a 24 hour guard outside the hospital room.

Steven decided to turn in early so I left. I told him I would be back at 8:00 a.m. the next morning. I was so tired that all I could do was take a taxi home and fall into bed.

The next three days Steven was like a sponge absorbing everything I showed him. Dr. Stone took him in for more tests. The swelling in the back of head had gone down but not a significant amount. The only indication Steven had been injured was a band-aid on his forehead. Steven asked

Dr. Stone when he could leave the hospital. Dr. Stone said he wanted to give it two more days but Steven could only go home, not work.

Another challenge was familiarizing Steven with his house. I understand wanting to sleep at home but as familiar as a person thinks he or she is in their own house, it is different when the person is blind. Everything has to be relearned. It was at this time I introduced Steven to the white cane with the red tip: the universal symbol of blindness. The cane would help him navigate in unfamiliar surroundings. I showed him how to use it by tapping it from one side to the next as he took a step.

Steven had a small two-bedroom beach house. I was grateful it wasn't larger so I wouldn't have to teach him more than necessary.

I arranged to have George come to the house to help him learn the shower area. To help things go smoothly, George brought a shower chair from the hospital.

Because Steven left the hospital and was living at his house, I was expected to be there 'round the clock. I had a choice of the sofa bed or the second bedroom. I chose the sofa bed because I didn't like sleeping in a small bedroom. Many nights, I would fall asleep on the sofa and stay there all night instead of going into the bedroom that I shared with Thomas. I hardly slept the first night even with my sleeping pill. At 5:45 a.m. I went into the kitchen and made coffee. The smell of fresh brewed coffee permeated the house. I opened the sliding glass door to get a better view of the ocean. The whiff of salt air cleared my head. As I sipped my coffee, I stared at the waves as they lapped against the shore and my thoughts drifted to my wedding day.

I heard a noise in the living room. When I turned around, I saw Steven walking toward the kitchen. He was tall, 6'2", slightly taller than Thomas and weighed about 180 pounds.

Aside from that, Steven and Thomas differed in every other physical characteristic except they both had hair on their chests. Steven had dark brown hair and green eyes. Thomas had blond hair and blue eyes. Steven was tall and slender and Thomas was tall and muscular.

"Hi, you're up early." Steven said.

"I'm sorry if I woke you," I said trying to cover my thoughts.

"You didn't wake me. The coffee did."

"Would you like a cup?" I asked as I went for the pot.

"Yes, thanks."

"Black, correct?

"Correct, how did you know? Am I a stereotype of cops – no cream or sugar?" chuckled Steven.

I smiled. "I was about to make breakfast. How about eggs, potatoes, and toast?"

"That sounds great."

I went to the cabinet, pulled out a fry pan, all the ingredients and made breakfast.

"Ok, eggs are at 10 o'clock, potatoes at 2 o'clock, toast is on a separate plate at 3 o'clock. I poured some juice and that is at 12 o'clock. Do you want some ketchup for the potatoes?"

"No ketchup, but I would like some salt."

"The salt shaker is at 1 o'clock. Take the salt and first put some in your hand. Then spread it over the eggs and potatoes."

Steven did as he was instructed. Lesson one, breakfast at home was complete. We talked little while we ate. My mind wasn't on eating. I was consumed with the ocean. It brought back even stronger memories of Thomas. He was holding me in his arms, saying how much he loved me.

"Marla? Marla?" Steven shouted.

"Yes, Steven," I said in a calm voice.

"Are you ok?"

"I'm ok."

"You seemed like you were a million miles away."

"I'm sorry. I was. It won't happen again," I responded unemotionally yet I could feel myself wanting to throw up.

"You want to talk about it?"

"Thanks, but maybe another time."

"Do you want to show me how to clean up?" Steven asked changing the subject.

"That's ok; we'll save that for later. George should be over in about an hour to familiarize you with the shower. After that, I will acquaint you with the kitchen. I want you to be able to make a basic meal, whether it is opening a can of tuna, or making a vegetable salad, eventually graduating to a more complicated meal by using the stove or barbeque. You have a beautiful patio that is perfect for barbequing."

"With the long hours I work, I don't have much time for anything including barbequing," Steven said sadly.

"I know what you mean. With the long hours I keep at the hospital, if I am lucky, I might barbeque once every two months on a Sunday. Dr. Fong is an expert with the grill. I take care of the salad and beer," I replied.

"Sounds like fun," said Steven politely.

There was a knock at the door.

"Come in," I yelled.

 It was George.

"You're early. Have you had breakfast?"

"Are you going to make me some whether I have or haven't?" said George inquisitively.

"How many?"

"Four, overeasy."

"Yes sir." I saluted and got out another fry pan.

While I cooked breakfast, Steven and George talked about sports and politics. In all the years I knew George, I never knew he was so up on politics. I listened for a while but my thoughts drifted back to Thomas. I just couldn't focus but I knew why. The cases were similar. The Navy assigned me to be Thomas' nurse; the constant one-on-one care. I had to teach Thomas to walk again; now I was tapped by the Navy once again this time to teach Steven to function while he was blind whether it was temporary or permanent. The déjà vu was overwhelming.

The breakfast was about to turn into a disaster until George yelled, "Hey Marla, over easy, not burnt."

"Sorry."

I poured the eggs into the plate and left. I went to the bathroom. Tears flowed. I wiped my eyes. I had a job to do. I needed to pull myself together, now. But how? That was another matter.

Chapter 44

After Steven dressed, we reviewed yesterday's lesson on the living room and dining room area and we completed the kitchen lesson just in time for lunch. I showed him how to construct a basic sandwich using a small paring knife and spreader.

After we ate, I suggested a walk down the beach. Two police officers were stationed outside Steven's house 24 hours a day, 7 days a week. They were our escort wherever we went. Until the police apprehend the person or persons who attempted to murder Steven, there would be body guards visible at all times. It made me feel somewhat better that the police were present, but I still felt anxious wishing they would catch the lunatic already.

It was a clear sunny day. Steven wore a large straw hat and sunglasses to cover his eyes. I put my hair in a ponytail, slipped on my sunglasses and baseball hat and off we went. I took a beach towel, sun block, a bottle of water and a small umbrella. We strolled leisurely for 10 minutes. Not much was said until I suggested we rest for a while. I found a semi-shady spot near the rocks. I opened the umbrella and laid the towel on the sand. I applied some lotion to my face and arms. Then turning to Steven, I gave him the sun block and he spread the white liquid all over his face, arms and legs.

While he was busy doing that, I took off my sandals and laid back on the towel. Steven handed the sun block back to me and sat down. It felt good to relax even if it was only for a few minutes.

"How long do you want to stay?" Steven asked.

"I'm flexible. As long as you do," I replied.

"I can't remember the last time I did this," Steven said as he laid next to me on the towel.

I felt a little uncomfortable but didn't say anything.

"I can and it was a long time ago," I responded as I pulled myself on my elbows and stared out into the ocean.

"When was that?"

"I'd rather not get into that right now," I said trying to change the subject.

"This morning at breakfast you were a million miles away even though you were sitting next to me. You said you would talk to me another time. I might not be able to see but I am a good listener," Steven turned on his side facing me with his head up. He pressed for information about something I was uncomfortable talking about.

"Steven, you deserve another nurse, one who would be able to give you her full attention. I am going to request the Navy appoint someone else to your case."

Steven looked stunned by the remark.

"Please don't. It was wrong for me to pry."

"It's not your fault. It's mine. I'm having problems concentrating because everything reminds me of my husband."

"I'm sorry. I didn't know you were married," Steven said even though George told him I was a widow. He wanted to hear it from me.

"I was married. I'm a widow now."

"I'm even sorrier. How did he die?"

"In NAM," I replied not wanting to go into details.

"How long has it been?"

"It will be 9 years next month. I've been told that time heals all wounds, that I will move on, find a new person to spend my life with. I loved Thomas with all my heart. We were soul mates. There isn't anything I wouldn't have done for him and he felt the same way. If I could have died in his place, I would have because living without him isn't living, it's existing. I just can't move on or forget our life together." I fought back tears as I spoke. I was grateful Steven was blind at the moment so he couldn't see me so emotional.

"Whoever told you to move on didn't mean it disrespectfully. I think they were trying to show that you needed to think of yourself. After a period of time it would be right for you to go out, date, live a little," commented Steven in defense of some unknown person dispensing advice.

"I didn't meet Thomas at a dance," I retorted. "He was a patient like you are. I don't date. I don't have the time to socialize. I work 12 hours a day, 6 days a week."

"If I didn't know you were a nurse, I would swear you were a cop," Steven said half-laughing.

I chuckled.

That broke the seriousness of the moment.

"Do you want to walk a little further down the beach?" I said.

"Sure."

I collected our stuff and gave Steven the towel to carry. I went barefoot so I could continue enjoying the sand beneath my feet. We walked for about a half mile before we turned around and went back to the house all the while being shadowed by two police officers. Nothing more was said about Thomas. Everything was peaceful for the moment.

Little did I know that things were about to change.

Chapter 45

We spent the afternoon making dinner. I acquainted Steven with how to use the stove. Our dinner was baked chicken breasts in olive oil and basil with a green vegetable salad and chocolate cake for dessert. After dinner, I instructed Steven on how to load the dishwasher.

It was time to take a break from learning. We went into the living room and I turned on some Barry Manilow. Steven asked me to read the newspaper to him. It was early, around 9:00 p.m., when we heard a noise outside. I got up from the sofa to look out the living room window to see if the police officers were still there. I could see one but not the other. I moved from the living room window to the side window by the front door. Before I could position myself, the first rock smashed through the window where I was standing. Glass flew everywhere. I tried to get my bearings but there wasn't time. A second rock pulverized the window I was standing next to. It hit me in the shoulder. Instinctively, I raised my arms to shield my face from flying glass.

Steven yelled, "What's happening?"

"Turn off the lights. Someone is trying to break in," I shouted.

There was a crash in the kitchen. A third rock had

broken the patio window. Two people were breaking into the house.

"Steven, get down on the floor as low as you can."

"Are you alright?" Steven screamed.

"Yes," I answered.

I lied. Glass shards had cut into each arm but I needed to keep Steven as calm as possible. A man entered the house through the broken living room window. He was a big guy, about 6'3", 230 pounds, carrying a knife in his waistband and a gun in a shoulder holster. He didn't see me behind him. As he moved forward, I approached cautiously. I had to do something but there was blood running down both arms so my only thought was to use my feet and kick him in the back of the knee. With all my might, I did a flying kick and hit his knee. He went down but only temporarily. To my chagrin, he rose up quickly, pulling a gun from his holster. I hit his hand knocking the gun to the floor. He bent down, picked up the gun and shoved it in his waist band. I dropped down and crawled by the bookcase getting as close to the wall as I could. As he came toward me, I blindsided him on the side where he had the knife and landed a punch on the bridge of his nose. He grabbed his nose and let out a scream. He turned around, grabbed me and punched me in my right eye. I staggered backwards for a moment. This gave him the opportunity to land another blow this time to my jaw. I fell to the floor. When I looked up, I saw him grab the knife from its holster.

He was coming to kill me. I rolled as best I could through the broken glass to the corner near the bookcase. I laid as still as I could and when he turned me over to shove the knife in my chest, I reached up, grabbed his genitals and pulled them down as hard as I could. He screamed, grabbed his groin and fell to the floor. The knife was next to his shoulder. I grabbed it and threw it across the floor. The bastard looked up, took his hand off his crotch, and pulled his gun from his waistband. I grabbed the umbrella from the stand next to the door and began beating him with the handle. I pummeled him everywhere and anywhere until he dropped the gun screaming, "You bitch," and stopped trying to get up. I grabbed the gun and turned my attention to Steven. I could see another figure creeping toward the living room. Steven was still on the floor where I told him to stay.

I screamed, "One o'clock. He's got a gun."

Steven jumped up scaring the second guy. The assailant pushed Steven to the floor. I could see Steven was pinned so I screamed as loud as I could, "I've got a gun," The second guy continued to fight so I shot a round past the idiot's head. He still wouldn't give up so I put a round into his shoulder. He stumbled backward but remained standing. As he went for his 45, I put the third round dead on in his forehead.

The first guy started to get up. I turned and said, "Get on the ground, you dirt bag, facedown, hands behind your back, or you will end up like your partner over there, dead." The first guy dropped to the floor. Steven got up and made his way towards me. I cocked the gun, put the barrel against the back of his head and gave it Steven to hold.

I walked to the garage and shouted, "Steven, if this guy so much as scratches an itch before I get back, shoot him. I'm going to get some rope." The guy never moved. I hog-tied his hands and feet together. Then I dialed the police and told them to bring an ambulance.

David and the paramedics showed up in 12 minutes and told me both cops had been ambushed and were dead.

While we were waiting, Steven asked, "Did he hurt you, Marla?"

"No Steven, I'm ok. Don't worry, everything's going to be fine now."

I didn't want Steven to know the extent of my injuries.

The glass shards were very deep which was good and bad. The good thing was the glass was embedded so deep that it acted as a band aid which slowed the blood loss. The bad thing was that all the glass had to be removed surgically. Any attempt to pull them out would cause massive hemorrhaging. The paramedics stabilized the glass from moving deeper into my arms and transported me to Oahu General. On the direction of the emergency room doctor, I was given a small dose of Demerol for the pain. Discretely, I asked that George meet me in emergency. A general surgeon was waiting for me when I showed up by ambulance.

"George, could you look after Steven while I am seen by the ER doctor?" I said as calmly as I could.

"Sure, Marla, no problem," replied George trying to stay as calm as I was but was about to pass out when he saw my arms.

"George," Steven asked with great consternation, "How bad is Marla, really?"

"I don't know, Steven, honest. I received a phone call to come and be with you while the doctor examined her. As soon as I know, I will tell you, ok?"

Steven was fine except for a cut on his forehead.

The surgery lasted four and a half hours with 23 stitches in the left arm and 8 in the right. I put the glass shards in a jar and kept them on my office desk. I wanted them as a reminder of the night I faced death and realized it wasn't my time. Maybe God had a plan for me after all.

My face was another story. It looked like I had gone 15 rounds with Muhammad Ali. After I was stitched up, both arms were wrapped from the elbow to the wrist and I was given antibiotics for 10 days.

Chapter 46

Admiral Hargrove put me in for a bravery commendation and the Purple Heart. I wasn't brave; at least I didn't think I was. I did what I had to do to survive. But it didn't matter what I thought, it only mattered what the Navy thought and they decided to raise me in rank to Captain.

After I recovered, I resumed teaching Steven. I wore long sleeves to cover the bandages on my arms and avoided talking to Steven about that night. Peter asked if I wanted to talk to a shrink about what I went through. I thanked him for his concern but decided if there was anyone I wanted to talk to, it would be Chaplain Cook.

Steven went back to work a few days after the incident. Just as I had taught him to get around at home, I taught him how to get around at work.

Two weeks later Steven's sight returned while waiting to be seen by the Ophthalmologist.

"Steven, I've got a couple of things to do so you wait here until you are called. I will be right back," I said nonchalantly.

I was gone about 20 minutes when he started seeing clearly.

Steven got up from the chair and walked down the hall. He went to the nurse's station.

"Are you Marla?" Steven inquired.

"Oh no," said the nurse.

"I've got to find Marla," Steven said with a sense of urgency.

"She could be in the therapy room or her office. I'd check therapy first," stated the floor nurse.

"I don't know where that is. Is Dr. Fong in?"

"Come with me. I will have someone ring his office."

"Hello Dr. Fong, Steven Roberts, here. I'm downstairs at your nursing station 1A. Could you come down and meet me?"

A few minutes later Peter arrived.

"Marla didn't tell me you regained your vision."

"Marla doesn't know yet. I want to surprise her. Would you take me to her office?" asked Steven.

"No problem," Peter started to move but Steven just stood there.

"Is there something more Commander Roberts?" said Peter inquisitively.

"Dr. Fong, I have feelings for her," he said whispering.

"Commander Roberts, many patients feel something for their nurse or doctor when they have been through a traumatic incident. In Marla's case, many men have fallen for her. It's perfectly normal. But now you have your sight and your life back."

"These feelings are real," he said sincerely.

"You haven't seen her yet."

"I felt her touch. I heard her voice of encouragement. She saved my life…. I know how I feel."

"Don't tell her what you told me, at least not yet. I don't know how much she has told you about her life but I know Marla. She has become extremely tightlipped about her feelings. What you have said to me is liable to cause great distress to her."

"Why?" asked Steven with surprise.

"She lost her husband in NAM. Did she tell you that?"

"Yes."

"I've known Marla for 19 years. I was Thomas' best man at their wedding. She has never gotten over his death and I doubt she ever will. If you charge in there like a bull in china shop, any chance at a relationship with her will go down the drain. It will be over before it begins."

"Thanks for the advice, Dr. Fong."

Peter started to leave when Steven cried out, "Don't go."

"Why not?"

"I still need you to take me to Marla. I don't know what she looks like."

"Oh, I forgot," said Dr. Fong half-laughing.

The two of them walked down the hall toward my office. Peter appeared in the doorway. Steven was in the corridor out of my line of vision listening.

"Hi," Peter said coyly.

"Hi. What's up?" I said looking up from a stack of week old reports.

"What are you doing here? I thought you were with Steven," replied Peter with a straight face.

"I was but he is waiting to be seen by Ophthalmology. I thought I would take the time to review my in-box."

"How are your arms?"

"Good. Dr. Hunter said I might need a little plastic surgery on the left arm scar. That took 23 stitches. The right arm was only 8."

"Your face looks better. The swelling around your eye is gone and the bruising around your cheekbone is a faded green color. Instead of 15 rounds with Ali, it looks like you only went 3.

"Ha Ha. It was a good thing Thomas wasn't there. He would have tortured the guys for hitting me and for amusement he would have shot both of them in the testicles before blowing them away. I only killed one because I was forced to. You know, I thought about that. Too bad the other guy didn't challenge me. That would have been one less dirt bag in the prison system. Besides, the whole situation could have been far worse. Each of them had a gun and one had a knife. Having a run-in with a broken window isn't so bad if you compare it to an encounter with a gun or a knife," I said touching my pen to my mouth.

"You're busy so I'm going back to my office. Let me know if you need anything," said Peter as he was leaving my doorway.

"Hey, where's my cup of Joe? You used to at least drop by with a little coffee now and then."

"When you come back to staff full-time, I'll have a steaming cup waiting. I promise."

"Yeah, promises, promises. Thanks...for nothing."

I went back to my work. A few seconds later there was a knock on the wall but no one was in the doorway.

"Yes, come in," I shouted, not looking up.

No response.

Another knock.

This time I looked up but no one was there.

"Hey, Peter, are you playing games?" I shouted. "I don't have time for them, at least not now, unless you have that cup of Joe in your hand. Then, I'll reconsider." I lowered my head to write into a patient's chart.

There was another knock on the wall.

Perturbed, I shouted, "Peter, either get your ass in here or leave me alone." I continued writing but I hadn't looked up.

Steven came in. He sat down on the sofa in front of my desk and cleared his throat.

"Ok wadda you ...." I stopped in mid-sentence. "Steven, you can see."

"Yes, I was sitting in the chair waiting to be called and everything became clear. I called Peter. He brought me over to see you.

"We need to go back to Ophthalmology so you can be examined."

"We will. I just want to look at you," he said staring at me.

"Me?"

"You."

"Please don't embarrass me."

"I'm not. For almost six weeks, I have been existing in total darkness living, the worst nightmare imaginable. The only reassuring person in my life was you."

"Steven, I was doing my job."

"I knew you were going to say that. You went beyond your job."

"No, I didn't. Changing the subject, I need to contact Admiral Hargrove to tell him my assignment is complete."

"Please tell me I was more than just an assignment," said Steven in a hurtful tone of voice.

"What do you want me to say?" I said trying not to give him any encouragement.

"Marla, I have feelings for you. I hope you have some feelings for me."

"Have feelings?"

"I already heard the speech from Dr. Fong but my feelings are genuine. I know that you probably see hundreds of men and they have said the same thing but I mean what I say. You are a beautiful woman, Marla. While I was blind, I kept imaging what you looked like. The warmth of your touch, the sweetness of your voice..."

"Steven, please stop," I begged.

"I need to tell you how I feel."

"I don't want to hear how you feel. Please, can't you respect my feelings?"

"What are you feeling?" Steven asked hoping that I would feel for him was what he felt for me.

"You don't want me to answer to that question," I replied. I wanted to be anywhere than in the same room with Steven Roberts.

"Yes I do," he said. His voice suddenly dropped realizing Peter was right. He now understood it had been a mistake to confront me with his feelings.

"So you really want to know? Ok…" I took a deep long breath. "I have felt dead inside ever since my husband was Killed In Action in a bloody God-forsaken place called Vietnam. Since his death, all I have is my job. The Government is cutting the funding to my program so how long I'll have it is anybody's guess. Then you come along. I see some of Thomas in you, enough to make me run and hide. I have been praying this assignment would end. Now it's over and I don't know what I feel. Honestly, I can't open myself up to another loss. I just can't go through it again."

"If you don't take a chance, you will be alone for the rest of your life. A pretty lady like you should be with someone. If not me, at least make a life with someone else," Steven replied.

"I have my work, my friends, and as sad as some think, my memories. Steven, I can't ask you to compete with a memory; I just can't," I said imploring him to understand.

"I would never try. Marla, what I ask is a chance to make new memories with you."

"I can't deal with this right now. We need to return to Ophthalmology."

The conversation ended. Ophthalmology gave Steven a clean bill of health.

Before he left the hospital, Steven asked me to dinner, no strings attached. He wanted to get to know me better. I tried to say no but when I looked into his all-consuming green eyes, I said yes.

We agreed to meet the following Saturday night.

Chapter 47

Steven went back to his job and I went back to mine. Prior to dinner, Steven asked me if I had a meal preference and I told him it had been a long time since I had surf and turf. He knew a place on Maui and made reservations. He called in a favor from a friend at HPD who flew us over to the island.

As much as I wanted to wear this tropical-flowered dress I had received as a birthday present last year, I borrowed a long sleeve dress from Maria to cover my bandaged arms. I went to the hair salon and had my hair trimmed and styled. It had been years since I had a basic manicure so I indulged myself. My hairdresser applied make-up to cover the still visible green marks on my face plus eyeliner and mascara.

A limo arrived promptly at 7:00 p.m. to take me to the helipad. Steven had already arrived. I heard him say to the driver to return at 10:00 p.m. The driver acknowledged and drove away.

Steven looked at me and said, "Wow, you look lovely."

"Thank you. You look quite handsome yourself in your suit and tie."

"You didn't have to wear the long sleeves. Where we are going, no one will notice the bandages."

"Just where are we going?" I asked in a curious voice.

"A little surprise," he said with a devilish grin.

The flight to Maui was short. Another limo was waiting to take us to the restaurant. Steven told the driver return for us at 9:45 p.m.

Steven led me into the foyer. "Two for Roberts," he said. The host led us to a reserved table on a platform facing the ocean. I saw Steven pull a $20 bill from his wallet and hand it to him.

"No, not that one," Steven said.

"This one sir?"

"Yes, this one," said Steven.

Steven pulled my chair back. I sat down and he sat down next to me so we both could look out at the waves crashing into the cliffs. The rainbow sunset slowly disappeared in streaks across the sky. The waiter brought menus and rattled off house specials. I was so taken with the ocean view I never heard a word he said.

Steven saw I was a thousand miles away. He woke me from my trance by asking me if wanted a drink.

"Yes," I replied. "White wine please."

"Jack Daniels on the rocks for me," said Steven.

"I can't get over the sight. It's beautiful," I sighed.

"I'm glad you like it. Do you know what you want to eat?"

"Steak and shrimp," I replied. "And you?"

"Salmon. Care for an appetizer?" he asked.

"Crab stuffed mushrooms sounds good."

"Good," said Steven. "Waiter, we're ready to order."

He ordered for the both us. I went back to gazing at the ocean.

For a moment, I was at peace. I saw Thomas' laughing face on our honeymoon at Diamond Head.

"Marla, Marla..." said Steven.

"I'm sorry. I was thinking about a place I was at years ago. I was away from my job, the military, the investigation, and the nightmares."

"Nightmares?"

"Not very many any more."

The rolls and butter were served with the stuffed mushrooms. I bit into one. They were heavenly but Steven didn't seem to like them very much. I ended up polishing them off. The salad arrived followed by dinner. We made small talk about how beautiful the scenery was. I ordered another white wine and he had another Jack Daniels.

"Steven, I know you didn't fly me here to Maui for the excellent food and the romantic atmosphere," I said sipping my wine.

"I did and I didn't. Aside from the wonderful food, I wanted a place for us to sit and talk. Not about the Navy Marla, nor the teacher Marla, nor the nurse Marla, but the real Marla. You taught me that I could still be a man when I couldn't see. I had my mind, my other senses, and my experiences. I needed to thank you but saying it wasn't enough."

I could see how sincere he was. "You already thanked me. What I did for you was my job. Granted it had been a while since I had a case like yours but rehabbing people and helping them get on with their life has been my life's work."

"You do it well," he said smiling.

"I have tried to keep up on the latest techniques. The problem with most professionals is that once they graduate they continue on with only what they learned in the past instead of being on the cutting edge of their specialty. It takes time and effort to stay on that edge. If someone has a family, time isn't in abundance. Being single gives me more time to devote to work and education. I hold my staff accountable to the same standards as I adhere to. If they can't keep up, then they don't work for me. Are you surprised to hear this?" I said unemotionally.

"No I'm not. I've interfaced with George extensively. He definitely knew his job. Both of you helped me face my fear of blindness, overcome self-pity and do what I had to do to survive because had I not learned the basics from you, I might I have died the night those two men broke into my house."

"I don't know if I would go that far."

Steven surprised me. He grabbed both my wrists and exclaimed, "Marla, look at your arms. That alone should remind you how wrong things went that night."

"The point is we prevailed," I said flatly.

"Are you always this detached?" he replied with surprise.

"Since Thomas died, frankly yes," I said coldly. "I have feelings but I do my best to keep them under wraps. After Thomas' death, I consciously decided that it is ok to care; I have to care but not too much."

"Are telling me you won't open up to anyone?"

"Yes, that's what I'm saying. If I open up as you put it, I run the risk of more pain. Look Steven, you are a kind, decent, man but you're a cop. Cops get ambushed, shot at, and yes, killed in the line of duty. We were brought together because of an attempt on your life. Years ago, I fell in love with and married a Special Forces Officer. I knew that if he returned to NAM, he could be crippled or Killed In Action but I took my chances and got involved with him. I wouldn't have traded our time together for anything in the world but I went against my better judgment. After 4 tours of duty, the day before he was to leave NAM forever, he was killed.

Vietnam was a lousy war. All wars are lousy but this one was especially horrible because we didn't have to be there. We fought a limited war, not like WWII where we fought to win at all costs against Japan and Germany. Vietnam was different. If we had fought an all out war, we would have won. To make matters worse, the Vietnamese people didn't want us there. After the French left, why did we go? Why? To stop communism? That's what the Government wants us to believe or was there another reason? I personally believe if a country wants to be communistic, who are we to mix in their politics? The Vietnamese kicked the French out and then kicked us out too as painful as it is to admit. The military along with Hollywood portrays war as glorious but all wars are unglorious. I wish our Government would come visit my ward sometime and see the casualties of war: men without legs, arms, paralyzed, blinded, deafened, new symptoms from a chemical defoliant used called "Agent Orange" and let's not forget the psychological scars. The mental and emotional toll sometimes far exceeds the physical ones. In previous wars, they referred to it as battle fatigue. The new term is Post Traumatic Stress Disorder (PTSD). Our Government officials deny its' existence. By denying it exists, they won't have to pay benefits to our soldiers. It does exist. I know because I've seen it first hand. Thomas had it. It was never diagnosed but I saw the symptoms. I heard him scream and felt his body shake when we slept.

No one needs to die over a difference of opinion on how to govern a population. There is no one right form of government even though our Government would differ with that statement, just as there is no one right form of worship. How many people have died over the centuries because of religion? How many have died in war? Over 58,000 men were killed and hundreds of thousands were injured and that's just the American statistics in Vietnam. That doesn't include the dead Japanese in the 1940s, or the French in the 1950s. Hell, it doesn't even count the dead Vietnamese."

I gulped down the rest my wine so I could finish, "Steven, you fight a daily war on the islands of petty and violent crimes, drugs, gambling, prostitution and whatever else is out there. If I dated you, came to love you, and something happened to you, I don't know what I'd do so just let sleeping dogs lie."

"What ifs are no reason to keep a relationship from

happening. Please, give it some time. All I ask is that you reconsider."

"I'll think about it but I don't think it will happen. Can we go back to Oahu now?" I said feeling very uncomfortable.

"Certainly." Steven waived for the waiter. "Waiter, check please."

We barely spoke all the way back to Oahu. I picked up my car at the hospital and thanked him for the meal.

"Can I call you in a couple of days?" said Steven.

"Sure."

As I was getting into my car, Steven ran over. "Marla, what are you doing tomorrow? I could pick you up for lunch. We could have a picnic. My friend has a yacht. He would let me borrow it. If you fish, we could drop a couple of lines and see what we catch."

"I'm sorry Steven. Sunday is the one day I have off and those days are planned. I go to Peter's house for a BBQ when he has one. He's having one next weekend. Tomorrow I have things to do. If you'd like to go to Peter's BBQ, I'll let him know to buy more food."

"With our busy schedules, it will be difficult to see each other during the week. Weekends are best and many times you and I have to work Saturdays," Steven said trying to convince me.

"I'm sorry but this has been my schedule for years. I can get someone to cover an occasional shift but as a manager, I have to be at the hospital Monday - Saturday. Sunday is my day off to do certain things. You of all people should understand this. Your schedule is as tight as mine," I said with a definitive tone in my voice.

"Yeah, I understand but I don't have to like it."

"Good night Steven. I had a nice time." I kissed him on the cheek, got in to my car and left.

I was exhausted from the later than usual evening I had

with Steven. I slept in until 9:00 a.m., showered, cleaned the condo, packed a picnic basket and drove to the cemetery. I stopped for flowers and proceeded to Thomas' grave. I had been doing this since Thomas died but on this particular day I saw an unfamiliar black sedan follow me from my house to the flower shop. After I picked up six white carnations, I stopped over to the grounds keeper booth and saw my friend, Ben Kanali.

"Ben, a black sedan has been following me since I left my house," I said. "After I set up lunch, could you see if you recognize it?"

Ben met me there each week to pull the vase and put water in it. He shined Thomas' headstone and took special care to edge around it. I always brought a blanket which Ben helped spread on the grass and a picnic basket which had sandwiches, some kind of salad and dessert. Today, I brought an Italian sub which was Ben's favorite for us to share. I also brought homemade potato salad and sliced pickles. I cut up some fresh fruit and made a large container of pink lemonade. Ben liked brownies so I baked a batch and left it with him, pan and all.

After Ben finished his work, he went over to the black sedan to see if he could get a license number or description of the man in the car. As soon as Ben walked toward the car, the man made a U-turn and drove out of the cemetery. Ben returned. He was sorry but he didn't get any information. I told him not to worry and gave him lunch. Ben thanked me and left. He left me alone because he knew I wanted to eat near Thomas without anyone around. As I finished my lunch, I looked at my wedding ring. I told Thomas that I went out with a man named Steven but it would never amount to anything except friendship. I made a vow to Thomas and Thomas alone.

After an hour, I cleaned up and packed the car. I called

Ben over. I gave him $10.00 which he promptly declined. He always refused but I insisted he take it. I told him I would leave his lunch at the gardener's shack next Sunday because I had plans and my visit would be shorter. I asked that he please pull the vase before I arrived. He told me everything would be ready when I arrived. He thanked me for the money.

I drove home, pulled the blinds and spent the next hour crying. After chastising myself that self-pity wouldn't get me anywhere, I pulled out my nursing periodicals. I read for a while. I must have fallen asleep because I awoke to the sound of the doorbell.

"Who is it?" I yelled.

"It's George and Maria," said George.

"Just a moment." I opened the door. "George, why didn't you call?"

"We were in the area. Can we come in?"

"Of course," I replied.

George and Maria brought steaks, corn, potatoes, fruit and a chocolate cake for desert.

The BBQ was on the patio. George took everything into the kitchen.

"How did you know I needed this?" I asked George.

"I wasn't sure. Since Steven entered the picture, your emotions have been all over the place. I thought after a visit to Thomas' grave, you might want some company. If I'm wrong, we'll go."

"No, please stay. What can I do to help?"

"Nothing. Maria and I will do all the work. Do you want to invite Steven?"

"No, I'll pass," I said in a low infuriated tone of voice.

"What happened?" asked George.

"I'm sure Steven sent someone to follow me to see where I was going today and he followed me all the way to Thomas' grave. When Ben went over to the car, the guy drove off in a hurry."

"Uh-oh. What do you plan to do?" said George with great concern.

"I plan to give Detective Roberts an earful."

"Maybe he was just curious…"

"And you know what happens to the curious…"

"Marla, try to see it from his side. He cares for you."

"And he needs to see it from my side. I told him I was busy today and what I was doing was none of his business. I don't report in or out to anybody, including Chief of Detectives Steven Roberts.

"I'm sure you will get your message across when you see him."

"Damn right. Now let's change the subject and let me help you cook."

Chapter 48

The next day Steven called me at 9:00 a.m. I was in my office reviewing a case for a 10:00 a.m. meeting. I told my secretary to take a message. Steven called back an hour later. He was told I was in a meeting. He called at 11:30 a.m. She told him I was in the PT room. Not a man to be deterred, Steven drove over to the hospital. He knew my schedule from his time in the hospital. At 12:30 p.m., I would be in the cafeteria.

Oahu General had a wonderful cafeteria. When entering the turnstile, the trays, plates, napkins and silverware were to left under the clock. The "Specials of the Day" board hung on the wall over the silverware area.

The hot food was to the left and the cold food such as the salad and sandwich bar was to the right. Further down on the right was the refreshments bar stocked with diet and regular soda, tea, lemonade, coffee and milk. Past the soda and coffee bar on the right were the deserts such as puddings, Jello, cakes and ice cream. To the left past the hot food was the cash registers. Employees received a discount when they showed their badge. After paying the cashier, there was a large eating area. To the right were double doors to enter the outdoor patio. Large umbrellas shaded visitors and staff as they ate. Since the cafeteria was on the first floor, not the basement like many hospitals, on a clear day you could see the ocean. To the left and around the corner inside the dining room was a carrousel for patrons to leave their dirty plates and silverware as they exited the room.

I was eating lunch with Peter when Steven arrived. Peter took one look at me and picked up his tray without saying a word. He walked to each of the tables and whispered something in each person's ear. He left. All the people sitting at each table picked up their trays and followed Dr. Fong out of the cafeteria.

There was dead silence as everyone left. It was just the two of us.

Steven watched this mass exodus in amazement and said, "What gives?"

"They know that a volcano named Mount St. Marla is about to erupt."

"I don't understand. I called this morning and left three messages. Did you get them? What's wrong?" Steven said still not comprehending what was amiss.

"I got your messages. You asked what's wrong. Since you asked, I'll tell you. I don't like to be followed. Don't deny it. You had one of your men follow me yesterday," I said looking through not at Steven.

"I won't deny it. It's true," replied Steven averting his eyes from mine.

I rose from the table and shouted, "How dare you?" I could feel the blood rush into my face. "You've got your gall, you know that?"

"When you told me you couldn't see me Sunday, I needed to know where you went."

"That was none of your business," I snarled.

"I know but Marla, you are an enigma. I have never met anyone like you."

"And you probably never will."

"I'm sorry if I offended you," Steven said softly.

"Offended?" I bellowed. "I don't know if I would call it offended. It's more like you are a nosy son of a bitch, you know that? Well let me lay it out for you, Chief of Detectives, Steven Roberts: I am consumed by my work and my heart and soul belongs to Thomas. That is as plain as I can make it. When will you understand this?"

"Not until you give me one chance to make you happy."

"Why? My life was fine until you entered it. Do all men have the idea that the harder she is to get, they have to do anything to win her over."

Steven stood across from me completely baffled. "I thought we had a nice time Saturday night," he said not comprehending what he did.

"We did but you couldn't leave it at that. You had to snoop and pry into my personal life. Everyone who knows me respects my privacy. If you can't respect that, any future friendship or whatever is over. Period." My voice was so loud it echoed through the empty cafeteria.

I picked up my tray, walked to the carousel, dropped it and left.

Steven sat alone; even the workers stayed in the kitchen too afraid to come out until they were sure I left.

A week went by. Not a peep out of Steven. It was good to have time to reflect. I decided if Steven called we would talk, perhaps meet again on a less formal basis. If he didn't call, I would put everything behind me and go on as if I had never met him.

Steven called at 2:00 p.m. I was in physical therapy. Maria asked me if I wanted to take the call. I told her I would take it in my office.

"Captain Bristol speaking," I said formally pretending not to know it was Steven.

"Marla, it's me. I thought about what you said and we need to start over. Wipe the slate clean. Can you do that?"

"There is only one problem with that. You need to keep in mind that I am in love with a man who is not here."

"I won't disrespect that. I would like to spend time with you. If things don't work out, at least we tried."

I thought for a moment.

"Marla, are you there?" Steven shouted into the phone

"Yes. Ok. How about pizza Friday night?" I said.

"Sure, pick you up at 7:00 p.m."

"No, let's meet at 7:30 p.m. at Georgio's on Kalahani Blvd. It's close to the hospital."

"Ok, see you there."

Steven was already there when I arrived. He wore a blue Hawaiian flowered shirt and white pants. I wore a Mumu. The evening went smoothly with the conversation confined to safe topics like the Navy, our jobs, and who could cook better.

We continued to see each other as schedules permitted. One Saturday we took off and went to Molokai. I hadn't snorkled since my honeymoon but Steven was an expert in snorkeling and diving. We rented equipment from Kaunakakai. The water was so clear. I was overjoyed when the fish came to me. After snorkeling, we changed and went up to the dock and sampled some raw fish. I loved Molokai so much that Steven took me back again to see St. Joseph Church and Our Lady of Sorrows located outside of Kalaupapa. Father Damien founded both churches. He helped the victims of leprosy on the island but unfortunately he contracted the disease and died at the age of 49. Seeing those churches and hearing about Father Damien really moved me especially the part on the tour when the tour guide said that Father Damien accepted his leprosy as "his cross to bear." I thought to myself that everyone had a cross to bear in some way, some not as drastic as Father Damien but some more painful like incurable cancer. In that perspective, I felt that my cross wasn't as severe as others. My cross was one of emptiness – the emptiness of missing my husband that nothing or no one could fill. As a PT nurse I had seen my share of suffering with our soldiers yet I was sheltered by never having to work with a dying child or cancer victim. I admired those people who did.

I worried that Steven would fall in love with me. There was nothing I could do if he did. I laid my cards on the table so to speak. I cared for him but it wasn't love, certainly not the feelings of love I had for Thomas. There was no pressure for sex. He knew how I felt but hoped to change my mind. I don't mean about sex; I mean to love him and marry him.

I tried several times to set him straight but mere words didn't work. He was a cop. He was used to getting what he wanted. "No" wasn't in his vocabulary.

Chapter 49

We had been seeing each other for about six months when Steven was injured at work.

It was around 10:00 a.m. I was in the PT room when George ran in. "Marla, I need Maria for a minute," he said between huffing and puffing.

"No problem," I replied and went over to relieve Maria all the while wondering what was wrong.

It wasn't five minutes later George, Maria and Peter came back to PT.

"Marla, I know you don't like the TV on during therapy sessions but there's something you need to see," Peter said in a half-calm voice.

"Ok," I replied. "What is it?"

George reached up and turned the set on. A reporter was doing a remote from the harbor area where the expensive yachts were anchored.

"There has been an explosion at the yacht of J. K. Tanner, a multi-million dollar land developer. Details are sketchy at the present time but what we do know is that Tanner is dead. There was a second person on the boat with him who was thrown clear of the wreckage. Someone from another yacht pulled this second person to safety. That person has been identified as Steven Roberts, Chief of Detectives for the

State of Hawaii. Why Roberts and Tanner were meeting has not being disclosed. It was rumored that Tanner contacted the police because of threats made on his life. If that's true, the killer succeeded in killing Tanner and nearly received a bonus with Detective Roberts being on the yacht at the time of the blast. The condition of Roberts is unknown at this time. Stay tuned to this station for any updates. This is…"

George shut off the TV.

Before I could get the words out, Peter said that Steven was in emergency as the station was airing the news. He had a possible concussion and right wrist fracture. Dr. Taylor was in with him. After Dr. Taylor looked at him, Peter said I could go and see him.

"Peter, I am going now," I said firmly.

Peter pulled me off to the side and said, "As much as you want to deny it, you are in love with him."

"No I have feelings for him. There is a difference."

"You had feelings for Thomas too – which turned into love."

"Peter, don't tell me what I feel for Steven is the same thing I felt for Thomas? What are you, my inner voice? I have feelings for him. That's as far as it goes."

"Look how you are acting. You are rushing to be at his side. I've wanted to say this for a long time. Marla, you are a young woman. It isn't right for you to be a widow at your age. All these years you have been alone."

"Single, widow – it's just a title. I'm married to my country, remember? I took that vow long before I met Thomas. Isn't that what Thomas did too? Our marriage came second."

"Marla…"

"Peter, I don't want to discuss my personal life with you any further. Just mind your own business." I stormed off to my office and slammed my door. My secretary buzzed and asked if I was alright. I told her yes but as far as Peter Fong was concerned, I was out for the rest of the day. I called over to emergency. I asked if I could be of assistance. Dr. Taylor requested I join him in Steven's room.

I ran to emergency. When I got there, I walked into ER #2.

"Hello Marla," said Dr. Taylor. "I have one of your old patients back. Could you please call x-ray and then prepare a suture tray."

"Yes Doctor," I replied as I picked up the phone on the wall.

Afterwards, I approached Steven. He was still in his wet clothes. He reached up to grab my hand. I gently touched it and carefully laid it at his side.

"Marla, would you please get the patient out of his wet clothes. I will be back in a few minutes."

I paged George to come to the ER #2 immediately. George showed up within a minute of the page.

I cut off his jacket, then his shirt mindful of his wrist injury. There was a large bandage on his left side and one above his left eye.

I went to the closet and retrieved dry linen for the bed. While I was gone, George disrobed Steven and put a gown on him. George assisted me in changing the bed linen on the bed by rolling him to one side and then the other.

Dr. Taylor re-entered the room. "I'm taking him to x-ray. Marla, you can go back to PT. I'll page you when we return," he said.

I left but instead of returning to PT, I went to the cafeteria for an iced tea. After 45 minutes and two teas later, I returned to emergency. The diagnosis was a concussion and two hair-line fractures to the right wrist. He also had a five inch laceration on his left side which required minor surgery of several stitches to close and a small gash above the left eye that required three stitches. After surgery he went to the 3rd floor for observation.

I sat with him for a few minutes after he returned from surgery thinking about how close he came to dying. There was no denying I had feelings for Steven. But love? And with love ultimately comes intimacy. Could I be intimate with another man? I felt afraid. I broke out in a cold sweat and shivered at the thought. Not the thought of his touch on my body but the fear of how I would react. How can I sleep with another man while still wearing the wedding ring of my soul mate?

Yes, I realize I took vows that said as long as we both shall live. I know that vow was broken years ago. I am free to seek the companionship of another but my heart and soul said something different. Thomas is gone; I am living. I am supposed to resume my life. But like Thomas never existed? I can't. As I looked at Steven in the bed, I saw Thomas lying there sedated. I needed to leave as quickly as possible. I was half out the door when I heard, "Hey pretty lady, can you stay a little longer?"

"Of course," I said as I walked to the bed. My thoughts were pulled back to Steven.

"Do you remember what happened?" I said.

"Yes, I was with Tanner on his yacht. One minute we were talking and the next minute I was being pulled out of the water. How's Tanner?"

I lowered my eyes and Steven instantly reacted. "He's dead, isn't he?"

"Yes, he was pronounced at the scene," I responded.

"Dr. Taylor wants you to stay a couple of days for observation. Are you in any pain?" I asked.

"My wrist hurts like a bastard," Steven replied.

"I'll get you something for that."

"Thanks."

Steven hated IV's but he needed a line to keep him hydrated. He also needed antibiotics. He spent three days at Oahu General and a week at home before he returned to work. Of course that didn't stop him from working while recuperating. This had become personal. The person or persons who killed Tanner almost killed him.

Eventually the psycho responsible was caught by HPD. Steven was in the wrong place at the wrong time.

While Steven was off from work, he asked me to go whale watching. I said yes. I had never gone whale watching and it was exciting to see the humpback whales swim off the coast of Maui.

Peter came into my office after we returned from Maui. I thought he came to apologize. That couldn't have been further from the truth. As soon as he opened his mouth about Steven, I told him to get out. When he wouldn't, I walked out of my office toward the PT room all the while Peter was gibber jabbering about how I needed to move on with my life. I didn't say a word. Just before I got to the PT room, I made a sharp left into the ladies room, slamming the door in Peter's face. He shouted through the door until one of the ladies yelled at him to leave as she walked out of the bathroom. He knew I could out-wait him so he left. This reminded me of a soldier who said to me many years ago during a therapy session that I must have the patience of Job because I never yelled or lost my temper while teaching. Chaplain Cook told me that was a compliment. Unfortunately I have found that the older I become, my tolerance for ignorance has shortened; however, if I have to, I found I can still out-wait a nemesis.

I decided to see Chaplain Cook for some advice. I was angry at Peter for telling me to move on with my life, telling me I loved Steven. What did he want me to do? Forget Thomas like he never existed? I'm fighting a war with the

Government over Thomas' death. I'm trying to give this investigation 100% of my time and energy and yet my job is taking 200%. I was unhappy about the budget cuts in my program. Do more with less is what kept coming back. How?

The pressure was too much. As I walked into the base chapel, Chaplain Cook was standing at the altar preparing the Bible for Sunday's Scripture Reading. Chaplain Cook looked up and for a moment he thought maybe this would be the right time to bring up the letter and the cross but first he needed to hear what I wanted to talk about.

"Hello Marla, what do I owe the pleasure of this visit?"

"Chaplain Cook, I'm not one to pull any punches. I'm angry at Peter. I hate my job. I am frustrated by the continued Government stonewalling of my case. I feel like I am being pushed into a relationship I can't handle with a man I care for but don't love," I said feeling like the weight of the world was on my shoulders.

Thinking to himself, today was definitely not the day to bring up the letter, Chaplain Cook softly responded, "Well, that's a lot to deal with at one time. How about we take each issue one by one?"

"You're angry at Peter, why?"

"He says I should be with Steven. I'm too young to spend the rest of my life alone."

"Forget what he says. How do you feel about living alone?"

"I'm fine with it."

"Then why do you feel like you are being pushed into a relationship you can't handle with a man you don't love?"

"Steven and I have gone out a few times."

"Ok, so what's wrong with that?"

"He loves me."

"I see and you are unsure of your feelings for him?

"No, I care about Steven but I don't love him."

"Then what is the problem. Don't get angry Marla but it is possible you have feeling for Steven you don't want to admit to, maybe feelings of love. It is perfectly human to have feelings of love for him but you know it isn't the same thing you felt for Thomas. The love for a parent is different than the love for a spouse or a sibling or a child. God gave us the capacity to love more than one person and there are many kinds of love."

Chaplain Cook continued, "I know you are frustrated with the Government's foot-dragging but see how far you have come since Thomas died. You have made great strides. There is more work to do but you will achieve your goal. Just keep focused.

Finally, you said you hate your job. I know you don't really mean you hate working with veterans. You hate the bureaucracy. We all do. Even chaplains have it. You can only do your best. Some things are out of your control and for those problems, you have to say to yourself, these things are not in my power to solve but I give them to God.

I have never preached to you, Marla. You either believe or you don't. If you believe in God, then trust Him. He will not fail you."

"Thank you Chaplain Cook."

"You're very welcome."

I hugged him and left.

I thought and thought about what Chaplain Cook said. I needed to believe. Thomas believed. He never once said anything about how strong his faith had become but he found God. This was a good first step. I will do what is in my power and trust Him with what I cannot do.

Chaplain Cook hoped he planted the seed of faith but only time would tell and until the right moment, the letter and cross would stay in his possession.

My attitude had changed. My will to press on became

stronger. I felt that since I had handed what I couldn't do to God, I could concentrate on what needed to be done to bring the newly promoted Lt. Colonel Lambello to justice.

I pressed forward with finding the men from that last mission. I tape recorded interviews with them. I compiled hours of recordings and hundreds of pages of facts from others who sent me signed sworn depositions of what happened on that final mission. I had at least enough evidence to charge Lt. Colonel Lambello on Article 107 – Filing False Reports but that was nothing but a slap on the wrist. I wanted the big ones – Article 99 – Misbehavior before the enemy and Article 134 – Negligence Homicide – for the deaths of my husband and the other men.

No one I talked to had any evidence to corroborate that Lt. Colonel Lambello was the mole but I had the evidence to show he caused the mission to go bust.

I handled my work pressures better. I knew the military would close the rehab department with or without my protests. It was up to me to prolong its' demise and then accept the end of the program with dignity. It was out of my hands and now in God's.

Chapter 50

Steven completely recovered in six weeks. He returned to work but he insisted that we continue to see each other. I had my concerns where this relationship would go and reluctantly agreed to see him all the while reminding him of my commitment to Thomas.

We went to the Big Island to visit the Lilluokalani Gardens. The centerpiece of the park is the Japanese gardens laid out around a series of lava flows and small lagoons with beautiful bridges. There were dwarf palms and stone pagodas that dotted the shore. Bamboo and mango trees were everywhere. There were places on the bridges to have picnic lunches. It was on one of the bridges that Steven asked me to marry him.

I told him no.

Two weeks later, Steven asked me to accompany him to Hilo – back to Lilluokalani gardens – this time to visit the volcano winery. The exotic wines flavored with tropical fruit were heavenly. There was guava, passion fruit, and honey. The winery produces about 1500 cases per month with most of it sold on the islands. Steven purchased a bottle of the passion fruit wine. After walking around for an hour, we left for the airport. When we got back to Oahu, he drove me to my house and asked to come in.

"Are you hungry?" I asked trying to figure out if I should throw a couple of steaks on the barbeque.

"A little but don't go to any bother. I'd rather talk," he replied.

"Uh-oh" I said under my breath as we sat down on the sofa.

"Would you like some wine?" he asked as he went for the corkscrew.

"No thank you," I replied.

Steven stopped, put the wine and corkscrew back in the bag.

"Marla, I know a couple of weeks ago you turned me down when I asked you to marry me? I wanted to know if you gave it any more thought. I mean, we have so much fun together. Why can't it be permanent?"

"You know why, Steven. Maybe down the road when the man who killed my husband is brought to justice, I might be able to think about a life with someone but I told you up front and have never lied to you, I love Thomas. He was my heart, my soul, the air that goes in and out of me. I know he isn't here any more but I loved him more than life itself. I can't think about being with another man. Please don't take offense. If we had met another time, another place, perhaps things would be different but all I can give you is what we have been doing. If it isn't enough, I understand if you have to say good-bye."

"Marla, I want to be with you. If it means continuing our friendship as it is to have your company, then I will have to be content with that."

Steven got up from the sofa. We walked to the door.

"Good night," he said as he opened the door and left.

I stood there for a minute thinking Steven isn't a man to give up so easily. This wouldn't be the last conversation we had about marriage.

Chapter 51

About three months later, Steven was involved in a revenge shooting by a man he put in prison 12 years before. The former prisoner wasn't supposed to be out for another five years but received time off for good behavior. He swore in court if he ever was released he would kill Steven Roberts but the Parole Board didn't take the threat seriously since he had been a model inmate from the first day and no threats were ever made since the trial. The first day out of prison this guy found out where Steven lived and watched his habits for two weeks.

Early every morning Steven jogged down the beach and back home. On that fateful day, the former inmate came out of the shadows and shot Steven three times. He would have died on the beach if it hadn't been for a woman in the area who heard the shots. She ran out, saw him on the ground and called the police. She returned and held pressure on his chest to slow the bleeding. The first two shots were superficial but the third bullet entered the chest cavity and lodged in his lung.

It was Saturday morning. I was running late to work when my pager went off and wouldn't stop. I thought ok, come on, give me a break, I'm not that late but the damn thing became a pain in the ass so I called the main switchboard.

"This is Captain Bristol. I have been paged several times. I know I am running a few minutes late but this is ridiculous."

"I'm sorry Captain but my orders were to page you until you called in or arrived. I'm connecting you to Dr. Fong."

Peter, what are you doing? Trying to give me a hard time? I said smugly.

"Marla, get to the hospital now," Peter replied in urgently.

"Why?"

"Just do it. I'll explain when you get here. Park in ER."

I finished dressing and arrived 11 minutes later all the while pondering what was so urgent. I entered the ER. Peter met me.

"Marla, Steven was shot this morning while jogging."

"What? Can't be. I spoke to him first thing this morning."

"It happened about 45 minutes ago. He's in surgery. It doesn't look good." Peter's head was down. He shook it back and forth.

"How bad is it?" I pressed Peter for information.

"He has a collapsed lung and internal injuries."

"I don't understand how this could happen," I said in disbelief.

"HPD is combing the area for clues and witnesses. Steven will get through this. He's strong," Peter replied trying to put a positive spin on the circumstances.

I said nothing. I couldn't if I wanted to. I wanted to be angry but all I felt was numb. I walked away from Peter, went to my office and closed the door. I felt like crying but I couldn't even muster that. I called upstairs to surgery. The nurse said to expect at least five hours.

At the five hour mark, I called again. I was told he was still in surgery but the word was they were nearly finished.

I went up to the surgical floor. Dr. Muller appeared.

"Captain Bristol?"

"Yes."

"I don't believe in sugar coating things. Detective Roberts was shot three times: once in the upper arm, once in the side and once in the chest. The first two were in and out. No serious damage. However the third bullet punctured his lung. He had severe internal bleeding. I was able to stop the bleeding and re-inflate the lung. We transfused four pints. He's in recovery and will be sent to pulmonary ICU. Overall his health is good which is a plus but his injuries were quite severe."

"Is he going to live?" I asked hoping for the best but preparing for the worst.

"Given his current condition, he has a 50/50 chance."

Steven was in a coma for four days. I stopped by every two hours checking on him when I was on shift and calling four times off shift.

At the end of the fourth day, I stopped by as usual. I walked by the nurse's station into his room. I liked to review his chart and check vitals. While I was listening to his heart and lungs, Steven made a moaning sound. I ran to the desk and had Dr. Muller paged. Dr. Muller responded immediately and checked Steven's vitals. He made it through the worst and was on his way to making a complete recovery. He left the hospital 10 days later to recuperate at home. He was still weak and needed help with his basic needs.

I called the Governor to ask him to cover the cost of Steven's recovery as private care was needed. The Governor assured the costs would be taken out of a special budget number. I hated to do this but I had to because my PT program was cut and money was an issue with the military. I started my lobbying efforts in Washington to save my program but I knew that within 3-5 years it would be dead.

I was no psychic but I saw the budget figures year after year. Since the Vietnam War had ended, the Government felt there wasn't a need for any rehab services. President Jimmy Carter wasn't only cutting my budget but was cutting the entire military budget. I thought, how did the President expect the country to survive without the military? You can't keep taking money away and not have problems. I got used to budget reconstructing. It became part of my job. Unless I found money in the private sector, layoffs would be in the immediate future.

George was assigned to help Steven during the day while I worked at the hospital. When I got off shift, George would leave and I would take over. Steven healed quickly. He was anxious to return to work. I had to remind him that due to his severe injuries, he couldn't go back too soon or he would relapse. I slept on the sofa bed so I could be closer to him in case he needed me in the middle of the night.

When Steven was better, he took me to Kona. I always wanted to see the coffee plantations.

Kona – The King of Coffee with an altitude of 800-2000' above sea level has rich volcanic soil, wind shelter rainfall and cloud shade from the hot afternoon sun. All this combined has given Kona the right conditions for producing coffee beans. Coffee was introduced to the island in 1928. Hawaii is the only place in the United States where coffee is grown commercially. The Big Island is by far the most famous producer.

We stopped at the Royal Kona Coffee Mill on Mamalahoa Highway. The shop was crammed full of tasty products. I had to try the chocolate dipped coffee beans and the Macadamia nut brittle. We were sitting on a rock overlooking the mills when Steven proposed again. This time he got down on one knee. For a moment, I thought back to that night with Thomas when he asked me to marry him. It was one of the happiest moments in my life. I looked down and realized that I was with Steven now. People were coming and going around us and a few stopped to look. One woman waited for my answer. I was extremely embarrassed.

In my mind, I needed another reason to refuse. It wasn't that Steven was unattractive. Quite the opposite! Those green eyes could melt butter. He was the epitome of tall, dark and handsome. He was sexy, attractive and had a hairy chest. I'm still a woman; I have eyes – I can see. I have feelings but my inner self said no. I knew my time with the Navy was short. If I married Steven and left the Navy, what would I do? Become a housewife? At 40? All I've known my entire working life is 12 hours a day, 6 days a week. I wouldn't know what to do if that suddenly stopped. Would I be in the house all day cooking, cleaning and washing? I would die in no time if that was my fate. If I retired in 5 years with 25 years of service at the age of 45, where would I work? With no PT programs on the island, I would have to go back to school for another specialty or go into floor nursing. None of these options appealed to me. My only choice was to leave the Navy and enter civilian life as a PT nurse or a Director of Nursing. I didn't have to make a decision on my future career now. What I had to do was convince Steven I couldn't marry him.

Chapter 52

The final incident came a few months after the shooting when Steven told me about the Governor's Ball. He was in charge of security. This year, there was a direct threat of assassination against the Governor. Lunatics are always threatening to kill high ranking officials. However, the Governor would be out of his security element. He would be in the open at a party. This party was the who's who of the state. State Senators, State Assembly people and their spouses, aides, distinguished guests from the military, and some big wigs from Washington would be there to represent the President of the United States. Canceling was not an option.

This was the perfect opportunity for me to lobby for funds for my PT program and talk about the evidence I had against Lt. Colonel Lambello. I needed help from the Governor, Senators and Congressman from Hawaii.

After a little coaxing, Steven asked me to attend as his date. Then he asked me to do the one thing I hated most – wear my dress uniform.

"Well Steven, that's going to cost you," I said.

"What's the penalty?" he replied.

"A BBQ steak dinner at your place with potato, corn, and rocky road ice cream for dessert."

Steven laughed. "You're on."

Steven needed to be at the hotel several hours before the event started to direct security procedures. All vacations were suspended. Additional officers were flown in from the other islands. There were officers in full riot gear guarding each entrance and exit. Every spare officer was assigned to protect the governor and guests. Invitations were checked off against a master list but before allowing any person to enter the ballroom, he or she had to go through a metal detector. When I showed up and saw all the security measures, my first thought was no one would be able to sneak through and injure the governor.

I went to the bar. I felt like imbibing a little before the grand evening started, so I ordered something different: a vodka martini with three olives. Not bad, I thought but I better eat to counter act some of the alcohol's effects. Hors d'oeuvres were being passed. I motioned for a waiter to come over. The choice of hors d'oervres varied: deviled eggs, shrimp cocktail, crab-stuffed mushrooms and egg rolls. As I sat there enjoying my food, I was fascinated to see who was there. David was in plain clothes. He saw me at the bar and waived as he made his way to the back of the ballroom.

An announcement was made that salad would be served in five minutes. Everyone was to proceed to their tables. Steven came over to escort me to the head table. I made a remark to the effect that I didn't think a spider could get through all the security.

"I am never that confident," Steven replied.

The salads were served with a creamy house Italian dressing.

Steven hardly touched his meal keeping in constant radio contact with his undercover men.

The main course arrived. Chicken in a brown mushroom

sauce, rice pilaf and asparagus with a touch of hollandaise sauce.

Dessert was a delicacy flown in from the mainland: New York Cheesecake. The only word to describe it was "heavenly."

After dessert, the Governor spoke for a few moments. Steven brought two men from the entrance to stand behind him with every exit covered on the main level. We were on the Mezzanine, one flight up from the ground level. This posed its own security risks by someone coming in from the dock area and making their way up to this level. Above us were conference rooms and additional ballrooms. The hotel staff was escorted to the kitchen until the speech was over.

The speech concluded. Short for a politician – only four minutes long. The Governor was ushered to the reception line guarded by Steven's men. He greeted guests and members of state government. Steven's men formed a semi-circle covering the back of the Governor. If the gravity of the situation wasn't so serious, the evening looked like a circus. The who's who of Hawaii was present. Each needed to be protected from a potential killer because no one could be sure if the threat was credible or a crank.

The night's entertainment was a variety of hula dancers and fire eaters.

Once the entertainment ended, it was customary for the Governor to lead the first dance. The Governor's date seemed uncomfortable and did not want to dance with him so I offered to fill in for her. He accepted.

As the Governor escorted me to the dance floor, he whispered, "Why do I get the feeling this dance will be more business than pleasure?"

"I like a man who gets right to the point," I whispered back.

"Governor," I began, "My budget has been severely cut

by the Navy. I have done everything including a personal appearance before Congress to lobby for needed funds. I am not blind to the fact that since the end of the Vietnam War, the need for rehab services has decreased but I believe the military wants to eliminate the program altogether which would be a disservice to every veteran living in Hawaii that needs physical therapy.

We have to ensure these men and women receive the care that they need," I said wearily, "I am about to celebrate my 20th year in the Navy. I can retire, go into civilian life and not deal with this crap anymore but I care about my veterans. I believe in this program. You saw what it did for Steven. Can't the State make up the short fall in the budget?"

"It would depend how much we're talking about. Come to my office Monday morning. We'll go over the numbers together."

"Governor, one more thing, I need help in pursuing my case with the military against Lt. Colonel Anthony Lambello. I've been stonewalled at every turn. Perhaps you could open a few doors with our esteemed Senators and Congressman."

"I would be delighted," he replied.

I was so happy I hugged him. The Governor was over six feet tall but bent down to return my hug. I looked up and saw a rifle aimed at his back. I pushed him backward as hard as I could. He fell to the floor. I heard the shot and thought I better get the hell out of the way but it was too late. I felt a burning sensation in my upper left chest. I fell backwards and hit the floor with the force of being hit by a car. People were screaming all around me. They were running for cover wherever they could find it: under tables, behind the bar. Everything was surreal. I couldn't move or catch my breath. I knew the bullet had done some serious damage. The Governor was closest to me. He crawled over, took off his jacket and laid it over me.

"Governor," I gasped, "Get some napkins and/or table-cloths and hold pressure against my chest. As the Governor was searching around for napkins, with my right hand I opened my dress uniform jacket. I was oozing blood from the wound. The Governor found napkins plus a tablecloth. I guided his hand where to hold pressure.

"Press hard. Don't take your hand off this area," I said breathing heavily.

Someone from Steven's team had made it to where we were.

"Governor, are you ok?"

"Yes, but Marla's been hit. Call an ambulance," the Governor shouted.

I grabbed his arm. In a whispered tone I said, "I'll bleed to death before it arrives."

"Forget the ambulance. Get my limo here immediately with police escort," the Governor shouted.

Steven's man radioed a person was down on the dance floor. Steven heard the message but didn't know it was me.

This is where I started to go in and out of consciousness.

Steven arrived. He said, "I'll pick up her up. Governor, continue to hold pressure on the wound."

The limo arrived. Steven carried me up the stairs and out-side to the waiting limo. The Governor got in first. Steven transferred me temporarily to the Governor until he got into the car with the Governor giving me back to Steven after he sat down. I was stretched out on Steven's and the Governor's laps with the Governor still holding pressure on my chest. There were two police motorcycle units in front and two behind us with lights and sirens blaring as we sped to Oahu General. My situation had already been phoned in. ER was standing by.

As the limo pulled up, two techs pulled me out, laid me on the gurney and rushed me through the double doors. I could vaguely see Steven and the Governor trying to keep up. Dr. Fong met them. There was a moment of silence while they watched the curtain close. I could hear Peter yelling outside the curtain.

"What the hell happened?" asked Dr. Fong. I heard his voice crack. Peter must be getting old. He actually showed some emotion.

"I was dancing with Marla," the Governor began. "She saw the shooter aiming at my back and pushed me out of the way. The bastard shot her instead. Is that as plain as I can make it? You think I'm happy about this? Damn it."

"I'm going in to get a status report," said Dr. Fong.

Peter entered the room. I was heavily sedated but I saw him come in. "Peter, is that you?"

"Yes Marla. Dr. Collier, How is she?"

"Not good. We're taking her up to surgery shortly. I'm waiting for the x-ray to confirm where the bullet is but from the loss of blood, it definitely nicked an artery. We need to stabilize her before we operate."

"Peter," I said softly.

"Yes, Marla." Peter came closer to the bed.

"Peter, you are my Medical Power of Attorney. If anything happens, I want you to carry out my wishes. Promise me you will do this."

"Yes, Marla. Not to worry. You need to concentrate on getting better."

Dr. Collier pulled Dr. Fong off to the side.

"Dr. Fong?" asked Dr. Collier.

"Yes, Dr. Collier," replied Dr. Fong.

"What are her wishes?"

"No heroic measures are to be used to keep her alive."

"Got it," said Dr. Collier.

Peter grabbed Dr. Collier's arm as he left the room. "Dr. Collier, I need to see you for a moment…."

Chapter 53

The x-ray showed the exact location of the bullet. As I was being prepped for surgery, Dr. Collier said I had a visitor waiting to see me. I told him there wasn't anyone I wanted to see. He replied it was Chaplain Cook. I agreed to have him come in for a minute.

"Hello Marla," said Chaplain Cook.

"Hi," I said weakly. "I guess my condition must be really bad if they got you out of bed at this hour. Are you going to give me last rites?"

"No, but I will pray for you while you are in surgery," replied Chaplain Cook in a calm voice.

"I appreciate you doing that but to be honest Chaplain, if it's God's will that I am to be with Thomas now, nothing would make me happier, so I'll give you something to think about – praying for my recovery which would make me miserable or praying for me to die on the table so I can be with Thomas which would make me very happy. That's your choice," I said sincerely.

Chaplain Cook wanted to respond; he wanted to tell me about the letter and the cross right now because he might not get another chance. He wanted to tell me that Thomas believed and I was so close in my journey in believing too, but he didn't respond. He left the room.

Dr. Collier came into the room and said it was time to go upstairs.

That was the last voice I remembered hearing until I woke up in Pulmonary ICU, 12 hours later with a tube down my throat, a Foley catheter and two IV bags in my right arm."

I couldn't speak because of the breathing tube. Dr. Collier was paged to remove it. He cautioned me that it would be difficult to talk for a day or two; I should use notes to communicate."

My first note to him was: "What happened when I went to surgery? I remember you saying things didn't look good."

"They weren't," he replied.

"Did I flat line on the table?" I wrote.

"Yes."

"Where was Dr. Fong?" My handwriting was getting worse with each pen stroke.

"He was there," replied Dr. Collier calmly.

"Why did you bring me back when my medical directive said no heroic measures were to be instituted especially on a code blue?" I was shaking.

"Because he overrode your directive."

"What? How was he able to do that?" I said in a high pitched whisper.

"He's the Chief of Medicine in this hospital. He took it upon himself to override your wishes. He said he would take full responsibility. You have two choices, Marla. You can pursue legal action against him or you can forget it, find another Power of Attorney and move on. I realize you are in quite a bit of pain both physically and mentally. You need rest. I don't want you to have visitors today and I definitely don't want you getting aggravated."

"That bastard," I squealed. My blood pressure jumped 20 points.

"Marla, if your blood pressure goes any higher, I'm going to have to give you a sedative.

"Just thinking of that son of a bitch makes my blood boil," I shouted in the loudest voice possible. The blood pressure machine beeped as my pressure went into the caution zone.

"Nurse, administer 1 milligram of Ativan with 1 milligram repeated as necessary up to three times per day."

"I am already on 2 milligrams of Valium. If you want to increase it to 5 milligrams that would be better," I wrote as I tried to calm myself down.

Dr. Collier changed the order.

Dr. Fong was standing in the hallway when Dr. Collier walked out of ICU. Dr. Fong started to go in when Dr. Collier grabbed his arm and said,

"I wouldn't go in there if I were you. I've seen hornets friendlier than she is right now. I've known you a long time, Peter. I find it hard to believe that you actually went against her written directive knowing how deeply she felt about this. Had I known how strongly she felt, I would have let her die on the table with or without your approval."

Dr. Fong attempted to go into the room when Dr. Collier pulled a note out of his pocket and handed it to Dr. Fong. It read, "Don't bother coming to see me now or in the near future."

The only people I wanted to see were George, Maria, Ben, Chaplain Cook and the Governor. In my mind, the Governor owed me and I planned to collect, big time. One of the nurses at the desk called the Governor's office and asked him to come over at his convenience. I needed to see Chaplain Cook. I had some raw feelings to deal with and all the Valium in the world wouldn't help me deal with them. I had to come to grips with my life and take back control.

Chapter 54

My day nurse, Hilda, was efficient and indispensable in my recovery. A rotund woman who stood 5'7" and weighed 190 pounds, she grew up in post war Germany and escaped when the Berlin Wall was erected. After spending a few years in Texas, she settled in Hawaii in 1970. She worked at a couple of other hospitals before coming to Oahu General.

It took three days before I was able to get out of bed. I was forced to use the dreaded bedpan. I thought back to what Thomas went through. Not the humiliation of using a bedpan but the reliance on another person for even the slightest personal function.

Late on the third day, Hilda helped me to the bathroom, IVs and all. My upper chest was bandaged heavily which affected movement of my left arm. Dr. Collier put my arm in a sling to relieve the pressure on my chest. I need help using the toilet, walking and bathing. I had no problem eating or holding anything on the right side because that was my dominant side. Breathing regularly was not a problem but God help me if I coughed. The pain cut through me like a knife. Hilda held a pillow against my chest so when I coughed, I wouldn't open my incision. Since this kind of injury was prone to infection, Dr. Collier had me on a high dose of antibiotics to try and guard against contracting pneumonia.

By the fourth day, Hilda helped me take short walks up and down the hall. I had to walk very slowly due to severe shortness of breath. There I was pushing my IV with my right hand, Hilda supporting me with her right hand and rolling the O$_2$ tank in her left. I kept a note pad and pen in the pocket of my robe because I still found it difficult to speak. We walked to the elevators and back to the room at least three times a day. On the final trip of today, we had just turned around to return to my room when I saw Peter approaching. He stopped. We stopped. When he got a couple of feet away, he started to mumble about being sorry. I took out my pad and pen and wrote, "Good-bye, Peter."

Peter said nothing more and walked away.

By the time I got back to my room, I was gasping for breath. Hilda called Dr. Collier. Call it bad timing but Steven showed up with flowers.

I heard Hilda yell, "This isn't a good time and no flowers in ICU. Leave them at the nurse's station."

Steven sat outside ICU for a minute. Just as he was about to leave, he saw Dr. Collier run in. There was fluid building up in my left lung. The only thing Dr. Collier could do was relieve it with a needle.

It was one of the most painful procedures I ever endured even with an anesthetic.

On the fifth day in ICU, I received a note from Ben. He mailed me the paper from the day following the shooting. He said he missed our picnic lunches and visits. Maria had come up to see me late in the day. I asked her to send Ben some money for flowers to put on Thomas' grave along with a thank you note. I also asked Maria to bring my paycheck to ICU so she could deposit it and take the money I owed her. Ben said he would take care of Thomas' grave with six carnations and would clean the stone every Sunday until I returned. Ben wrote, "Things are not the same without you, Marla. Get well soon." That really made my day.

I spent 10 days in the hospital, 7 in ICU. I recuperated at home for 2 additional weeks. It turned out 2 weeks wasn't long enough because I relapsed and had to be re-admitted for walking pneumonia. This time I stayed 6 days. During that time I received a call from Admiral Hargrove congratulating me for saving the Governor's life. He also called to tell me that I would be receiving the Purple Heart and the Bronze Star for bravery.

"Thank you Admiral Hargrove but the attention is hardly necessary," I replied.

Admiral Hargrove said, "Nonsense, no one is more deserving of this honor than you, Marla."

The following month I was awarded my medals. My mind drifted by to what Thomas would have said: "Whoopee, more medals for the collection."

My feelings of betrayal deepened against Peter. I needed to talk to Chaplain Cook about these feelings. Chaplain Cook came to visit me several times during my first hospitalization but I wasn't up to speaking to him. When I was admitted the second time, he came by to see how I was. This time I wanted to talk. I needed to heal my mind and soul in addition to my body.

"Chaplain Cook, do you know that Peter overrode my medical directive? Because of him I have been suffering since the operation. You know I should have died on that table," I said looking for a reaction.

"Marla, have you thought there are too many people who love you and want you to live? Besides, you haven't fulfilled Thomas' last wish."

"Maybe I never will be able to," I retorted.

"I wouldn't have expected so much pessimism from you.

Marla, God works in mysterious ways. I know you have heard that before but it's true."

"Tell me Chaplain Cook, how can I get past the feelings of betrayal? Will I be able to forgive Peter Fong?"

"Marla, I know you don't want a sermon but the best story of betrayal comes from the Bible. Jesus was betrayed by Judas for 30 pieces of silver and denied by Peter before the cock crowed 3 times. Jesus foretold these events.

You asked how you can forgive Dr. Fong for what he did to you. Jesus was crucified on the cross and yet, while he was dying, Jesus asked forgiveness for the men casting lots for his garments beneath the cross. 'Jesus said, Forgive them Father! They don't know what they are doing. They divided his clothes among themselves by throwing dice.' Luke 23:24 (GNT)

I guess what I am getting at is that your feelings of betrayal are not much different than what Jesus felt when he was betrayed by Judas for money and Peter when he denied Jesus to save his own life because the Romans were after anyone that were disciples of Christ. You want to forgive Dr. Fong but you feel you can't; however, if Jesus could ask for forgiveness on behalf of the soldiers who were casting lots for his garments at his crucifixion, then maybe you can find it in your heart to forgive Dr. Fong for not carrying out your instructions as Power of Attorney. Forgetting is not the same as forgiving. You may not be able to forget but let the anger go so you can move on with more important things in your life. Don't waste your time or life on being angry with Dr. Fong."

"Thank you Chaplain Cook. You have given me something to think about."

I watched Chaplain Cook leave. As Chaplain Cook walked down the hall, he knew the next conversation would be the right time to show me the letter and the cross.

After I got out of the hospital, I stopped by Peter's office. I told him that all was well. We should let bygones be bygones. I knew in my heart that I would never forget but I forgave him and that was the most important thing I could do.

I appointed Admiral Hargrove as my new Power of Attorney. Under Navy rules and regulations, I knew that Admiral Hargrove would carry out my wishes if the need arose.

My relationship with Steven needed to end. He proposed to me again in the hospital and again I said no. I told him he needed to find a woman that could give herself completely to him and I wasn't that woman.

Over the next five years, the Governor did what he could for my PT program and as promised, he assisted me in my case against Colonel Anthony Lambello who recently was promoted from Lt. Colonel to Colonel.

He earmarked funds from the state budget money to fund my program. For three years following the shooting he made up the military shortfall. Maybe he felt he owed me. I thanked him for all he did. Two years ago, the state money ran out. I was forced to close all the PT programs except Oahu General. Only the day program was left. Any person that required long term physical therapy had to be flown to the mainland. After 25 years, my program was dead. It was time to retire.

The Governor and Hawaiian Senators and Congressman signed a formal letter asking for an official investigation into Thomas' final mission. A joint Senate and House Committee met and asked me to fly to Washington to present my case. Armed with over 10 hours of recorded phone conversations and written declarations of the mission plus Thomas' diary which contain pertinent facts of events leading up to the mission, I faced the committee. Over the course of two days,

I presented the evidence. I showed that General Lambello and his son deliberately covered up the truth.

The committee took 40 minutes to recommend a military court-martial for Colonel Lambello. General Lambello was dead but pending the outcome of his son's trial, there would be some notations made in the General's military record.

My heart leaped for joy. Fifteen years of hard work had finally come to fruition.

I returned to Hawaii. I had just arrived at my condo when I received a call from Washington. Charges were being drawn up. Colonel Lambello would be notified along with the witnesses against him. I would be notified of a time, date and place of the court- martial. Colonel Lambello was about to receive the shock of his life.

Chapter 55

Colonel Lambello had been stationed in Kentucky for the past seven years. His Commanding Officer (CO) had reluctantly been involved in preparing the court-martial papers and was now ready to serve them to Colonel Lambello. Two Military Police (MP) Officers escorted the CO to Colonel Lambello's house.

The CO stood there for a moment, hesitating before ringing the bell. He shook his head not believing what he was about to do, rang the buzzer and waited for someone to answer the door. Colonel Lambello answered the door.

"May we come in, sir?" said his CO.

"Yes, come in, Colonel Becker. What is this all about?" said Colonel Lambello surprised by the intrusion.

Colonel Lambello invited everyone into the family room. His wife appeared with their three children. He asked his wife to take the kids to the bedroom and give them some privacy.

"Please be seated, sir," said Colonel Lambello to his CO. "Can I get you anything?"

Shaking his head no, his CO began, "Under Rule 101, I have a report of offenses committed by you that are considered detainable. You are to be extradited to Hawaii immediately. Upon arriving in Hawaii, you will be confined to base

"

waiving the pre-trial confinement in the brig under Rule 305. Under Rule 307, you will be advised of the charges. Under Rule 305 d1 – you are entitled to know your rights (Miranda vs. Arizona). Rule 305 g1 – sets forth three rules. First, you have the right to remain silent, if you give up the right to remain silent anything you say can and will be used against you. Second, you have the right to an attorney. Third, if you cannot afford an attorney one will be appointed by the military at no charge.

"Do you understand your rights?" said his CO.

"Yes, but I still don't understand what is going on," said Colonel Lambello completely bewildered.

"Do you want a lawyer? If so, do you want a military, civilian or both?"

"Yes, but…"

The CO cut him off. "Are you willing to make a statement?"

"No," replied Colonel Lambello in a near whisper.

"Since you want a lawyer, no questioning will take place at this time. You may have a lawyer appointed by the military and/or hire an attorney at your expense or both. What do you desire?"

"I wish to consult with outside legal counsel."

"So be it. I will allow you one phone call at this time. Colonel Lambello, these are your formal court-martial papers. Please pack a duffle bag. You are to leave for Hawaii immediately."

Colonel Lambello was stunned trying to comprehend everything he just heard but couldn't. He went into to the bedroom to pack. His actions were that of a robot shoving his clothes into a duffle bag. His wife came over and asked what was wrong but all he could say was he would call her from Hawaii.

Colonel Lambello picked up the phone and called Roger

Miller Esq. Miller was the best military defense attorney money could buy. Miller told Lambello that as soon as he arrived in Hawaii he should leave a message for him at the Windham Suites Hotel in Oahu. Miller would contact him and arrange a meeting.

He finished packing. The MPs accompanied him to the airplane and on the long flight to Hawaii where he was restricted to barracks.

According to Rule 405, Attorney Miller was given access to all the evidence against his client. During the pre-trial investigation, he sifted through everything: phone logs, tape recordings, sworn statements, and Thomas' diary. The defense had nothing – no character witnesses, no friends, and no colleagues willing to speak on Colonel Lambello's behalf.

Attorney Miller arranged a meeting with his client.

"Tony, I'll be honest. This doesn't look good."

"What the hell does that mean? You are my lawyer. I'm paying you good money. Do something," screamed Colonel Lambello.

"Do what? You got yourself in this stinking mess 15 years ago. All the survivors of the mission have given statements – both written and taped. They have agreed to fly to Hawaii to testify in person. Then there is Lt. Colonel Smith's diary, his dying declaration witnessed by his wife, statements made to his doctor and the Captain of the Ship 'Mercy.' All swore statements of what was said. Look, I'm good. I've been on both sides of the table for more years than I can count but you have to tell me something to build a defense on. The thing they can't charge you with is treason because they can't prove you were the mole but on the other counts, they have you cold," said Roger Miller with conflicted emotions.

"What can you do?" pleaded Colonel Lambello.

"I don't know. I have a meeting scheduled with the

prosecutor but don't hope for much. If this goes to trial, you could be looking at life."

"Life? Oh my God, Roger, you have to do something. I have a wife, kids, a career to think about," said Colonel Lambello shaking.

"Your father dug a nice hole for you 15 years ago and you didn't do anything to stop it. The military doesn't want old cover-ups coming back to life. It makes them look bad. They will distance themselves from you as much as they can." Attorney Miller looked at Colonel Lambello hoping he had grasped the reality of the situation.

"What do you recommend?" replied Colonel Lambello as the sweat formed on his brow and upper lip.

"Under Rule 406, my pre-trial advice is to let me work out a plea agreement."

"What kind of plea?"

"I don't know. I have to talk to the prosecutor but don't expect a slap on the wrist. I feel like this is a five-card stud poker game and the man sitting across from us has a royal flush. You can't possibly win. All we can do is minimizing the damage. I'll get back to you." Attorney Miller picked up and left the room.

Colonel Lambello was escorted back to his barracks.

Roger Miller called Trent West, the prosecutor in the case. They set up a meeting in West's office the next day.

"Roger, good to see you. Have a seat. Care for a cigar?" Trent said trying not to gloat.

"No thanks," replied Roger opening his briefcase.

"Roger, I can't believe you agreed to take this case," Trent said in a surprised voice. "I've known you for over 10 years. This case isn't something you would become involved with in unless you were the prosecutor. The evidence against your client is insurmountable." Trent paused for a moment and then rubbed it in, "You *have* seen everything, haven't you Roger?"

"I have and I want to cut a deal," Roger said matter-of-factly.

"Are you kidding?" replied Trent half-laughing. "This has to be the finest case of my military prosecutorial career and you want to cut a deal?"

"You know it would be better for everyone not to have a long trial," said Roger Miller this time his voice was half-pleading.

Captain West put down his cigar, stood up and looked Roger Miller in the eye. "Maybe for your client but what about Lt. Colonel Smith's widow who fought the system for 15 years obtaining evidence against your client? What about the survivors of the ill-fated mission who have waited 15 years to see Colonel Lambello brought to justice? What about the men who never returned?" Captain West's anger bubbled over to the point he slammed his fist on the table.

"Isn't it enough he's going to jail? Why air dirty laundry in court?"

"Maybe it's necessary to air 'dirty laundry' as you call it so it never happens again. Look, I could go after life without parole for what he did and get it in a heartbeat, maybe even the death penalty under Article 99. What do you want to offer?"

"Twenty-five with possible parole after 20 with good behavior, no benefits and bad conduct discharge."

"Have you told him this?"

"Not yet. I wanted to talk to you first."

"Let me think about it. Talk to your client. See what kind of reaction you receive on your proposal. My bet is he isn't going to like it."

"Like it or not, he has to face reality."

The two men shook hands and Miller left to see Colonel Lambello.

Attorney Miller arrived at the base. Colonel Lambello was ushered into a private room off the regular meeting area.

"Well?" said Colonel Lambello.

"He wants to go to trial. He could push for the death penalty but I doubt he could get it; however, he almost certainly could get life without parole. I told him 25, with parole in 20 with good behavior, a bad conduct discharge and no benefits."

"Shit Roger, is that the best you could do?" replied Colonel Lambello not understanding the gravity of the situation.

"You arrogant son of a bitch…you are nothing but an ingrate!" Roger shouted. "Are you listening? He could try for the DEATH PENALTY on an ARTICLE 99 OFFENSE. If he couldn't get the death penalty, you would be facing LIFE WITHOUT PAROLE. Twenty-five with five off for good behavior is better than life. At least you'll be out before you're dead. LIFE means that you will die in a military prison, get it!"

"I'm sorry," said Colonel Lambello sobbing.

It was a pathetic sight to see a grown man cry. After a minute he stopped and looked at Attorney Miller. "This just comes as such a shock. Take the deal, Roger. Take the deal."

"One more thing," said Attorney Miller. "I recommend a military court-martial by a judge only."

"Why?"

"Shorter trial, less publicity. I will try but I cannot promise to have you serve your sentence in a minimum security military prison on the mainland. I will contact the prosecutor, work out the details and advise you but don't expect 'Club Fed.' During your incarceration, you will have a job. There won't be any favors. You serve your time; you do the job your assigned and you stay out of trouble."

Chapter 56

Work continued to go downhill. I notified Admiral Hargrove I would retire before the trial. He offered me a position any place in the world we had troops but I declined. It was time to move on. I needed a new beginning. I sent resumes to five hospitals on the mainland. All five wanted me. I decided on San Francisco. It was by the ocean and I needed to be near water.

I told Admiral Hargrove I wanted to retire on July 14th, 1984, five days before the trial. He told me that he wanted to have a small ceremony for me. No wasn't an option.

The day of my retirement had arrived.

Admiral Hargrove rose from his chair to speak. I thought to myself I hope this is brief.

"It is my honor to introduce Captain Marla Sydney Bristol. Captain Bristol has spent the last 25 years of dedicated service to the Navy. Today we are bidding her farewell and good luck as she moves on to a career in civilian life. The Navy has lost a fine officer but San Francisco Memorial Hospital has gained a knowledgeable and committed professional. Captain Bristol, would you please say a few words to our invited guests?"

I rose to the podium. I kept thinking I'm a nurse not a public speaker. I'll keep it short.

"Thank you Admiral Hargrove and everyone else for attending today's ceremonies. It has been a privilege to serve my country. I have trouble believing 25 years have passed. It feels like yesterday I graduated nursing school and joined the Navy. It has been an honor to work closely with many of you during my tenure. It wasn't that long ago I was involved in rehabilitating soldiers coming back from Vietnam. I've had a good career with the Navy. I wouldn't have traded it for anything else in the world but time moves on. After 25 years, I must move on too. I appreciate this send off to civilian life."

The audience stood up and gave me a standing ovation.

Admiral Hargrove stood up and stated, "This concludes our ceremony. The receiving line will be to your left. From there, you may proceed to the buffet. Two full bars are located on each side of the picnic tables."

I left the stage. I always felt uncomfortable in my dress uniform. I didn't wear it much, thank God. Because of my height and weight, 5'3" 115 pounds, I didn't feel I looked good in it. My two bronze stars and two purple hearts were properly hung from my jacket. Around my neck, I wore the wedding band of my beloved husband, Lt. Colonel Thomas Smith.

Admiral Hargrove escorted me to the receiving line. All the people I worked with at Oahu General over the years were there. Some who had been laid off years before and had taken jobs on other islands or the mainland made sacrifices to be here. I was touched by their presence. Former nurses told me I was special. They wouldn't have missed this for the world. There were a few Admirals and Generals in attendance, one was Admiral Lewis (retired); the other was General Butterfield (retired).

Admiral Hargrove was the first to congratulate me. "Nice short speech," he said.

"Thanks."

I excused myself and went over to get a drink at the bar. Steven came over.

"Thanks for coming," I said.

"I wouldn't have missed it for the world," Steven replied.

"Will you be at the trial Wednesday?"

"Now that is one place you couldn't keep me from even if I had to swim from Maui to get there." he said seriously. "Changing the subject, when do you leave for the mainland?"

"Next Friday, after the trial."

"How do you know the trial will be over that quickly?"

"I know. I have this guy so far in the hole he can't see daylight."

"Are you selling the condo?"

"No, George and Maria are moving in. It's almost paid off. It didn't make sense to sell it. I think it's time for me to make a quiet exit."

"Can I take you anywhere?" asked Steven.

"No thanks. I'm going home to rest. It's been an exhausting few weeks. I still have a few boxes left to pack."

I left and went to the cemetery to see Thomas. It wasn't Sunday but I just felt I needed to see him today. After an hour, I grabbed some take-out Chinese and went home. Time was growing short.

The next day, I received a call from Trent West. "Marla, I shouldn't be informing you of this but I felt you should know that an agreement was reached. This will be brought up at the trial."

"You bastard. You're nothing but a sellout out. Didn't you think you could win with the evidence I provided?" I screamed.

"Marla, that's not it at all."

"You would deny the survivors their say in court."

"No, you don't understand. It just saves us from dealing with a long drawn out trial."

"If you do a plea, the story of what happened won't be told. These men will never get to tell their side of the story of what the 'green' Lt. Lambello did to them all those years ago. You can't cop a plea."

"Marla, what if I write into the agreement that just prior to sentencing anyone who wishes to speak, can. Ok?"

"If you can get Colonel Lambello to agree to that, then ok but I hope he pays dearly for what he did to the men on the mission and you didn't sell us out."

"I don't think you will be disappointed, Marla."

Chapter 57

I went to the cemetery at my normal time on Sunday. Since my VW had already been shipped to San Francisco, Ben didn't recognize me when I showed up in a rental car. I had conflicting emotions because I was visiting Thomas' grave for the last time. In 15 years, I only missed coming here when I was in the hospital recuperating from the shooting. Now I was leaving the island not knowing when I would visit Thomas again.

I gave Ben a check for $500 and requested he keep half for himself and spend the other half on flowers for Thomas' grave. I handed him my new address in San Francisco and told him that when the flower money ran out he should write and I would send another check. He balked at my persistence about taking the money for doing a job he loved but finally agreed. He said he would keep the stone polished and fresh flowers would be placed in the pot every Sunday. I hugged him and told him that I would miss him dearly.

When I left the cemetery, I drove to Diamond Head. What a spectacular view! It was as gorgeous as the day Thomas and I went there on our honeymoon. After I left Diamond Head, I drove around for about an hour ending up again in Chinatown. I walked around Chinatown for a while, had a bowl of soup and drove home. The air cargo company was coming Thursday afternoon to pick up my belongings for delivery to San Francisco. As soon as the trial ended, my life in Hawaii was over. I would begin a new life in a new city. After all these years, everything was happening at once. The trial, my retirement, a new job: I felt scared and excited at the same time.

Chapter 58

"Colonel Lambello, how do you plead?" said Judge Beecham.

"Guilty, your honor," said Attorney Miller.

"Colonel Lambello, your plea of guilty will not be accepted unless you understand its meaning and effect. I am going to discuss your plea of guilty with you now. If you have any questions, please say so. Do you understand?"

"Yes sir," replied Colonel Lambello.

"A plea of guilty is the strongest form of proof known to the law. On your plea alone, without receiving any evidence, this court-martial could find you guilty of the offenses to which you are pleading guilty. Your plea will not be accepted unless you understand that by pleading guilty you admit every element of each offense and you are pleading guilty because you are guilty. If you do not believe that you are guilty, you should not plead guilty for any reason. You have the right to plead not guilty and place the burden upon the prosecution to prove your guilt. Do you understand that?"

"Yes sir."

"By your plea of guilty you waive, or in other words, you give up certain important rights. These rights that you give up are: the right against self-incrimination, that is the right to say nothing at all about these offenses; the right to a trial of the facts by the court-martial, that is, the right to have this court-martial decide whether or not you are guilty based on evidence presented by the prosecution and if you chose to do so, by the defense and the right to be confronted by the witnesses against you, that is to see and hear the witnesses against you here in the court-martial and to have them cross-examined, and to call witnesses in your behalf. Do you understand these rights?"

"Yes sir."

"If you plead guilty, there will not be a trial of any kind as to the offenses to which you are pleading guilty so by pleading guilty you give up the rights I have just described. Do you understand that?"

"Yes sir."

"Defense counsel, what advice have you given Colonel Lambello as to the maximum punishment for the offenses to which the accused pleaded guilty?"

"I informed him of the penalties associated with each count of the indictment," responded Roger Miller.

"Trial counsel, do you agree with that?"

"Yes, Your Honor," said Trent West.

"Colonel Lambello, by your plea of guilty this court-martial could sentence you to the maximum authorized punishment for Article 134 is a Dishonorable Discharge, three years in prison and total forfeiture of benefits, Article 107 is a Dishonorable Discharge, five years in prison and total forfeiture of benefits and Article 99 is Dishonorable Discharge or Death, or Life in prison and total forfeiture of benefits."

The people in the court room gasped.

Judge Beecham banged his gavel. "Order in the Court or I will have the Sergeant at Arms remove everyone immediately." There was instant silence.

"Colonel Lambello, do you understand that?"

"Yes sir."

"Do you feel you have had enough time to discuss your case with your counsel, Attorney Roger Miller?"

"Yes sir."

"Colonel Lambello, are you satisfied with Attorney Miller as your defense counsel and do you believe his advice has been in your best interest?"

"Yes sir."

"Are you pleading guilty voluntarily?"

"Yes sir."

"Has anyone tried to force you to plead guilty?"

"No sir."

"In a moment, you will be placed under oath and we will discuss the facts of your case. If what you say is not true, your statements may be used against you in a prosecution for perjury or false statement. Do you understand?"

"Yes sir."

"Please rise," said Judge Beecham.

"Trial counsel, will you administer the oath?"

"Do you swear that the statements you are about to make shall be the truth, the whole truth and nothing but the truth so help you God?" stated Trent West.

"I do," replied Colonel Lambello.

Judge Beecham continued, "I am going to explain the elements of the offenses to which you have entered pleas of guilty. By 'elements' I mean the facts which the Government would have to prove by evidence beyond a reasonable doubt before you could be found guilty if you plead not guilty. When I state each of these elements ask yourself if it is true, and whether you want to admit that it's true. Then be ready to talk about these facts with me."

"Please look at your copy of the charges and specifications. Do you understand those elements?"

"Yes sir."

"Do the elements correctly describe what you did?"

"Yes sir."

"Do you admit that you are Colonel Anthony Joseph Lambello Jr., the accused in this case?"

"Yes sir."

"On May 8th, 1969 were you a member of the United States Marine Corps., Special Forces on active duty and have you remained on active duty since then?"

"Yes sir."

"Is there a pre-trial agreement in this case?"

Roger Miller Esq. responds, "Yes your honor. Under Rule 910, Pleas: Trial counsel and defense counsel have reached an agreement."

"Mark the plea agreement as Appellate Exhibit 1 and the sentence agreement as Appellate Exhibit 2," said Judge Beecham.

"So noted," said the court reporter.

"Colonel Lambello, I have here the Appellate Exhibit 1 which is part of a pre-trial agreement between you and the Government, the convening authority. Is this your signature that appears on the bottom of page 2?"

"Yes sir."

"Did you also read and sign Appellate Exhibit 2 which is the second part of the agreement?"

"Yes sir."

"Do you believe you fully understand the agreement?"

"Yes sir."

"I don't know, and I don't want to know at this time the sentence limitations you have agreed to. However, I want you to read that part of the agreement over to yourself once again. Without saying what it is, do you understand the maximum punishment the convening authority may approve?" asked Judge Beecham.

"Yes sir."

"In a pre-trial agreement, you agreed to enter a plea of

guilty to the charges and specifications and in return, the convening authority agrees to approve a lesser sentence than what the maximum sentence is. Do you understand that?"

"Yes sir."

"If the sentence adjudged by this court-martial is greater than the one provided in the agreement, the convening authority would have to reduce the sentence to one no more severe than the one in your agreement. On the other hand, if the sentence adjudged by this court-martial is less than the one in your agreement, the convening authority cannot increase the sentence adjudged. Do you understand that?"

"Yes sir."

"Colonel Lambello, is this agreement, Appellate Exhibits 1 and 2 the entire agreement between you and convening authority? In other words, is it correct that there are no other agreements or promises in this case?"

"Yes sir."

"Do counsels agree?"

"Yes, Your Honor," said the prosecutor.

"Yes, Your Honor," repeated the defense.

"Colonel Lambello, do you understand your pre-trial agreement?"

"Yes sir."

"Does each counsel disagree with my explanation or interpretation of the agreement in any respect?"

"No, Your Honor," they replied in unison.

"Attorney Roger Miller, did the offer to make a pre-trial agreement originate with the defense?"

"Yes, Your Honor."

"Colonel Lambello, are you entering this agreement freely and voluntarily?"

"Yes sir."

"Has anyone tried to force you to enter this agreement?"

"No sir."

"Have you fully discussed this agreement with your counsel and are you satisfied that Attorney Miller's advice is in your best interest?"

"Yes sir."

"Colonel Lambello, although you believe you are guilty, you have a legal and moral right to plead not guilty and to require the Government to prove its case against you, if it can by legal and competent evidence beyond a reasonable doubt. If you were to plead not guilty, then you would be presumed under the law to be not guilty, and only by introducing evidence and proving your guilt beyond a reasonable doubt can the Government overcome that presumption. Do you understand?"

"Yes sir."

"Do you have any questions about your plea of guilty, your pre-trial agreement, or anything we have discussed?"

"No sir."

"Do you still want to plead guilty?"

"Yes sir."

"I find that the accused has knowingly, intelligently, and consciously waived rights against self-incrimination, to a trial of the facts by a court-martial, and to be confronted by the witnesses against him; that the accused is in fact guilty; and his plea is accepted."

"Colonel Lambello, you may request to withdraw your plea of guilty anytime before sentence is announced in your case and if you have a good reason for your request I will grant it. Do you understand?"

"Yes sir."

"Colonel Lambello, in accordance with your plea of guilty, this court-martial finds you guilty of all charges."

"After a 10 minute recess we will proceed with sentencing." Judge Beecham hit his gavel once and disappeared through the door behind his desk.

Chapter 59

The court audience sat nervously during the break.

Judge Beecham appeared through the door after the recess.

"Court will come to order," he bellowed. He banged his gavel twice. The courtroom was so quiet you could hear a pin drop. Everyone held their breath as they awaited the sentence.

"Your Honor," said Attorney West. Before you pass sentence on the accused, it has been agreed upon by both the prosecution and the defense that one man from each of the three missions be allowed to speak on behalf of everyone connected to the case. Since you have already made your decision on the defendant's sentence and our plea agreement has been signed, this would change nothing in the trial's outcome."

"This is highly unusual but so is the entire case so I will grant the motion. Who is the first to speak?"

A voice came from the second row. "I am, Your Honor. My name is Joshua Washington. I was a Sergeant on the 1st recon team, May 8th, 1969. The recon team I was part of was called in to rescue a downed pilot east of the Trail inside Laos. We assembled at the helicopter. It should have been a standard retrieval but things went wrong from the very beginning. After we took off, it started raining like hell. The pilot decided to turn back to base to wait for the storm to blow over but Lt. Lambello, the senior officer on board, balked. Lt. Lambello argued with the pilot and said the mission would go forth as scheduled. No one wanted to relieve the Lieutenant from duty because we were all afraid of his father, General Lambello. The pilot continued to follow the homing beacon of the downed pilot. We arrived at the correct landing coordinates but were unable to land because of the poor visibility. The pilot landed one kilometer north of the signal. As soon as we touched down, we were in immediate trouble. As I said, visibility was zero. The Lieutenant insisted on being in the 1-0 position or point position which was my position. This was the Lieutenant's first mission. He didn't know what to do but he felt he had to prove something. We made our way to the downed pilot and were trying to make it back to the landing zone when we were surrounded by NVA. We called back to HQ informing them we were pinned down. Some of us were already hit and one was dead. The Lieutenant sat frozen, too afraid to issue an order. Headquarters acknowledged our problem and sent a 2nd recon team out. We were sitting ducks waiting for the 2nd recon team." Sergeant Washington sat down.

The next speaker stood up. "My name is Corporal Lance McBride. Your Honor, I was on the 2nd recon team. The leader of our squad died in battle. Here is what happened to our team. We took off 15 minutes after receiving the distress call of the 1st recon team. The rain was coming down worse than ever. We were given the wrong coordinates and we ended up landing three kilometers north of the 1st recon party. HQ informed us that a Marine recon squad was five kilometers west of us but they had their own problems fighting the NVA. We were on our own. We had inadvertently sandwiched some NVAs between the 1st recon and us. There were twelve of us total, some already dead, some wounded, against two hundred NVA. Aside from trying to miss the punji sticks and other booby traps the NVA had set in the area, we were fighting a vicious ground war. Our Lieutenant radioed HQ before he getting hit that we needed back up or all of us would be dead. The Lieutenant specifically requested that Major Thomas Smith lead the 3rd recon team. It was an unspoken fact that Major Smith had been a POW in this area and knew every square inch of the terrain intimately.

Major Smith died in the extraction but it was his expertise that saved all the other men on the mission. From the 3rd recon team, I introduce Sergeant Leonard Fernandez."

Sergeant Fernandez rose to speak.

"Your Honor, we were sitting in the tents when the loud speaker went off requesting that Major Smith come to the Colonel's office immediately. Everyone, including the Major, had an immediate sick feeling that another recon team was in trouble. Major Smith related his conversation with the Colonel.

'Major, we have an urgent situation with one recon team pinned down at these coordinates. The rest of the men are near these coordinates but we have no idea if they are alive or dead. Communications with both recon parties have been cut off. They were trying to pick up a downed pilot when they got into trouble. Five kilometers west of the 2nd recon team is a platoon of Marines but they are having an all out battle with the NVA. There is no way they can help. I need you to lead the 3rd extraction team.'

'Colonel, meaning no disrespect but isn't there anyone else you can get to lead this recon team,' said Major Smith.

'I thought about that before I asked you to come to my office. I realize you leave tomorrow for Hawaii after 4 tours of duty here. However, there is no one more qualified to do this. You are the best at what you do. The main reason I want you is this area is the area you wandered around in after your escape from the POW camp. Your intimate knowledge of the terrain is invaluable and the 2nd recon team requested you personally.'

'Yes, sir. I will assemble my team. We'll take off in 10 minutes.'

'Thank you Major. Good luck.'

Thomas saluted the Colonel and left.

Major Smith assembled his team. He explained the situation in detail and told us to over pack our sacks accordingly. Usually, the men carry 50 pound backpacks but he wanted us to increase the load to 80 pounds carrying extra claymore mines, ammo and grenades. Major Smith bore a larger load of a 100 pound pack because he wanted to make sure he had an extra radio, battery and more ammo. Two hundred NVAs against a handful of us weren't exactly the best odds. He also had each team member carry a machete, a hand gun with extra clips, canteen of water, gas mask, serum albumin, (a blood expander to counter severe blood loss,) morphine sticks and assorted smoke grenades to signal the helicopters in case the rain stopped. The most important thing was our CAR-15 and as much ammo as we could carry.

Our helicopter took off with one following us to pick up the dead and wounded. The weather was miserable. Visibility was still zero because of the continued rains. The storms were coming through one after the other with no break.

Headquarters radioed that another recon team was coming but gave no details. Per Major Smith, we observed radio silence. Major Smith knew there was still an undiscovered mole in camp and didn't want to compromise the mission.

Major Smith had the pilot drop us one kilometer east of the coordinates given. With no landing zone available, we repelled down as quickly as possible. Being east took us out of the sandwich position and put us on the side between the fighting. It was hoped that we would take them by surprise but no such luck. We were in radio silence but someone – possibly the mole – had leaked the information to the NVA that we were coming.

As soon as we landed, they were all over us. We pulled out our machine guns and shot everything in sight until it was clear. Major Smith assumed the 1-0 position. I was in the 1-1 with the rest of us proceeding in formation until John took up the rear position. We made our way to the first landing zone where we saw the dead and injured lying in the open. The only one who had no injuries was Lt. Lambello cowering behind a tree. Major Smith and I went into the area north of the LZ and encountered a pocket of NVA. We threw grenades and set some claymore mines to clean them out. Once out, the 2nd recon team group came south to reunite with the rest of us.

They said another group of NVA was close behind them. Major Smith called in an air strike to stop the wave of NVA behind us and to allow the helicopter to land and get us out of there. The bombers hit the coordinates and cleaned out the NVA temporarily. One helicopter landed. The dead and injured were loaded along with Lt. Lambello and the downed pilot. It took off. The other copter landed. By that time, more NVA had made their way to where we were and started firing. Major Smith couldn't call in another strike so we had to use machine guns and grenades. We provided cover for the unit to get into the copter. We were low on ammo and the rain continued to hamper our visibility. The pilot screamed he needed to take off. Major Smith told me to get into the helicopter while he covered. The NVA continued firing on us. Major Smith fired back and as he backed into the aircraft, the pilot took off. Major Smith wasn't completely in; I was holding on helping him in and the NVA shot up at him and got him under his flack jacket. He died a later aboard the hospital ship, 'Mercy.' If it hadn't been for Major Smith, none of the guys would have made it out of there alive." Sergeant Fernandez stopped speaking and just stood there in silence. He had just relived the most traumatic moment of his life. Tears were rolling down his face.

After a few moments, the Judge asked, "Anything else, Sergeant Fernandez?"

"No, Your Honor."

"You may be seated. I have reviewed the charges and maximum sentences associated with those charges. I do not know what the pre-trial agreement was between the prosecution and defense counsel. Based on the seriousness of the charges, I would have to believe it was a reduction of time served in a military prison.

As judge in this case, I am not given the right to see the pre-trial agreement until I sentence you, Colonel Lambello. However, I was deeply disturbed that you pled guilty to such serious charges. I had to believe that the prosecution must have overwhelming evidence against you and my belief was confirmed.

I have been a judge for 13 years. Prior to my becoming a judge, I have served 12 years as both prosecutor and defense counsel. I was selected to serve at this court-martial for my impartiality toward the prosecution and defense. Gentlemen, I have been on both sides of the table and I know how this game is played.

Therefore, it is time to announce the findings of the Court.

Will the accused please rise with counsel?

Colonel Anthony Joseph Lambello, Jr., this court-martial sentences you to life in prison with parole in 25 years, a dishonorable discharge and total forfeiture of all benefits."

There was clapping coming from the gallery in the court. I gave a sigh of relief.

"Order in the Court," exclaimed Judge Beecham banging the gavel.

Will the defense counsel please reveal the pre-trial agreements as indicated in Appellate Exhibits 1 and 2?

Roger Miller stood and addressed the Court. "Your Honor, it was agreed upon that the accused would receive 25 years in prison but with good behavior he would be released in 20, receive a dishonorable discharge, and accept a forfeiture of all benefits."

"You may be seated."

"As stated earlier, as the convening authority, I cannot increase the sentence to equal the pre-trial agreement. I can only lessen the sentence that is imposed by the court."

"The pre-trial agreement will stand."

"Do you have any questions Colonel Lambello?"

"No sir."

"This court-martial is adjourned. Remove the defendant from the court room."

Chapter 60

It was over. I was happy and sad at the same time. Colonel Lambello would finally pay for what he did but it didn't bring back my Thomas or the other men who died on that final mission.

People came over to shake my hand to congratulate me for putting Colonel Lambello in jail where he belonged. I felt sorry for his wife and kids but I had no feelings for him whatsoever. My anger melted away when the judgment was read.

I had invited all my close friends for a going away party. The caterers were already at the condo setting up the food and decorations. I wanted it to be housewarming for George and Maria too since they would be moving in the day after tomorrow.

Steven came over. He gave me a big hug and congratulated me on my victory.

"It was a victory in name only, Steven. Thomas isn't coming back. I'm left to carry on without him," I said feeling empty and sad.

"It doesn't have to be that way," said Steven. He pulled out a ring box. In it was the biggest diamond I had ever seen.

"Marla, marry me, please. I will make you a wonderful husband. I will take care of you and love you for the rest of our lives. I know someone at the Hall of Records who could issue a marriage certificate. Chaplain Cook could marry us at the condo. All you have to do is say yes," pleaded Steven.

I looked into those beautiful green eyes of his and knew that what I was about to say would crush him.

"Steven, even though things are now over with the man responsible for my husband's death going to prison, I can't marry you. I realize that I do love you and care for you but not the way a woman should love a man. Maybe it would grow into that over time but what would I do for a career. My nursing career in Hawaii is over. My future is in San Francisco. How fair would it be for me to ask you to give up your career and move to San Francisco?" I replied gently. "You knew this was coming for years. I told you to move on with your life," I said with a tinge of sadness because my future wasn't in Hawaii or in being his wife.

"I couldn't move on because I have always loved you almost from the moment we met and most certainly when I saw you," Steven said softly.

"Another time, another place dear sweet Steven and I know things would have been different," I replied as I touched his face.

He put his hand on mine and looked at me with puppy dog eyes.

He began to pull me closer to his lips when I pulled back and asked, "Are you coming to the house to eat?"

"Yes, I will be there."

"Good. See you there."

Chaplain Cook had waited for Steven to leave so he could give me a big hug and congratulate me on a job well done.

"Marla, I have something for you, something I have saved for the past 15 years."

Chaplain Cook had laid the cross on the bottom of the box with the letter neatly folded on top. Around the box was a small white ribbon. He handed me a small box and said, "Marla, open this alone, in a quiet place so you can meditate on what it says and means. I will be available if you want to talk."

I was puzzled. Steven proposes marriage again and now this. I left as fast as I could. When I got to my car, I started to cry.

I couldn't believe how many people showed up at the condo. It was almost wall to wall people eating and drinking, celebrating the justice all the men finally received. I was glad everyone was having a good time but I couldn't stand the commotion. I decided to take a walk on the beach. I figured no one would miss me. I grabbed my umbrella, a large towel, the little box and left.

I took off my shoes and walked barefoot on the sand for what seemed an eternity but was in reality only 10 minutes. I could still see my condo in the distance; however, only the sound of the ocean rang in my ears.

I felt so tired. All I wanted to do is sleep. An enormous weight had been lifted off my shoulders. I pitched my umbrella on the sand and arranged my towel under it taking as much advantage as I could of the shade it provided. I wanted to sleep but I was too curious to know what was in the box. I undid the ribbon, removed box top and pulled out the letter. Beneath the letter, I saw the small cross. I opened the letter and began reading it. "Dear Chaplain Cook…," it began. As I finished the letter, tears ran down my face. In the years since Thomas died, while I was seeking God, God was there with me, through everything. I took Thomas' cross and put it around my neck. I still had questions but they could wait. I laid back on the towel and fell asleep. At last, I finally found peace.

The End.

Author's Biography

Maxine Flam has been a guest columnist for the Los Angeles Daily News since 1999 writing about issues that affect the community.

She has an Associate of Arts Degree from Los Angeles Valley College and was on the Los Angeles Valley College and California State University Northridge Speech Teams winning numerous trophies and awards for her speeches.

Maxine has been involved with veteran organizations since her father's death in 1995. She is on the Board of Directors of "Veterans for Constitutional Law Ltd." and formerly on the Board of Directors of "The Veterans Advisory Board" both are 501c3 non-profit organizations. She is a member of the Firebase Network and an Associate Member of the 5th Armored Division. Maxine has been an outspoken veteran's rights advocate on television, radio and in newspaper editorials.

Maxine lives in Southern California with her mother, Florence.